Interactive Reader and Study Guide

HOLT

American Anthem

HOLT, RINEHART AND WINSTON

A Harcourt Education Company

Orlando • **Austin** • New York • San Diego • London

ISBN 0-03-039393-0

9 10 11 12 13 14 1689 14 13 12 11 10 09

Contents

Interactive Reader and Study Guide

Contents

Interactive Reader and Study Guide

Contents

Interactive Reader and Study Guide

How to Use this Book

The *Interactive Reader and Study Guide* was developed to help you get the most from your American history course. Using this book will help you master the content of the course while developing your reading and vocabulary skills. Reviewing the next few pages before getting started will make you aware of the many useful features in this book.

Chapter Summary pages help you connect with the big picture. Studying them will keep you focused on the information you will need to be successful on your exams.

Graphic organizers help you to summarize each chapter. They are a valuable study tool to help you prepare for important tests.

Answering each question will help you to understand the graphic organizer and ensure that you fully comprehend the content from the chapter.

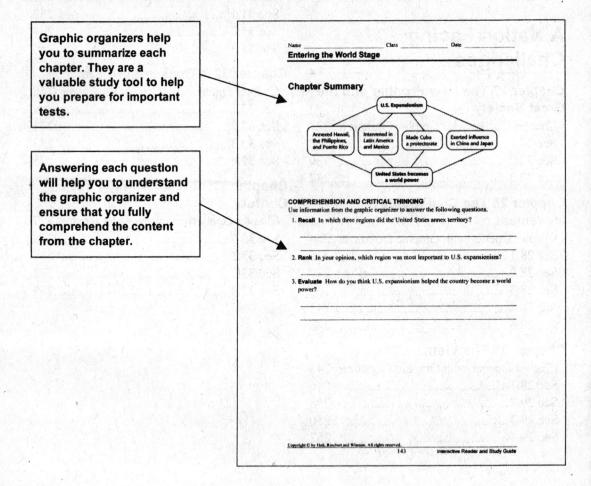

Name _____ Class _____ Date _____
Entering the World Stage

Chapter Summary

U.S. Expansionism

Annexed Hawaii, the Philippines, and Puerto Rico

Intervened in Latin America and Mexico

Made Cuba a protectorate

Exerted influence in China and Japan

United States becomes a world power

COMPREHENSION AND CRITICAL THINKING
Use information from the graphic organizer to answer the following questions.

1. **Recall** In which three regions did the United States annex territory?

2. **Rank** In your opinion, which region was most important to U.S. expansionism?

3. **Evaluate** How do you think U.S. expansionism helped the country become a world power?

Copyright © by Holt, Rinehart and Winston. All rights reserved.
143   Interactive Reader and Study Guide

Section Summary pages allow you to interact easily with the content and key terms from each section.

Clearly labeled page headers make navigating the book very simple.

The Main Idea statement from your textbook focuses your attention as you read the summaries.

The Key Terms and People from your textbook are provided with their definitions, making studying them easier.

Headings under each section summary relate to each heading in the textbook, making it easy for you to find the material you need.

Simple summaries explain each section in a way that is easy to understand.

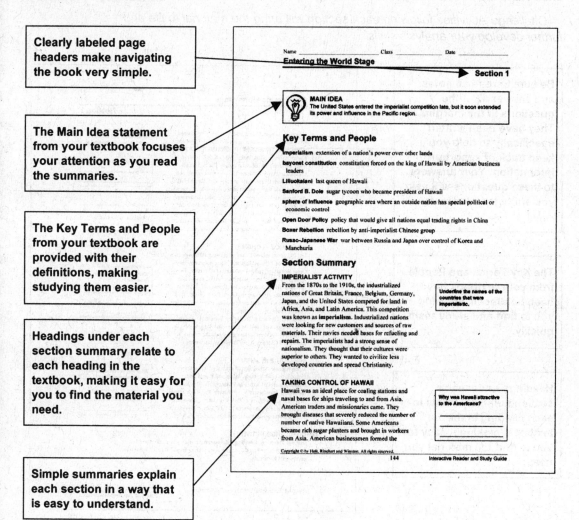

Name _____ Class _____ Date _____

Entering the World Stage

Section 1

MAIN IDEA
The United States entered the imperialist competition late, but it soon extended its power and influence in the Pacific region.

Key Terms and People

Imperialism extension of a nation's power over other lands

bayonet constitution constitution forced on the king of Hawaii by American business leaders

Liliuokalani last queen of Hawaii

Sanford B. Dole sugar tycoon who became president of Hawaii

sphere of influence geographic area where an outside nation has special political or economic control

Open Door Policy policy that would give all nations equal trading rights in China

Boxer Rebellion rebellion by anti-imperialist Chinese group

Russo-Japanese War war between Russia and Japan over control of Korea and Manchuria

Section Summary

IMPERIALIST ACTIVITY
From the 1870s to the 1910s, the industrialized nations of Great Britain, France, Belgium, Germany, Japan, and the United States competed for land in Africa, Asia, and Latin America. This competition was known as **imperialism**. Industrialized nations were looking for new customers and sources of raw materials. Their navies needed bases for refueling and repairs. The imperialists had a strong sense of nationalism. They thought that their cultures were superior to others. They wanted to civilize less developed countries and spread Christianity.

Underline the names of the countries that were imperialistic.

TAKING CONTROL OF HAWAII
Hawaii was an ideal place for coaling stations and naval bases for ships traveling to and from Asia. American traders and missionaries came. They brought diseases that severely reduced the number of number of native Hawaiians. Some Americans became rich sugar planters and brought in workers from Asia. American businessmen formed the

Why was Hawaii attractive to the Americans?
_____
_____

Copyright © by Holt, Rinehart and Winston. All rights reserved.

144

Interactive Reader and Study Guide

Notes throughout the margins help you to interact with the content and understand the information you are reading.

Challenge Activities following each section will bring the material to life and further develop your analysis skills.

Be sure to read all notes and answer all of the questions in the margins. They have been written specifically to help you keep track of important information. Your answers to these questions will help you study for your tests.

The Key Terms and People from your textbook have been boldfaced, allowing you to find and study them quickly.

Headings under each section summary relate to each heading in the textbook, making it easy for you to find the material you need.

Name _____ Class _____ Date _____

Entering the World Stage

Section 1

Hawaiian League to take over Hawaii. They forced King Kalakaua to sign a new constitution at gunpoint. It was called the bayonet constitution. It gave Pearl Harbor to the United States. When Kalakaua died, his sister **Liliuokalani** became queen. The American minister to Hawaii ordered U.S. marines ashore and forced Queen Liliuokalani to surrender. **Sanford B. Dole** became the president of the Republic of Hawaii. An investigation by President Cleveland condemned the revolt. However, Dole refused to step down. In 1898 President McKinley annexed Hawaii. It became the 50th state in 1959. In 1993 Congress apologized for the U.S. role in overthrowing Liliuokalani.

What action was ordered by the American minister to Hawaii?

Circle the date when Congress apologized to Hawaii.

INFLUENCE IN CHINA

In 1895 Japan seized China's Liaotung Peninsula and the island of Taiwan. Russia, France, Germany, and Great Britain carved out **spheres of influence**. These were geographic areas where an outside nation had special political or economic influence. In 1899 the United States proposed the **Open Door Policy**. This would give all nations equal trading rights with China. Many Chinese were unhappy with the foreign influence. This led to the **Boxer Rebellion**, during which a group of Chinese rebels laid siege to the city of Beijing. Western nations put down the rebellion and forced China to sign a humbling settlement.

What caused the Boxer Rebellion?

INFLUENCE IN JAPAN

Japan became industrialized after the United States forced it to open to trade. Japan and Russia both wanted control of Korea and Manchuria. This led to the **Russo-Japanese War**. President Roosevelt helped negotiate a peace treaty. With this victory, Japan became the strongest power in East Asia. It rivaled the United States for influence in China and the Pacific.

What was the result of the Russo-Japanese War?

CHALLENGE ACTIVITY

Critical Thinking: Drawing Inferences How do you think that imperialism contributed to later events such as World War II? Write two paragraphs to explain.

145   Interactive Reader and Study Guide

The World Before 1600

Chapter Summary

The World Before 1600

Early Native American Cultures	North American Cultures in the 1400s	Africa	Europe
• Scientists disagree on when and how the first Americans arrived • One theory is that the first Americans crossed a land bridge from Asia to North America • Early Mesoamerican cultures include Olmec, Maya, and Aztec • Early North American cultures include Hohokam, Anasazi, Adena, Hopewell, and Mississippian	• Native Americans in North America establish diverse cultures based on geography • Some North American cultures share characteristics, including social structure, religious beliefs, and technology • Trading networks allow North American groups to share goods and ideas	• Major kingdoms include Ghana, Mali, Songhay, Benin, and Kongo • Portuguese traders arrive in Africa in 1400s • European slave trade begins in late 1400s	• Magna Carta establishes basic principles of government in 1215 • The Renaissance begins around 1300 • The Age of Exploration begins in the late 1400s • Christopher Columbus voyages to the Caribbean in 1492 • The Reformation begins in 1517

COMPREHENSION AND CRITICAL THINKING

Use information from the graphic organizer to answer the following questions.

1. **Identify** What were the three early Mesoamerican cultures?

_____

_____

2. **Explain** On what were the different cultures of Native Americans in North America based?

_____

_____

_____

3. **Recall** When did the European slave trade begin?

_____

_____

4. **Analyze** Why is the Magna Carta important?

_____

_____

_____

The World Before 1600

MAIN IDEA
People arrived on the American continents thousands of years ago and developed flourishing societies.

Key Terms and People

nomad person who moves from place to place in search of food

hunter-gatherer way of life where some food is hunted and some is gathered

agricultural revolution change that occurred when people started farming and settling in villages

Olmec the first major Mesoamerican society; grew up around 1200 BC

Maya Mesoamerican society that grew up around 400 BC

Toltec society that took over in Mexico as the Maya began to decline

Aztec warlike society that took over central Mexico in the 1400s

Inca group that built a large empire that grew up in the Andes Mountains of South America

pueblo Spanish word for "town"; applied to the adobe buildings built by the Anasazi that were several stories high

clan group of people related by blood

Section Summary

MIGRATION TO THE AMERICAS

Archaeology is the scientific study of what is left of past human life. Archaeologists look for information about people who lived before history was written down. During the Ice Age, a land bridge existed between Asia and North America. Between 12,000 and 40,000 years ago, **nomads** came over this bridge. These first Americans were people who lived by moving from place to place in search of food. They followed a **hunter-gatherer** way of life. This meant that women gathered nuts, berries, wild plants, and birds' eggs. Men hunted animals. When the animals moved, so did the people. Over time, Native Americans began to plant and harvest crops. They settled in villages. This change was called the **agricultural revolution**. The main crops were corn, beans, and squashes, such as pumpkins. Men still hunted, but they also began raising animals for food.

> When did nomads come over the land bridge from Asia to North America?
>
> _____
>
> _____

> What did women do in a hunter-gatherer way of life?
>
> _____
>
> _____

Interactive Reader and Study Guide

The World Before 1600

CULTURES OF CENTRAL AMERICA AND SOUTH AMERICA

The area from central Mexico into Central America is called Mesoamerica. The **Olmec** was the first major Mesoamerican society. It began around 1200 BC. The Olmec were engineers and artists. They made huge sculpted heads. Their religion, art, and agriculture influenced later peoples. Around 400 BC, the **Maya** society grew. Their cities were religious centers with stone pyramids. The Maya studied the stars and made calendars. They had a writing system and a number system that included the idea of zero. In AD 900 the **Toltec** ruled central Mexico. In the 1400s the **Aztecs** came to power. Beginning in the 1100s the **Inca** rose to power in the Andes Mountains of South America. They built an empire connected by roads and bridges.

> How did the Olmec influence later peoples?
>
> _____
>
> _____
>
> _____

> Underline the accomplishments of the Maya.

THE EARLIEST CULTURES OF NORTH AMERICA

There were many different environments in North America. These included forests, deserts, and fertile land. Native Americans adapted the ways they lived to these areas. In the Southwest, the Anasazi built **pueblos**. These were adobe buildings several stories high. In eastern North America, people lived in small farming villages. These were probably ruled by the leaders of **clans**. A clan is a group of people related by blood. Groups known as Mound Builders lived in the Ohio River Valley. They traded with other peoples over a large area. The most advanced farming society north of Mexico was the Mississippian culture. They built towns with temple-mounds, plazas, and pyramids. Their most populated city was Cahokia.

> What did the Native Americans in North America have to adapt to?
>
> _____

CHALLENGE ACTIVITY

Critical Thinking: Elaborate Choose an accomplishment of Maya culture that interests you. Make a poster that illustrates its importance.

Interactive Reader and Study Guide

The World Before 1600

MAIN IDEA
A variety of complex societies existed in different regions of North America before European explorers arrived in the early 1500s.

Key Terms and People

Pueblo Native American group of the Southwest

Kwakiutl Native American group of the Pacific Northwest

Iroquois Native American group of the Northeast

longhouse large wooden buildings in which the Iroquois lived

kinship blood relations

matrilineal system where possessions are inherited through the mother

division of labor system where different people do different kinds of work

shaman person thought to have spiritual and healing powers

barter exchange of goods without using money

Section Summary

REGIONAL DIFFERENCES AMONG NATIVE AMERICANS

Different Native American groups had different cultures. The **Pueblo** of the Southwest inherited many traditions from the Anasazi. They grew corn, beans, squash, and cotton. They made pottery and baskets. In the Pacific Northwest, the **Kwakiutl** and other Native American groups became skilled woodworkers. They fished and hunted wild game. They carved totem poles. They liked to show their wealth by giving valuable gifts to their guests. Inuits and Aleuts live in present-day Canada and Alaska. They were probably the most recent migrants from Asia.

East of the mountains of the Pacific Coast lay the dryland areas of the Great Basin and the Plateau. In these areas there was little rain, few trees, no large rivers, and little wild game. Still, some Native Americans lived there. They were hunter-gatherers. Some of the best-known Native Americans lived on the Great Plains. These included the Sioux, Pawnee, and Cheyenne. Farming was difficult. The Plains Indians depended on hunting buffalo. In the Northeast, the **Iroquois** lived in large villages. **Longhouses**

> From whom did the Pueblo people inherit their traditions?
>
> _____

> Where did the ancestors of the Inuits and Aleuts come from?
>
> _____

The World Before 1600

provided shelter. These were large wooden buildings. In the Southeast, most Native Americans lived in settled farming villages. Some of them carried on the culture of earlier mound-building peoples.

> **How did most Native Americans in the Southeast live?**
>
> _____

NATIVE AMERICAN CUSTOMS

Families were at the heart of Native American cultures. Most villages and nations were organized into clans. These were based on **kinship**, or blood relations. Kinship ties could come through either the mother or the father. Iroquois society was **matrilineal**. This meant that possessions were inherited through the mother. Among the Hopi in the Southwest, a man went to live with his wife's family after he married. Some cultures had strict social classes. In other groups there was more equality.

> **What was at the heart of Native American cultures?**
>
> _____

Native Americans did not believe that land should be bought or sold. Some viewed the land as a gift from the Great Spirit. Even in the earliest groups, certain people did certain kinds of work. This is called **division of labor**. For example, women wove cloth and men carved wood. Native Americans shared some spiritual and religious ideas. One was a spiritual link to the natural world. Many Native Americans believed that a tree stood at the center of the earth. Animals, especially bears, were thought to be powerful spirits. Hunters honored the spirits of animals they killed. Native Americans told many stories. In many cultures, **shamans** were people thought to have spiritual and healing powers.

TRADING NETWORKS LINK NATIVE AMERICAN SOCIETIES

Native Americans traded goods using a **barter** system. This meant they exchanged goods without using money. They traded extra food, minerals, shells, pearls, cotton, baskets, and pottery. Traders traveled by canoe or on foot. Along with trade goods, ideas moved from place to place through the trade networks.

> **Underline the things Native Americans traded.**

CHALLENGE ACTIVITY

Critical Thinking: Elaborate Choose one of the Native American nations mentioned in the chapter and write a two-page report on their way of life.

The World Before 1600

MAIN IDEA
Trade was a major factor in the development of African societies south of the Sahara.

Key Terms and People

Islam religion founded by the prophet Muhammad

oral tradition history passed down through people telling stories

Mansa Musa ruler of Mali from about 1307 to 1332

Muslims followers of Islam

Askia Muhammad ruler of Songhai from 1493 to 1528

lineage ancestry

plantation large-scale farm

Section Summary

WEST AFRICAN TRADING KINGDOMS

The Sahara is the largest desert in the world. It divides North Africa from the southern part of the continent. Trading caravans have crossed the Sahara since ancient times. Trading empires in West Africa grew along the trade routes for gold, ivory, and salt. Desert traders also brought **Islam** to West Africa. Islam is a religion that was founded by the prophet Muhammad in Arabia in the 600s. The earliest West African trading state was Ghana. What we know of Ghana's history is largely from **oral tradition**. This is history passed down by storytellers. In about 1240 a great warrior conquered Ghana and started the new state of Mali. The most famous ruler of Mali was **Mansa Musa**. He was in power from about 1307 to 1332. The people of Mali were **Muslims**, or followers of Islam.

By the mid-1400s the kingdom of Songhai ruled a larger area than either Ghana or Mali. Its most famous ruler was **Askia Muhammad**. He was in power from 1493 to 1528. By about 1300 Benin was becoming a powerful state. It grew rich from foreign trade. It was famous for its artists who created beautiful bronze statues. Farther south, Kongo grew up along the Congo River in Central Africa. It exported salt and palm oil.

> Underline the things that were traded in West Africa.

> What is our main source for knowledge about Ghana's history?
>
> _____

The World Before 1600

KINGDOMS IN EAST AFRICA

People in East Africa looked to Egypt, India, and the Middle East for trading partners. Their ships sailed the Red Sea and crossed the Indian Ocean. East Africa exported gold, cinnamon, rhinoceros horn, and tortoise shell. Traders also shipped enslaved Africans abroad. Many Arab merchants settled on the shores of East Africa. Several Muslim city-states grew up. The blending of African and Arab influences created a new culture.

> Underline the things that East Africa exported.

AFRICAN SOCIETY AND THE SLAVE TRADE

Strong families were a central feature of African society. People were loyal to those with the same **lineage**, or ancestry. They also felt loyalty to their village. The biggest class division was between those who were free and those who were not. Slavery was a common practice. In most African societies, however, slaves could work their way to freedom. They could rise to a higher social class. Then the Europeans came. The Portuguese established trading posts and forts on the Atlantic coast. They—and later the Spanish—set up **plantations**. These were large-scale farms. When the Americas were discovered, they set up plantations there, too. Plantations needed many workers. The slave trade arose from the demand for labor. The Portuguese traders convinced a few African rulers and merchants to supply them with slaves. The slave trade went on for 400 years. It destroyed societies in West Africa. As many as 20 million enslaved Africans may have been shipped to the Americas. Several million more were sent to Europe, Asia, and the Middle East. Countless others died on the trip. Slave hunters took the strongest young people—Africa's future leaders. Parts of Africa suffered great losses in population.

> What was the biggest class division in African cultures?
>
> _____
>
> _____

> Underline the ways that the slave trade hurt West Africa.

CHALLENGE ACTIVITY

Critical Thinking: Elaborate Choose one of the African nations mentioned in this section and write a two-page report on its history.

The World Before 1600

MAIN IDEA
Renaissance ideas changed Europeans' medieval outlook and inspired them to explore the world.

Key Terms and People

Middle Ages period in Europe from about AD 500 to 1500

Crusades wars in which Christians tried to take the Holy Land from the Muslims

Magna Carta English document signed by King John in 1215; put limits on royal power

Renaissance a new era of creativity and learning in Europe

Martin Luther German monk who criticized the Catholic Church

Reformation reform movement that split the Catholic Church

Protestants people who joined in protesting against the Catholic Church during the Reformation

Queen Isabella Spanish queen who wanted to unite Spain as a Catholic country

caravel a fast, strong ship developed by the Portuguese and used by explorers

Section Summary

THE MIDDLE AGES

The period in Europe from about AD 500 to 1500 is known as the **Middle Ages**. It is also known as the medieval period. In the early Middle Ages, no government was strong enough to protect people. As a result, feudalism developed. This was a system in which nobles, or lords, gave land to vassals. These were nobles of lower rank. In return, the vassal pledged loyalty to fight for his lord.

Muslim Turks ruled the Middle East. There were many places there that Christians considered holy. The Catholic Church declared wars called **Crusades**. Their purpose was to capture the Holy Land. At first the Crusades were successful. However, the Muslims eventually won back the right to rule the land.

The Crusades boosted trade between Europe and the Middle East. Europeans wanted goods such as fruits, spices, sugar, silks, perfumes, and carpets. In time, a middle class of merchants grew up in the towns. They gave their loyalty to the king. Strong rulers began to unify their lands. They created nation-states. These were countries with strong central

> **When did the Middle Ages take place?**
>
> _____

> **What effect did the Crusades have on trade between Europe and the Middle East?**
>
> _____

The World Before 1600

governments. In England, some nobles forced King John to sign the **Magna Carta**. This document put limits on royal power. It also gave the nobles certain rights. These included no taxation without representation and the right to trial by a jury of one's equals. Later these rights were given to ordinary people.

> Underline the principles of government stated in the Magna Carta.

THE RENAISSANCE AND THE PROTESTANT REFORMATION

In the 1300s a new era of creativity and learning began. It was called the **Renaissance**. Rich merchants supported artists who created works that are still admired today. A German monk named **Martin Luther** criticized some practices of the Catholic Church. This led to a movement for reform known as the **Reformation**. People who joined the movement were known as **Protestants**. By 1600 Protestants controlled most of northern Europe. The Catholic Church was still strong in the south. **Queen Isabella** and her husband King Ferdinand wanted to unify Spain as a Catholic country.

> Circle the name of the man who started the Reformation.

THE AGE OF EXPLORATION

During the Middle Ages, Marco Polo traveled to China and India. In 1419 Prince Henry of Portugal established a school and a naval observatory. He wanted to encourage exploration. His shipbuilders designed a new kind of ship called a **caravel**. It was faster and more manueverable than earlier ships. New and improved instruments like the compass helped sailors find their way. In 1488 a Portuguese explorer named Bartolomeu Dias sailed down Africa's west coast. A storm blew him off course. He sailed around the southern tip of Africa before turning back. Ten years later Vasco da Gama rounded the tip and went on to India. Other Portuguese explorers later saw the coast of what is now Brazil. This sighting gave Portugal a land claim in the Americas.

> Why was the caravel better than previous ships?
> _____
> _____

CHALLENGE ACTIVITY

Critical Thinking: Elaborate Choose one of the explorers mentioned in this section and write a two-page biography of him.

The World Before 1600

 MAIN IDEA
Columbus's voyages to the Americas established contact with Native Americans and led to European colonies and an exchange of goods and ideas.

Key Terms and People

Vikings the Norse from Scandinavia; sea raiders who attacked the people living on the coasts of western Europe

Leif Eriksson Viking who probably landed on the coast of Canada in about 1000

Christopher Columbus explorer whose landings in the Americas led to colonization

Tainos Native Americans who lived on the island where Columbus first landed in 1492

colonization process of starting colonies

Columbian Exchange exchange of plants, animals, languages, and technology between Europe and the Americas, and later Africa

Section Summary

VIKINGS VISIT NORTH AMERICA

The **Vikings** were people from Scandinavia. They were sea raiders who attacked the people living on the coasts of western Europe. In about 1000 **Leif Eriksson** headed for Greenland. He sailed west, probably landing in Canada. He named where he landed Vinland because there were many grapevines. Later, other Vikings tried to establish a colony at Vinland. That led to the first known European contact with Native Americans. According to Scandinavian legends, the Native Americans were not friendly. The Vikings left after three years. They returned for wood, but never tried to settle there again.

> Circle the name of the European group who made the first contact with Native Americans.

COLUMBUS VOYAGES TO THE CARIBBEAN

In the 1400s other Europeans did not know of the Vikings' visits to North America. Not knowing the Americas blocked the way, **Christopher Columbus** thought he could get to India by sailing west. Backed by Queen Isabella of Spain, Columbus set sail on August 3, 1492. On October 12, his men sighted land. The local people, **Tainos**, greeted him. However, Columbus called them Indians because he believed he was in the Indias. The Tainos lived simply in thatched

> Circle the date when Columbus set sail.

> Why did Columbus call the Tainos Indians?
> _____

The World Before 1600

huts in the jungle. Columbus was disappointed not to find the rich cities and treasures he expected.

IMPACT ON NATIVE AMERICANS

Columbus's trips started a wave of European **colonization** of the Americas. In the first settlement he started, Columbus's men behaved wildly. This angered the Tainos and they killed them. Columbus started another colony on the island of Hispaniola. Columbus captured some of the Indians to sell as slaves. Then he conquered the whole island. Spaniards enslaved many Indians and made them work at mining gold. The Indians received harsh treatment from the Europeans. Not everyone wanted to see the Indians enslaved. Queen Isabella said that the Caribbean Indians belonged to her and Ferdinand and could not be owned by anyone else in Spain. Spain passed laws to protect the Indians. However, the laws were hard to enforce.

> What type of work did the Spaniards make the enslaved Indians do?
> _____

THE COLUMBIAN EXCHANGE

Contact between Europeans and Native Americans led to valuable exchanges. Because all of these exchanges took place as the result of Columbus's travels, they were called the **Columbian Exchange**. Corn, beans, squash, chocolate, and peanuts were some of the American food products taken to Europe. Europeans brought certain foods to the Americas. They also brought animals and technology. They brought horses, which became a big part of Plains Indian culture. Native Americans also learned about guns from Europeans. However, the Europeans also spread deadly germs among the Native Americans. Diseases such as smallpox and measles wiped out thousands of Native Americans.

> Underline what the Europeans brought to the Americas in the Columbian Exchange.

CHALLENGE ACTIVITY

Critical Thinking: Elaborate Do research on Leif Eriksson's voyage. Write a one-page report on the voyage and where he may have landed.

European Colonies in America

Chapter Summary

Spain
- Major explorers in North America: Ponce de León, Cabeza da Vaca, de Soto, Coronado
- Colonies founded in American Southeast and Southwest

England
- Major explorers in North America: Cabot, Drake, Raleigh
- Colonies founded along Atlantic coast

European Colonies in America

France
- Major explorers in North America: Cartier, Champlain, la Salle
- Colonies founded in Quebec and Louisiana

The Netherlands
- Major explorer in North America: Hudson
- Colonies founded in New Netherland and Delaware (both later become English colonies)

COMPREHENSION AND CRITICAL THINKING

Use information from the graphic organizer to answer the following questions.

1. **Identify** Who were the major Spanish explorers of North America?

_____

_____

2. **Identify** Where were the French colonies located?

_____

_____

3. **Recall** Where were England's American colonies located?

_____

_____

4. **Recall** What happened to the Dutch colony of New Netherland?

_____

_____

_____

European Colonies in America

 MAIN IDEA
In the 1500s and 1600s, European nations, led by Spain, continued to explore, claim territory, and build settlements in America.

Key Terms and People

Treaty of Tordesillas agreement dividing the New World between Spain and Portugal

conquistador Spanish explorer of the 1500s; Spanish word for "conqueror"

Juan Ponce de León first Spanish explorer to reach mainland North America

Hernán Cortés conqueror of the Aztec Empire in Mexico

Francisco Vásquez de Coronado explorer of the American Southwest

missionary church members who teach and convert others to Christianity

Popé leader of the Pueblo Revolt against the Spanish

Sir Francis Drake English naval captain who raided Spanish ships and coastal towns

Section Summary

SPANISH CONQUISTADORS

In the late 1400s Spain and Portugal divided the Americas between them in the **Treaty of Tordesillas**. England, France, and Holland did not accept the treaty. Spanish explorers were called **conquistadors**. **Juan Ponce de León** was the first Spanish explorer to touch mainland North America. He named Florida and claimed it for Spain. In 1519 **Hernán Cortés** conquered the Aztec Empire in what is now Mexico. Others explored the region around the Gulf of Mexico. They also explored as far north as the Carolinas and Tennessee. In 1540 **Francisco Vásquez de Coronado** explored the American Southwest. Still others visited the coast of California.

> **Who did not accept the Treaty of Tordesillas?**
> _____
> _____
> _____

> **Underline the names of the places the Spanish explored.**

SPAIN BUILDS AN EMPIRE

To govern its American colonies, Spain divided them into provinces called viceroyalties. A new social order developed. At the top were those who came from Spain. Then came people of pure Spanish blood born in America. Below them were people of mixed Spanish and Native American blood, then people of mixed Spanish and African descent, pure-blooded Native Americans, and Africans.

Spain sent Roman Catholic **missionaries**. These were church members who taught and converted others to Christianity. Spanish colonists first used Native Americans as workers on the land. They often treated them as slaves. After the Native Americans died of European diseases, Spanish landowners used enslaved Africans to work the land. Native Americans and Africans were also forced to work in silver mines. In 1680 the Pueblo Indians revolted. They were led by a shaman named **Popé**. In the Pueblo Revolt, the Native Americans attacked Santa Fe and tried to wipe out Spanish culture. Spanish soldiers later took it back, but Pueblo culture stayed strong.

> **What groups did the Spanish enslave or try to enslave?**
> _____
> _____

OTHER NATIONS EXPLORE

John Cabot led England's first voyage of exploration to North America in 1497. He landed in Newfoundland. He claimed the land for England. England did not act on the claim until the reign of Elizabeth I, when it became a major naval power. England's ship captains attacked Spanish ships to steal their gold and silver. **Sir Francis Drake** was a famous captain. He raided Spanish ships and towns in Central and South America. In 1588 the Spanish king sent a fleet of ships to attack England. England's navy defeated it.

> **Circle the name of the queen in whose reign the English began to act on their claims.**

In 1524 the French king sent Giovanni de Verrazano to explore the Atlantic coast. Jacques Cartier discovered the St. Lawrence River. He claimed what are now Quebec City and Montréal for France. The French found the area rich in furs and fish. In 1666 Sieur de la Salle explored the Great Lakes region and the Mississippi Valley to the Gulf of Mexico. He claimed the land at the mouth of the Mississippi for France and named it Louisiana.

> **What riches did the French find in the New World?**
> _____
> _____

The Netherlands also explored North America. It sent Henry Hudson, who found what is now called the Hudson River. The Dutch started a colony called New Netherland, now known as New York.

CHALLENGE ACTIVITY

Critical Thinking: Summarize On a world map, draw the line created by the Treaty of Tordesillas. Mark the explorations and claims of all countries.

European Colonies in America

MAIN IDEA
After several failures, the English established a permanent settlement at Jamestown, Virginia.

Key Terms and People

joint-stock company business in which people pool their money hoping to make a profit

John Smith a leader of the Jamestown colony

Powhatan Native American leader in whose territory Jamestown was settled

Pocahontas Powhatan's daughter who helped keep peace between the settlers and the Powhatans

John Rolfe first tobacco grower in Virginia; married Pocahontas

headright 50-acre grant of land that colonists could obtain in various ways

House of Burgesses Virginia assembly that was America's first legislature

indentured servant people who worked for a certain number of years in return for food, shelter, and the voyage to America

Bacon's Rebellion Virginia revolt that resulted from differing views on westward expansion into land reserved for Native Americans

Section Summary

THE FIRST ENGLISH COLONIES

England's first colony was at Roanoke, in present-day Virginia. It did not last. In 1606 King James I gave a charter to two companies, the London Company and the Plymouth Company. These companies were **joint-stock companies**. This meant that investors pooled their money in hopes of making a profit. The companies were responsible for governing and maintaining their colonies.

> **Where was England's first colony?**
> _____

THE JAMESTOWN COLONY

In 1606 the London Company sent three ships with male colonists to Virginia. One of the leaders was Captain **John Smith**. The settlers built Jamestown. The place they chose was low and swampy. It was in the territory of a powerful group of Native Americans. The group went by the name of its leader, **Powhatan**. Many Jamestown settlers died of malaria or dysentery. The settlers spent more time looking for gold than

> **What was wrong with the site of the Jamestown colony?**
> _____
> _____
> _____

European Colonies in America

farming. John Smith helped trade for food with the Native Americans. He was captured by some Powhatans. Smith said Powhatan's daughter **Pocahontas** begged her father to save him. Pocahontas helped keep peace between the settlers and the Powhatans. The company sent more settlers. During the winter of 1609–1610 there was little to eat. The Powhatans attacked the colonists' livestock and kept them from hunting. The settlers called it "the starving time." Many colonists died that winter.

One crop made money for the colony. It was tobacco. The first tobacco grower was **John Rolfe**. He married Pocahontas. Their marriage brought peace between the settlers and the Powhatans. After Pocahontas died, the Powhatan attacks began again.

> **What was 'the starving time"?**
> _____

> **What was the first crop to make money in Virginia?**
> _____

VIRGINIA GROWS AND CHANGES

The king took back the company charter and made Virginia a royal colony. Virginia started to offer **headrights**. These were 50-acre grants of land. The head of a family received a headright for each family member and servant. Skilled artisans and women were brought in. In July 1619 representatives from the communities in Virginia met in an assembly. This was called the **House of Burgesses**. It was America's first legislature.

Settlers sometimes brought in **indentured servants**. These people had to work from four to seven years in return for food, shelter, and their voyage to America. In 1619 the first enslaved Africans were brought to the colony. This was the beginning of slavery in the future United States. As Virginians moved west, there were conflicts with Native Americans. The governor wanted good relations with the Native Americans. The western settlers wanted land reserved for Native Americans. A tobacco planter named Nathaniel Bacon started **Bacon's Rebellion**. He took over Jamestown. When he fell ill and died, the rebellion collapsed.

> **Underline the date when slavery began in the future United States.**

CHALLENGE ACTIVITY

Critical Thinking: Drawing Inferences Develop a list of all the artisans and workers that would be needed to develop a healthy colony.

Interactive Reader and Study Guide

European Colonies in America

MAIN IDEA
The Pilgrims founded colonies in Massachusetts based on Puritan religious ideals, while dissent led to the founding of other New England colonies.

Key Terms and People

Puritans people who wanted to "purify," or reform, the Church of England

William Bradford leader of the Pilgrims who sailed on the *Mayflower*

Mayflower Compact rules that the Pilgrims wrote to keep order in the new settlement

John Winthrop leader of the Massachusetts Bay Colony

Great Migration the moving of 20,000 English people to New England between 1620 and 1643

Roger Williams radical minister who started the settlement of Providence

Anne Hutchinson woman thrown out of Massachusetts for saying people could be spiritual without the help of ministers

royal colony colony under direct control of the king

Pequot War 1637 conflict over land and trade in the Connecticut River Valley

King Philip's War 1675 conflict between Native Americans and settlers; left southern New England open to white settlers

Section Summary

PURITANS FLEE TO FREEDOM

Some English Protestants wanted to reform the Church of England. They were known as **Puritans**. A group of merchants formed a joint-stock company to support Puritans going to America. Members of the first group to go were called Pilgrims. They were led by **William Bradford**. They sailed to the New World on the *Mayflower*. They were supposed to land near the Hudson River, but instead landed near Cape Cod. There they started Plymouth Colony. They wrote and signed the **Mayflower Compact** before they left the ship. It set rules to keep order. The colony's success drew more Puritan colonists. They started a new settlement called the Massachusetts Bay Colony. Its leader was **John Winthrop**. It grew faster than Plymouth. The success of the two colonies led to the **Great Migration**. This brought 20,000 English people to New England between 1620 and 1643.

> **Where were the Pilgrims headed for? Where did they land?**
> _____
> _____
> _____

> **Underline the names of the two colonies formed by Puritans.**

European Colonies in America

DISSENT AMONG THE PURITANS

The Puritans wanted religious freedom for themselves. However, they would not put up with anyone who wanted to worship differently. One minister, Thomas Hooker, and his followers decided to leave the Massachusetts Bay Colony. They went west and settled in the Connecticut River Valley. **Roger Williams** believed that church and state should be separate. He thought that settlers should buy their land, not just take it from the Native Americans. He started a settlement in what is now Rhode Island. **Anne Hutchinson** believed that people did not need a minister's teachings to be spiritual. She was imprisoned and sent away for stating her views. Her brother-in-law started a settlement in what is now New Hampshire. In the late 1600s, most of the colonies came under the direct control of the king. They were then known as **royal colonies**. In 1692 some girls accused several women in Salem of being witches. There were trials and 19 people were executed.

> How did the Puritans feel about religious freedom for people who disagreed with them?
>
> _____
>
> _____
>
> _____

> What did Anne Hutchinson believe?
>
> _____
>
> _____
>
> _____

LIFE IN NEW ENGLAND

The American public school system began in the New England colonies. Boys were better educated than girls. By the early 1700s New England had two colleges. People met in town meetings to choose delegates to colonial assemblies, set taxes, and deal with local issues. At first, the settlers had good relations with the Native Americans. The Native Americans helped the early settlers to survive. However, as the settlers kept taking more land, the Native Americans began to resist. In 1637 a conflict broke out over land in the Connecticut River Valley. The **Pequot War** ended with a massacre of the Pequot people. In 1675 the Wampanoag and other groups attacked and destroyed towns in **King Philip's War**. Most of the Native Americans in the area were killed. This left southern New England open to white settlers.

> Why did the Pequot War and King Philip's War happen?
>
> _____
>
> _____
>
> _____

CHALLENGE ACTIVITY

Critical Thinking: Analyze Find a copy of the Mayflower Compact and write two lists: How is it like the laws we know today and how is it different?

Interactive Reader and Study Guide

European Colonies in America

 MAIN IDEA
Events in England during and after the English Civil War led to a new wave of colonization along the Atlantic coast south of New England.

Key Terms and People

Restoration reign of Charles II of England from 1660 to 1685; restored the monarchy

proprietary colonies grants of land to loyal friends of the king

James Oglethorpe English general who started the colony of Georgia

Quaker member of a Christian group that believed in equality of men and women and direct, personal communication with God

William Penn Quaker who started the colony of Pennsylvania

Lord Baltimore Catholic who started the colony of Maryland

Toleration Act law passed by the Maryland colonial assembly giving all Christians the right to practice their religion

Section Summary

A NEW ERA OF COLONIZATION

In 1660 the English Parliament invited Charles II to be king. His reign is called the **Restoration**. The king owed money to many people. To repay them, he gave them land in America. These new colonies were called **proprietary colonies**. They were ruled by their owners. The king gave his brother James the territory that included the Dutch colony New Netherland. By 1674 the colony was in English hands. It was renamed New York. James gave part of his territory to a friend who called his land New Jersey. Soon ownership of the colonies returned to the crown.

> Why did Charles II give grants of land to his friends?
>
> _____
>
> _____

NEW SOUTHERN COLONIES

Charles II gave the land known as Carolina to a group of eight men. They attracted settlers by offering religious freedom to Christians and a say in government. The southern part of the territory had the port of Charles Town (now Charleston) and large plantations. Rice and indigo were the most important crops. Settlers from the West Indies brought enslaved Africans with them. The northern part of the territory was settled mainly by small farmers who did not

> What were the most important crops in the southern part of Carolina?
>
> _____
>
> _____

Interactive Reader and Study Guide

European Colonies in America

import slaves. There were tensions between the two areas. In 1729 seven of the owners sold their land back to the king. He divided it into North and South Carolina.

Some English military experts wanted to make the colonies more secure by creating a buffer between Spanish Florida and the Carolinas. In order to create the buffer the king gave a charter to **James Oglethorpe**, an English general. He established the colony of Georgia. Oglethorpe wanted the colony to be a home for honest people who had been sent to prison for debt. Slavery was legalized there in 1751. Georgia became a royal colony the next year.

QUAKERS SETTLE PENNSYLVANIA

Of all the groups who did not follow the Church of England, the **Quakers** upset people the most. They believed in direct, personal communication with God. They believed in the equality of all men and women. They also refused to fight in wars. A Quaker named **William Penn** got a grant from the king to form a new colony. He called it Pennsylvania. He advertised the colony widely. Penn recognized the Native Americans' right to land. He bought land from them. In 1701 he gave the colony a charter that set up a representative assembly. Penn also received land from the duke of York to give his colony access to the sea. That land later became Delaware.

> Underline the beliefs held by the Quakers.

THE FOUNDING OF MARYLAND

English Catholics were a minority, but included some important families. **Lord Baltimore** was a Catholic convert. He asked for a grant for land in the Chesapeake Bay area. After he died, his son got the grant and named his colony Maryland. In 1649 the colonial assembly passed the **Toleration Act**. It protected the right of Christians to practice their religion.

> What form of Christianity did the founders of Maryland practice?
>
> _____

CHALLENGE ACTIVITY

Critical Thinking: Drawing Inferences Write three paragraphs describing how experiences in the early colonies might have led to the Constitution's separation of church and state.

Interactive Reader and Study Guide

Colonial Life

Chapter Summary

```
                          ┌─────────────────┐
                          │      Life       │
                          │  in the Colonies│
                          └─────────────────┘
```

Political
- The Navigation Acts and the Dominion of New England: two attempts by England to gain more control over the colonies
- Salutary neglect of the colonies brought about colonial self-government

Economic
- Northern economy: farming, shipbuilding, trade, commerce
- Southern economy: plantation farming (tobacco, rice, indigo)
- Slavery in the northern and southern colonies provided agricultural workers, servants, and artisans

Social
- The European Enlightenment spread to the colonies, bringing ideas of law and individual rights
- The Great Awakening increased church membership
- Immigration from other countries increased diversity in the colonies

Military
- The French and Indian War (1754–1763): France and Great Britain clash over territory in North America
- Treaty of Paris (1763) redraws lines in North America, with England and Spain claiming the most territory

COMPREHENSION AND CRITICAL THINKING
Use information from the graphic organizer to answer the following questions.

1. **Identify** What were two ways in which England attempted to gain more control over the colonies?

_____

_____

2. **Recall** What treaty gave England more territory in North America?

_____

3. **Compare and Contrast** What similarities and differences were there in the economies of the northern and southern colonies?

_____

_____

_____

4. **Predict** What effect will the Enlightenment most likely have on the English colonies?

_____

_____

MAIN IDEA
British mercantilist policies and political issues helped shape the development of the American colonies.

Key Terms and People

mercantilism economic policy that said that a nation's power was directly related to its wealth

balance of trade the relationship between a country's imports and exports

Navigation Acts group of laws aimed at controlling colonial trade and making sure that the colonies made money for England

Dominion of New England a kind of supercolony created by King James II that included all of New England, New York, and New Jersey

William and Mary Protestants who became King and Queen of England in the Glorious Revolution

Glorious Revolution change of English monarchs from James II to William and Mary

English Bill of Rights document that gave Parliament the right to control taxes and set limits on the monarch's powers

confederation a group in which each member keeps control of its own internal affairs

salutary neglect a policy under which England did not control the colonies very strictly and they benefited from being left alone

Section Summary

MERCANTILISM

According to the economic policy of **mercantilism**, a nation's power came from its wealth. England made a profit on its American colonies because the colonists supplied raw materials. They also bought English goods. Another goal of mercantilism was a favorable **balance of trade**. This is the relationship between a country's imports and exports. Exports should be greater than imports to be favorable. England wanted to keep the colonies from trading with other countries. The colonists disliked England's attempts to control them.

England passed a group of laws called the **Navigation Acts**. These laws controlled ships, their crews, and their destinations. They placed taxes on many goods. Most colonists disliked the laws. Many ignored them. Some took part in smuggling.

> **Underline two ideas linked to mercantilism.**

> **How did the colonists react to the Navigation Acts?**
> _____
> _____
> _____

Colonial Life

THE GLORIOUS REVOLUTION AND
THE ENGLISH BILL OF RIGHTS

When the English restored King Charles II to rule, many Puritans refused to accept him. King Charles made Massachusetts a royal colony. When he died, his brother, King James II, created the **Dominion of New England**. This was a kind of supercolony that included all of New England, New York, and New Jersey. Its governor made the colonists angry. Meanwhile, James also angered the English. They replaced the Catholic James II with two Protestants, **William and Mary**. This peaceful change was called the **Glorious Revolution**. William and Mary accepted the **English Bill of Rights**. This document let Parliament limit the monarchs' powers. It also protected freedom of speech for members of Parliament and gave them control of taxes. The colonists did not hear of the Glorious Revolution until the next spring. After a small rebellion, they brought an end to the Dominion of New England.

> **Underline the names of the rulers of England during this time period.**

> **What happened to the Dominion of New England after the Glorious Revolution?**
>
> _____

GOVERNMENT IN THE COLONIES

Colonists wanted to claim their rights as English citizens. In 1643 several colonies formed the New England Confederation. A **confederation** is a group in which each member keeps control of its own internal affairs. The British set up a Board of Trade to handle colonial affairs. However, the colonies did have some say in their government. Rule over the colonies was not strict. It was called **salutary neglect**. This means that the colonies benefited from being left alone. Local governments were more important in colonial life than faraway English officials. Nearly all the colonies had colonial assemblies. Each colony had a governor. Governors were either appointed by the monarch or the colony's owner. Most governors had no way of enforcing their decisions.

> **Why might the colonies benefit from being neglected?**
>
> _____
>
> _____
>
> _____

CHALLENGE ACTIVITY

Critical Thinking: Drawing Inferences Develop a Bill of Rights that you think should apply to all students.

Interactive Reader and Study Guide

MAIN IDEA
A commerce-based economy developed in the northern colonies, while the southern colonies developed an agricultural economy.

Key Terms and People

triangular trade trade routes that linked the Americas, Africa, and the West Indies

Middle Passage name used for the horrific trip that enslaved Africans made across the Atlantic Ocean

cash crop a farm product grown to be sold

Eliza Lucas first person to grow a successful indigo crop

Olaudah Equiano former slave whose memoirs describe the Middle Passage

yeoman an independent small farmer

Stono Rebellion the major slave revolt of the colonial period

Section Summary

NORTHERN COLONIAL ECONOMIES

It was hard to farm in New England. Many colonists could only grow what they needed. In the middle colonies farming was easier. Farmers grew wheat and raised cattle and hogs. They were able to produce enough to export. The most productive farmers lived in Pennsylvania. The thick forests and fur-bearing animals of North America were valuable resources. So were timber and fish. Shipbuilding became important to many coastal towns. New Englanders started the whaling industry. However, under the Navigation Acts, colonial industries were not supposed to compete with England. This slowed industrial growth. However, some small industries developed to meet local needs.

Trade routes connected the Americas, Africa, and the West Indies. They were called the **triangular trade**. Ships from New England carried rum to Africa to trade for enslaved Africans. The Africans were traded to the West Indies for sugar and molasses. These were then shipped to New England to be made into rum. The horrible trip that enslaved Africans made across the Atlantic was called the **Middle Passage**. This was the middle leg of the triangle.

> Underline the items that were grown and raised in the middle colonies.

> Which places made up the triangular trade?
>
> _____
>
> _____

SOUTHERN COLONIAL ECONOMIES

The southern economy was based on agriculture. The southern colonies produced **cash crops**. These are farm products grown to be sold. One cash crop was tobacco. Others included indigo and rice. Indigo is a plant used to make blue dye. Southerners also produced naval stores such as rope, tar, and turpentine. These were used to maintain ships.

> Underline the three cash crops grown in the South.

The plantation system grew in Virginia and Maryland and spread south. A plantation is a large farm with an unskilled labor force. It produces a cash crop such as sugar or tobacco. Plantations needed workers. This encouraged slavery.

Rice and indigo were the chief crops in South Carolina. Rice growing was difficult and dangerous. Free workers would not do it. Many enslaved Africans already knew how to grow rice. The first successful indigo crop was grown by **Eliza Lucas**. She was only 17 years old when she experimented with the crop on her father's plantations.

> Who was Eliza Lucas?
> _____
> _____
> _____

THE IMPACT OF SLAVERY

By the 1600s Portugal, Spain, France, Holland, and England were involved in the slave trade. Some Africans who later gained their freedom described how horrible the Middle Passage was. One of them was **Olaudah Equiano**. He wrote about his terrible experiences as an enslaved African.

Slavery existed in all the English colonies. Slaves made up a small part of the population in New England, Pennsylvania, and Delaware. Most people in those colonies were yeomen. A **yeoman** is an independent small farmer. Most of the enslaved Africans were in the plantation states. Many Africans resisted slavery. Some ran away. Others found ways of rebelling. The major revolt in the colonial period was the **Stono Rebellion**. This took place in South Carolina in 1739.

> Why were there fewer slaves in the northern colonies than in the southern ones?
> _____
> _____
> _____

CHALLENGE ACTIVITY

Critical Thinking: Elaborate Do research on slave ships. Find out how many people were packed into how much space. Mark a similar space in your classroom.

Interactive Reader and Study Guide

MAIN IDEA
Enlightenment ideas and the Great Awakening brought new ways of thinking to the colonists, and a unique American culture developed.

Key Terms and People

Enlightenment European movement involving new ways of thinking

social contract the understanding that a government should protect its people's rights

Benjamin Franklin famous American of many talents; revised the Declaration of Independence and was the oldest delegate to the Constitutional Convention

Great Awakening a religious revival in the colonies

Jonathan Edwards Puritan clergy who was one of the leaders of the Great Awakening

George Whitefield British Methodist minister who preached in the colonies during the Great Awakening

Section Summary

THE ENLIGHTENMENT AND THE AMERICAN COLONIES

In the late 1600s Europeans came up with new ways of thinking about government and human rights. Their new ideas brought about the **Enlightenment**. This was a movement that stressed the search for knowledge. Scientists began using the scientific method. They observed nature and conducted experiments to learn. Other thinkers admired this new approach to science. They wanted to use logic and reason to make the world better.

English philosopher John Locke said that people had a **social contract** with their government. This meant that the government should protect its people's rights. If it didn't, the people had the right to overthrow the government. Some of Locke's thoughts were used in the Declaration of Independence. Philosophers looked at education, religion, and social reform in new ways.

In America, the Enlightenment affected **Benjamin Franklin** and others. Franklin was a man of many talents. He was interested in science and inventions. He revised the Declaration of Independence. He also served as an ambassador and as a delegate to the Constitutional Convention.

> **Underline what the Enlightenment stressed.**

> **Circle the name of the man whose thoughts appeared in the Declaration of Independence.**

Colonial Life

THE GREAT AWAKENING

A religious revival took place in the colonies. It was called the **Great Awakening**. One of its leaders was **Jonathan Edwards**. He was a Puritan. His preaching appealed to people's fears and emotions. Another leader was **George Whitefield**. He was a British Methodist minister who preached to large crowds in America. The Great Awakening increased church membership. It also linked the colonies together.

> What did Jonathan Edwards appeal to?
> _____
> _____

THE COLONIES BECOME MORE DIVERSE

At first, the colonists were mostly English. Then large numbers of Scots and Scots-Irish came. Religious unrest in Europe brought Germans, French Huguenots, and Jews. Many of the people in these new groups were skilled farmers and artisans.

> Circle the names of the new groups of people who came to the colonies.

LIFE IN COLONIAL AMERICA

Colonial cities were lively and exciting. There were libraries, bookshops, and large public buildings. There were plays and concerts. People enjoyed horse racing, hunting, and dancing.

Printers printed and distributed newspapers, books, advertisements, and political announcements. Ben Franklin helped improve the postal service between colonies. In 1734 a newspaper publisher was arrested for printing material that criticized the governor. The publisher went on to win the first court victory for freedom of the press.

Enslaved Africans created their own culture in spite of their hardships. Families were often broken up by the sale of members. Strong kinship ties helped those who were separated from their real families.

> What were some of the activities available to the colonists?
> _____
> _____
> _____

CHALLENGE ACTIVITY

Critical Thinking: Drawing Inferences Research colonial life in a colony of your choosing. Write a letter to a friend or relative in another colony describing what your life is like.

MAIN IDEA
The French and Indian War established British dominance in North America but put a strain on the relationship with the colonists.

Key Terms and People

Iroquois League an alliance of Native Americans who sided with the British against the French

George Washington leader of Virginia militia sent to try to get the French to leave the Ohio Valley; later took command of British troops in French and Indian War

Albany Plan of Union plan proposed by Benjamin Franklin to unite the colonies

William Pitt British secretary of state during the French and Indian War

Treaty of Paris peace treaty that ended the French and Indian War and gave Britain all French land east of the Mississippi

George Grenville British prime minister after the war who wanted to be strict with the colonies

Pontiac chief of the Ottawa nation in Michigan; headed an alliance that tried to drive the British out of Native American lands

Proclamation of 1763 British document that gave the land west of the Appalachian Mountains to Native Americans

Section Summary

FRANCE IN NORTH AMERICA

The first permanent French settlement in North America began in 1608. Later, the French claimed the Mississippi Valley. English and French fur traders started fighting in the 1600s. Both sides had Native American allies. By the early 1700s French forts formed a ring around the English colonies. There were almost constant battles along the frontier.

> **When did the English and French start fighting?**
> _____
> _____

SPAIN AND ENGLAND CLASH

Both Spain and England claimed territory in the area of Florida, Georgia, and South Carolina. Spanish missionaries started missions along the Georgia coast. English colonies expanded southward and threatened the missions. Carolina slave raiders attacked the Spanish missions. By 1700 Spain had a presence in only St. Augustine and Pensacola.

> **In what area were Spain and England in dispute?**
> _____
> _____

Colonial Life

THE FRENCH AND INDIAN WAR

The French and Indian War lasted from 1754 to 1763. It was part of a larger war between France and Great Britain called the Seven Years' War. Spain and its colonies also joined forces with Britain. The **Iroquois League** sided with the British. This league had been formed nearly 200 years before. Its members were Native Americans who lived in upstate New York. It had a constitution and a council of leaders.

In 1754 **George Washington** led troops that tried to move the French out of the Ohio Valley. England claimed this area. The mission was unsuccessful.

To help unite the colonies, Benjamin Franklin proposed the **Albany Plan of Union**. However, it was never approved.

The war at first went badly for the British. Then **William Pitt** became secretary of state. British officers began forcing colonists to help in the war. Pitt sent more British troops to America. The British won the war. The **Treaty of Paris** was signed in 1763. England gained all French territory east of the Mississippi River. Spain won the Louisiana Territory from France.

> How old was the Iroquois League at the start of the French and Indian War?
>
> _____

> Underline the areas that England and Spain got in the Treaty of Paris.

EFFECTS OF THE WAR

The war had forced the colonists to work together. It had been an expensive war for England. There was a new prime minister, **George Grenville**. He wanted the colonies to help pay for the war. He also wanted to be stricter with them.

The Treaty of Paris gave Britain control over the Great Lakes region. An alliance of Native Americans under the leader **Pontiac** resisted the British. There was a war. The **Proclamation of 1763** gave Native Americans the land west of the Appalachian Mountains.

> How did Native Americans react to British control over the Great Lakes region?
>
> _____
>
> _____
>
> _____

CHALLENGE ACTIVITY

Critical Thinking: Elaborate Do research on the Iroquois League. Write a report for your class on its constitution and council of leaders.

The Revolutionary Era

Chapter Summary

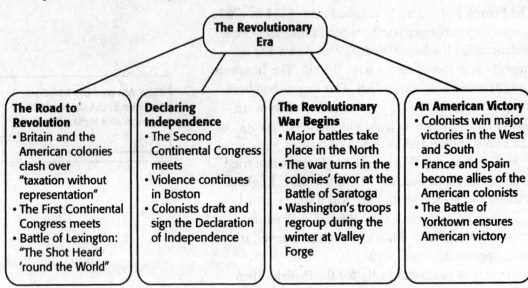

The Revolutionary Era

The Road to Revolution
- Britain and the American colonies clash over "taxation without representation"
- The First Continental Congress meets
- Battle of Lexington: "The Shot Heard 'round the World"

Declaring Independence
- The Second Continental Congress meets
- Violence continues in Boston
- Colonists draft and sign the Declaration of Independence

The Revolutionary War Begins
- Major battles take place in the North
- The war turns in the colonies' favor at the Battle of Saratoga
- Washington's troops regroup during the winter at Valley Forge

An American Victory
- Colonists win major victories in the West and South
- France and Spain become allies of the American colonists
- The Battle of Yorktown ensures American victory

COMPREHENSION AND CRITICAL THINKING

Use information from the graphic organizer to answer the following questions.

1. **Identify** Where was "The Shot Heard 'round the World" fired?

_____

2. **Explain** Over what issue did Britain and the American colonies clash?

_____

_____

_____

3. **Identify** What was the turning point in the Revolutionary War?

_____

_____

_____

4. **Recall** Which two European nations became allies of the Americans?

_____

_____

The Revolutionary Era

MAIN IDEA
A series of increasingly restrictive laws angered many American colonists, leading to rebellion against Britain.

Key Terms and People

Samuel Adams prominent Boston rebel

Stamp Act British law that required a government tax stamp on all legal documents

writs of assistance British law that gave customs officers the right to search colonial homes without a search warrant

Boston Massacre fight between Bostonians and British soldiers that left five colonists dead

Committees of Correspondence groups formed to spread news of British injustices from colony to colony

Intolerable Acts set of four British laws intended to punish colonists; one law closed the port of Boston

First Continental Congress meeting in 1774 of delegates from all the colonies

minutemen colonial soldiers who would be ready to resist a British attack at short notice

Section Summary

BRITAIN PASSES NEW LAWS

The French and Indian War left Britain with huge debts. It also left 10,000 British soldiers in America. The British thought the Americans should pay the costs. They passed a law that taxed sugar and molasses imported from the French and Spanish West Indies. **Samuel Adams** of Boston declared that it was wrong to make colonists pay taxes when they had no representation in Parliament. In 1765 Britain passed the **Stamp Act**. This said that all legal documents had to have a government tax stamp. The Quartering Act forced colonists to find living space for British soldiers in America. These laws angered the colonists. More laws were passed. One allowed **writs of assistance**. These gave customs officers the right to search houses without a search warrant.

> **What war left Britain with huge debts?**
> _____
> _____

> **What was the Stamp Act?**
> _____
> _____
> _____

THE COLONISTS RESPOND

Merchants in Boston, New York, and Philadelphia agreed not to import taxed items. Except for the tax on

Interactive Reader and Study Guide

tea, most of the taxes were repealed. People were still angry with the British. In 1770 colonists began throwing snowballs at British soldiers. The soldiers shot at them and killed five people. This was known as the **Boston Massacre**. Samuel Adams came up with the idea of **Committees of Correspondence**. These groups would spread news of British injustices from one colony to another. To punish the colonists, the British passed the **Intolerable Acts**. One of these laws closed the port of Boston.

> How many people were killed at the Boston Massacre?
> _____

THE FIRST CONTINENTAL CONGRESS

In 1774 delegates from all the colonies met in the **First Continental Congress**. This brought the colonists some unity. The Congress protested British actions. They issued a Declaration of Rights. They also agreed not to import or use British goods and to stop most exports to Britain. They formed a force of **minutemen**. These were colonial soldiers who would be ready to resist a British attack at short notice. The Congress agreed to meet again the following spring.

> Underline the things that the First Continental Congress did.

THE BATTLES OF
LEXINGTON AND CONCORD

Before the Continental Congress could meet again, war began in Massachusetts. The British tried to seize gunpowder the colonists had stored in Concord. Paul Revere and others rode to alert the colonists. The minutemen met the British at Lexington. This was the first battle of the Revolutionary War. The British then went to Concord. After an exchange of gunfire, the British retreated toward Boston.

> Where was the first battle of the Revolution?
> _____

CHALLENGE ACTIVITY

Critical Thinking: Elaborate Read Henry Wadsworth Longfellow's poem *The Midnight Ride of Paul Revere*. Write another stanza for it.

The Revolutionary Era

MAIN IDEA
As a revolutionary ideology grew and conflicts with Britain continued, the Second Continental Congress declared American independence.

Key Terms and People

Second Continental Congress meeting in 1775 of delegates from all the colonies

Thomas Jefferson Virginia delegate to the Second Continental Congress; wrote the first draft of the Declaration of Independence

Continental Army colonial army formed by the Second Continental Congress

John Adams Massachusetts delegate to the Second Continental Congress; suggested Washington should lead the Continental Army

Battle of Bunker Hill first major battle of the American Revolution

Loyalist colonist on the side of Britain

Thomas Paine influential writer who supported American independence

Common Sense Paine's pamphlet that argued in favor of independence

Virginia Declaration of Rights first official call for American independence; issued by the Virginia Convention in 1776

Abigail Adams wife of John Adams who became famous for her letters to her husband

Section Summary

THE SECOND CONTINENTAL CONGRESS TAKES ACTION

The **Second Continental Congress** met in 1775. Members included Benjamin Franklin, John Hancock, and **Thomas Jefferson**. Some delegates wanted independence. Others were loyal to Britain. However, since war had already begun in New England the Congress formed a **Continental Army**. **John Adams**, from Massachusetts, suggested that George Washington command the army. The Congress agreed. It issued two documents. One explained why the colonists took up arms. The other asked the king to use his authority to settle differences. The king declared the colonies to be in rebellion.

> Who commanded the Continental Army?
>
> _____
> _____

> How did the king respond to the colonists' petition for reconciliation?
>
> _____
> _____
> _____

MORE VIOLENCE IN BOSTON

Fighting was going on in several places. The Green Mountain Boys, a colonial force, captured Fort

The Revolutionary Era

Ticonderoga from the British. The British occupied Boston. This led to the **Battle of Bunker Hill**. It was the first major battle of the Revolutionary War. The British won. However, the colonists had fought well. This raised their confidence. In March 1776, with Washington in command, the colonists gained control of Boston. The British and many **Loyalists** fled. Loyalists were people who sympathized with Britain. In the winter of 1775–1776 Benedict Arnold led an unsuccessful colonial attack on Quebec. In the South, the colonists were able to stop a British invasion.

> Underline the name of the first major battle of the American Revolution.

THE DECLARATION OF INDEPENDENCE

The ideas of natural rights and the social contract were important to many colonial leaders. **Thomas Paine** helped make these ideas clear to ordinary Americans. He wrote a pamphlet called *Common Sense*. It persuaded many Americans to support independence. In May 1776 the Virginia Convention of Delegates issued the **Virginia Declaration of Rights**. It called for American independence. In June a Virginia delegate presented a resolution in favor of independence to the Continental Congress. Thomas Jefferson was chosen to write the first draft of a declaration. Other men made some changes. The Congress approved the Declaration of Independence on July 4, 1776.

> Circle the date when the Declaration of Independence was approved.

REACTIONS TO INDEPENDENCE

About one-fourth of the colonists stayed loyal to Britain. Loyalist sympathies were especially strong among former government officials and members of the Anglican Church. Several regiments of Loyalists fought with the British. Some Loyalists left the country. **Abigail Adams** described the Patriot celebrations in Boston. She wrote many letters to her husband, John Adams. He was a delegate serving in the Continental Congress in Philadelphia.

> Who was Abigail Adams?
> _____
> _____

CHALLENGE ACTIVITY

Critical Thinking: Elaborate Read a selection of Abigail Adams's letters to her husband. Make a quote board containing some of her ideas.

Interactive Reader and Study Guide

Section 3

> **MAIN IDEA**
> While the colonies and the British began with different strengths and weaknesses,
> the Revolutionary War demonstrated Washington's great leadership.

Key Terms and People

Redcoats British soldiers who wore red coats

Battle of Saratoga battle won by the Americans; considered the turning point of the
Revolutionary War

Valley Forge place where the Continental Army survived a bitter winter

inflation a fall in the value of paper money, accompanied by a rise in prices

Marquis de Lafayette French noble who came to help the American cause

Section Summary

THE PEOPLE BEHIND THE
AMERICAN REVOLUTION

When the war began, Britain was a world power. It
had a well-trained army of soldiers, known as
Redcoats for their red uniforms. However, the British
army also hired many German soldiers. The Americans
had fewer soldiers. They were not well trained. There
was no navy. The Continental Congress was short of
money. It was hard to get arms and supplies.

Patriot women found ways to take part in the war.
A few disguised themselves as men and became
soldiers. Others helped the troops. Some served as
couriers, scouts, and spies. Some turned their homes
into hospitals. Some raised money. Some knit wool
stockings and made bandages.

African Americans also participated. They fought
on both sides. Sometimes the British offered them
their freedom if they would fight on their side. There
were African Americans in the New England forces.
James Middleton led a Massachusetts regiment. He
was the only black commissioned officer in the
Continental Army. Most African American soldiers
were given lowly duties.

Some Native Americans supported the British.
Others supported the Americans.

From where did the British hire soldiers?
_____

Underline the ways that women served the Patriot cause.

The Revolutionary Era

Section 3

REVOLUTIONARY BATTLES IN THE NORTH

The British captured New York. The American soldiers were forced across the river into New Jersey and then Pennsylvania. In traditional European warfare, armies did not fight in the winter. Washington did not follow those rules. On Christmas night of 1776 he and the army crossed the Delaware River and occupied Trenton, New Jersey. Next, he and the army captured Princeton. British troops under General Howe captured Philadelphia. The Continental Congress fled the city.

How did Washington break the rules of warfare?
_____
_____

A BRITISH SETBACK AT SARATOGA

British General Burgoyne led a campaign in upstate New York. He planned to meet other British troops at Albany. At Saratoga, Burgoyne and his troops found themselves surrounded by American troops. On October 17, 1777, the British were forced to surrender. The **Battle of Saratoga** is considered the turning point of the war.

What battle was the turning point of the Revolutionary War?
_____
_____

WASHINGTON'S LEADERSHIP AT VALLEY FORGE

The winter of 1777–1778 was a low point in the Revolution. The American army wintered at **Valley Forge**. It was bitterly cold. Food was scarce. The men wore ragged uniforms and lived in tents. Washington's character and common sense held the forces together.

Paying for the war was a problem. The Congress did not have the power to tax. The value of paper money fell, and prices rose. This is called **inflation**. Some farmers and merchants chose to sell to the British, who had gold. This caused food shortages at Valley Forge. However, the American cause found support in Europe. One European who came to help was the **Marquis de Lafayette**. He was a French noble who became Washington's aide.

Why was paying for the war a problem?
_____
_____

CHALLENGE ACTIVITY

Critical Thinking: Drawing Inferences Do research on Generals Gates, Schuyler, and Arnold. Write a two-page report on the roles they played during the Battle of Saratoga.

The Revolutionary Era

Section 4

MAIN IDEA
A strengthened Continental Army, along with European allies, helped the colonists achieve a victory at Yorktown.

Key Terms and People

George Rogers Clark Kentucky pioneer who led colonial forces against the British in the West

Nathanael Greene commander of colonial forces in the Carolinas

Charles Cornwallis British commander in the South

Count de Rochambeau general who led 6,000 French soldiers on the side of the Americans

Bernardo de Gálvez Spanish governor of Louisiana who attacked British forts

Battle of Yorktown battle that led to Cornwallis's surrender

Treaty of Paris 1783 treaty that ended the American Revolution

Section Summary

REVOLUTIONARY BATTLES IN THE WEST AND SOUTH

After the Battle of Saratoga, military action shifted to the South and the West. **George Rogers Clark** led an expedition against the British. Clark was a Kentucky pioneer. He led a small force down the Ohio River. Clark's men captured British settlements in present-day Illinois. Later he captured Vincennes.

In 1778 the British shifted their strategy. They planned to campaign in the South. Loyalist sympathies seemed to be strongest there. However, the British soon found that the Patriots were just as strong there as in New England. The British faced many surprise raids. A new American general took over colonial forces in the South. His name was **Nathanael Greene**. His troops fought the troops of **Charles Cornwallis** at Guilford Court House. The British won, but with very heavy losses.

> **Why did the British move their campaign to the South?**
> _____
> _____
> _____

> **Circle the name of the American general in the South.**

AMERICA'S EUROPEAN ALLIES

France became America's strongest ally. Spain and the Netherlands also gave aid. At first the French government sent guns and ammunition. After the

The Revolutionary Era

Battle of Saratoga, France formally recognized the United States as a nation. They sent an army. It was led by a French general, the **Count of Rochambeau**. Spain joined the war in 1779. The Spanish governor of Louisiana was **Bernardo de Gálvez**. He attacked British forts on the Mississippi and the Gulf Coast of Florida. He defeated the British in Baton Rouge, Natchez, Mobile, and Pensacola.

> **Who was the Count of Rochambeau?**
> _____
> _____

VICTORY AT YORKTOWN

Washington sent Lafayette to Virginia to stop Cornwallis. In July 1781 Cornwallis built a fort at Yorktown. He thought British ships would come to take his troops to Charleston or New York. However, France's Caribbean fleet blockaded the sea around Yorktown. Lafayette kept Cornwallis trapped on the peninsula until Washington and Rochambeau got there. The **Battle of Yorktown** lasted about three weeks. Cornwallis surrendered on October 19, 1781. This was the end of the war. It took two years to negotiate a peace treaty. The **Treaty of Paris** was not signed until 1783.

> **Why did Cornwallis go to Yorktown?**
> _____
> _____

REVOLUTION CHANGES AMERICA

After the war, politics became more democratic. More men got to vote. There was a new idea of equality. However, women did not gain any rights. Married women still could not sign contracts or own property. In 1780 Pennsylvania passed a law for the gradual end of slavery. In the 1780s the New England states also ended slavery. Change came more slowly to the South. Many states passed laws separating church and state. There were many economic problems as a result of the war. It had cost a lot of money. The Continental Congress had borrowed to pay for it. Soon it would meet again. It would discuss economic issues and a new system of government.

> **Which states ended slavery after the war?**
> _____
> _____

CHALLENGE ACTIVITY

Critical Thinking: Elaborate Read Thomas Jefferson's Statute of Religious Liberty. Summarize what you read in one page.

Interactive Reader and Study Guide

Creating a New Government

Chapter Summary

┌─────────────────────────────────────┐
The Articles of Confederation
(ratified 1781)

• America's first written constitution

• A loose union of sovereign states

• Designed to make the central
government weak because early leaders
feared tyranny
└─────────────────────────────────────┘

┌─────────────────────────────────────┐
The U.S. Constitution
(ratified 1788)

• Replaced the Articles of Confederation

• Provided representation for all states

• Established three branches of
government (executive, legislative,
judicial) with separation of powers
to avoid tyranny

• Created checks and balances among the
three branches

• Included the Bill of Rights (ratified 1791)
└─────────────────────────────────────┘

COMPREHENSION AND CRITICAL THINKING

Use information from the graphic organizer to answer the following questions.

1. **Identify** What was the name of America's first written constitution?

_____

_____

2. **Explain** Why did early leaders make the central government weak in the Articles of
Confederation?

_____

_____

3. **Recall** What three branches of government did the Constitution create?

_____

_____

4. **Summarize** How did the Constitution keep one branch of government from
becoming too powerful?

_____

_____

_____

Creating a New Government

MAIN IDEA
In order to carry on the war and build a new nation, Americans had to create a framework of government, but their first attempt had many weaknesses.

Key Terms and People

legislative branch the part of government that makes laws

judicial branch the part of government that interprets the laws

executive branch the part of government that carries out the laws

republic a form of government without a king or queen

Articles of Confederation America's first national constitution

Land Ordinance of 1785 plan for settling and dividing the Northwest Territory

Northwest Ordinance law that governed how territories could become states

Section Summary

THE AMERICAN REPUBLIC

While Americans were fighting the Revolution, the states were also setting up new governments. Their state constitutions were similar. Each called for three branches. The **legislative branch** made the laws. The **judicial branch** interpreted the laws. The **executive branch**, the governor, carried out the laws. The states limited governors' power. They gave more power to the elected legislatures. Americans wanted a **republic**. This is a form of government that does not have a king or queen. No nation in the world at that time had such a government.

The Revolutionary War brought a change in women's roles. Many people believed in republican motherhood. This idea encouraged mothers to raise their sons to be patriotic future leaders. Mothers were to raise daughters to be intelligent, patriotic, and competent. The daughters would in turn educate their own children.

> **What branch of government had the most power under the state constitutions?**
>
> _____

> **Did any other countries have a republic for their government at this time?**
>
> _____

A NEW NATIONAL GOVERNMENT

America's first national constitution was the **Articles of Confederation**. The states kept most of their power, but a weak national government was established. The national government had only one

> **Who had the most power under the Articles of Confederation?**
>
> _____

Creating a New Government

branch, the Continental Congress. The Congress could make national policies and handle foreign relations. It could borrow and coin money. It also had the power to create an army and declare war.

THE CONFEDERATION FACES PROBLEMS

The new government had problems with money. The end of the war brought economic problems to all areas of the country. There were large war debts. The Congress did not have the power to tax. It asked the states for money. However, they did not give as much as they were asked for. Some soldiers who fought in the war were not paid. Paper money that had been issued during the war was not backed by gold or silver. States refused to accept it for payment of taxes. Poor farmers were hurt by the taxes. They began rebellions in several places. Congress could not settle disputes between states. The new government also had problems dealing with foreign governments.

> **What power did the Confederation lack that kept it short of money?**
> _____

THE NORTHWEST TERRITORY

Under the Articles of Confederation, the government created a pattern for settlement of the western lands. A plan was needed to settle the Northwest Territory. This was the area north and west of the Ohio River. The Congress passed the **Land Ordinance of 1785**. Under that law, the land was to be divided into a grid of townships. Each township would be six miles square. Each township would be divided into sections. The government would own some of these. As the United States expanded westward, other territories followed the same plan. In 1787 the Congress passed the **Northwest Ordinance**. This law governed how territories could become states. It guaranteed religious freedom and other civil rights. It also prohibited slavery in the Northwest Territory.

> **What did the Northwest Ordinance say about slavery?**
> _____
> _____

CHALLENGE ACTIVITY

Critical Thinking: Analyzing Primary Sources Read 10 pages of John Locke's *Two Treatises on Civil Government*. Summarize your reading in one page.

Creating a New Government

MAIN IDEA
The Constitutional Convention tried to write a document that would address the weaknesses of the Articles of Confederation and make compromises between large and small states and between the North and South.

Key Terms and People

James Madison American leader; often called the Father of the Constitution

Constitutional Convention 1787 meeting to write a new constitution

Virginia Plan plan for a government with a two-house legislature

New Jersey Plan plan for a government with a one-house legislature and two or three executives

Great Compromise plan for a government with a two-house legislature; in one house the number of representatives would be based on the state's population, and in the other house each state would have the same number of representatives

Three-Fifths Compromise agreement to count three-fifths of the slave population for purposes of taxation and representation

checks and balances system that keeps one branch of government from getting too much control

Section Summary

THE CONSTITUTIONAL CONVENTION

There was much frustration with the Articles of Confederation. There were also small rebellions. In fall 1786 George Washington and **James Madison** called a meeting of five states to discuss the problems. In 1787 Congress called all states to meet to revise the Articles of Confederation. This meeting was the **Constitutional Convention**. Delegates from 12 states came. Madison kept a detailed diary of what went on in the meetings. He played a big role in planning and writing the final document. Because of this, Madison is often called the Father of the Constitution.

All the delegates were men. Many were well-educated, and most were wealthy. Some famous Patriots did not attend because they did not want a strong central government. One difficulty was finding a balance between large states and small states. The **Virginia Plan** called for a two-house legislature. Members of the lower house would be chosen in proportion to each state's population. The members of

> Underline the date when the Constitutional Convention began.

> Why did some Patriots not attend the Constitutional Convention?
>
> _____
>
> _____

Creating a New Government

the lower house would choose the members of the upper house. The **New Jersey Plan** called for a one-house legislature where each state would have the same number of representatives. It also suggested that there be two or three top executives.

> Underline the proposals under the New Jersey Plan.

COMPROMISES AT THE CONVENTION

The Connecticut delegates came up with a compromise. They suggested a two-house legislature. In one house the number of representatives would be based on a state's population. In the other house, each state would have the same number of representatives. This **Great Compromise** was accepted. However, there were still other disagreements. Southern states wanted to count slaves for purposes of representation. They did not want to count them for purposes of taxation. The **Three-Fifths Compromise** called for counting three-fifths of the slave population for both purposes. The delegates went on to consider many other questions, such as how the executive would be chosen.

> What was the result of the Great Compromise?
> _____
> _____
> _____
> _____
> _____

CHECKS AND BALANCES

An important point for the writers of the Constitution was keeping the balance between the Congress and the executive, who would be known as the president. They were also concerned with balancing the powers of the states with those of the federal government. They had to work out a new compromise for selecting the president. The writers decided to have the state legislatures choose electors. These in turn would select the president. This took away some power from Congress. Then the office of vice president was created. These last-minute changes helped set up a system of **checks and balances**. These ensured that no one branch of government would get too much control. Benjamin Franklin urged everyone to sign the finished document. However, some writers refused because the Constitution did not have a bill of rights.

> What was the result of the compromise regarding how the president was selected?
> _____
> _____
> _____

CHALLENGE ACTIVITY

Critical Thinking: Solving Problems Develop a constitution for your family. Include the rights and responsibilities of each member.

Creating a New Government

 MAIN IDEA
Federalists and Antifederalists struggled over the principles of the new Constitution. But the promise of adding a Bill of Rights brought about ratification.

Key Terms and People

Federalist supporter of the Constitution

Antifederalist opponent of the Constitution

Alexander Hamilton young leader of the Federalists

Brutus name under which Robert Yates wrote anti-Constitution essays

Bill of Rights addition to the Constitution that would spell out and protect basic rights

John Jay one of the writers of *The Federalist*

Publius name under which several Federalists published pro-Constitution essays

The Federalist book in which pro-Constitution essays were collected

delegated powers powers given by the Constitution to the national government

reserved powers powers not specifically given to the national government and therefore belonging to the states or the people

Section Summary

FEDERALISTS AND ANTIFEDERALISTS

Delegates to the Constitutional Convention were expected to revise the Articles of Confederation. Instead, they wrote a new document. Some people were surprised and angry when it was published. There was a 10-month struggle over its approval. People in favor of the Constitution came to be called **Federalists**. People against it were called **Antifederalists**. The Federalists had strong leaders, including James Madison, John Dickinson, and **Alexander Hamilton**.

The Antifederalists were less organized and less unified. They did not trust any central authority. Their leaders included Samuel Adams, Patrick Henry, and Richard Henry Lee. Robert Yates of New York wrote anti-Constitution essays under the name **Brutus**. Antifederalists demanded that a **Bill of Rights** be added to the Constitution. This would spell out and protect some basic rights. Special conventions in nine

> Underline the names of the leaders of the Federalists.

> Circle the names of the Antifederalists.

> What would a Bill of Rights do?
>
> _____
>
> _____

states had to ratify, or approve, the Constitution before
it could take effect.

THE FEDERALIST PAPERS

James Madison, Alexander Hamilton, and **John Jay**
wrote a series of essays under the name of **Publius**.
These essays discussed and defended each part of the
Constitution. They were collected in a book called
The Federalist. The essays covered political theory
and practical arguments for a strong government. In
them, the authors tried to calm people's fears about a
strong national government.

> Underline the name of the book of essays written by Madison, Hamilton, and Jay.

ADDING A BILL OF RIGHTS

The Federalists were organized and took control of
several state conventions. On December 7, 1787,
Delaware became the first state to ratify the
Constitution. Ten states followed, the last being
Virginia and New York. North Carolina and Rhode
Island did not join the Union until after the new
government was already at work. Several states
ratified only because they were promised a bill of
rights. The Federalists did not oppose a bill of rights.
They simply did not think it was necessary. Madison
took charge of getting a bill of rights through
Congress. Congress approved 12 amendments in
September 1789. By 1791 the states had approved 10
of them. The first eight dealt with individual civil
liberties. The Tenth Amendment defined two kinds of
powers. **Delegated powers** were those specifically
given to the national government. Some powers were
not specifically given to the national government.
These **reserved powers** belonged to the states and the
people.

> What was the difference between the two types of powers defined in the Tenth Amendment?
>
> _____
> _____
> _____
> _____

CHALLENGE ACTIVITY

Critical Thinking: Analyzing Primary Sources Read an essay from *The
Federalist*. Write a one-page paper explaining how the ideas in the essay
apply to modern America.

Chapter Summary

Government
- President Washington forms his cabinet
- Judiciary Act of 1789 establishes the Supreme Court; *Marbury* v. *Madison* defines the Court's role
- Congress creates the Bank of the United States

Forging the New Republic

Conflicts
- Native Americans fight against white settlement in Northwest Territory
- United States and Great Britain fight the War of 1812

Expansion
- Louisiana Purchase roughly doubles the size of the United States
- Lewis and Clark explore the West

COMPREHENSION AND CRITICAL THINKING

Use information from the graphic organizer to answer the following questions.

1. **Identify** What court case defined the Supreme Court's role?

_____

_____

2. **Recall** What two conflicts took place during this period?

_____

_____

3. **Identify** What purchase roughly doubled the size of the United States?

_____

_____

4. **Explain** Why was the Judiciary Act of 1789 important?

_____

_____

Interactive Reader and Study Guide

Forging the New Republic

MAIN IDEA
President Washington and other leaders tried to solve the new nation's economic problems. This led to the rise of political parties.

Key Terms and People

cabinet heads of executive departments who serve as the president's advisers

Judiciary Act of 1789 act that organized the judicial branch of the government

strict construction belief that the government could do only what the Constitution said it could do

loose construction belief that the government could take any reasonable action that was not specifically forbidden by the Constitution

Bank of the United States national bank created by Congress in 1791

Whiskey Rebellion 1794 uprising in which farmers attacked tax collectors

two-party system political system that includes two opposing groups

Democratic-Republicans Jeffersonian Republicans; favored democratic government

Section Summary

ORGANIZING THE GOVERNMENT

Washington was inaugurated as the first president on April 30, 1789. John Adams was vice president. Washington chose the heads of the first executive departments. They became known as the president's **cabinet**. Henry Knox was secretary of war. Thomas Jefferson was secretary of state. Alexander Hamilton was secretary of the treasury. The Constitution contained many compromises, but there were still many questions to be answered. There were only 10 states, so the first Congress was small. Congress quickly passed a Bill of Rights. It also passed the **Judiciary Act of 1789**. This organized the judicial branch of the government. It set up a six-person Supreme Court. It also created district courts and appeal courts.

> **Who was the first vice president?**
> _____

> **Underline two things that the first Congress accomplished.**

SETTLING THE NATION'S DEBTS

The new government owed money to foreign nations. It also owed money to private lenders and former soldiers. Hamilton wanted the federal government to take on all debt from the Revolutionary War. Paying

Interactive Reader and Study Guide

off the government bonds would benefit speculators.
These were people who had bought bonds at a lower
price, hoping to make a profit. Some people thought
this was unfair. To raise money for the government,
Hamilton placed a tax on imports and certain other
products. These taxes were very unpopular. To get the
southern states to agree to help pay the nation's debts,
Hamilton had to make another compromise. The
capital of the nation was moved south from
Philadelphia to what is now Washington, D.C.

> **Why did some people think that paying off the bonds would be unfair?**
>
> _____
>
> _____

DEBATING A NATIONAL BANK

Hamilton wanted a national bank. Some people said
the government did not have the right to start a
national bank. These people believed in **strict
construction**. This meant that the government could
do only what the Constitution said it could do. Those
in favor of the bank believed in **loose construction**.
This meant that the government could take any
reasonable action that was not specifically forbidden
by the Constitution. In 1791 Congress passed the bill
that created the first national **Bank of the United
States**.

> **Why did some people think the government did not have the right to establish a national bank?**
>
> _____
>
> _____
>
> _____

FIRST POLITICAL PARTIES FORM

Hamilton's tax on liquor made many people angry. In
1794 there was an uprising called the **Whiskey
Rebellion**. Farmers in western Pennsylvania attacked
tax collectors. They threatened Pittsburgh. They even
talked of forming an independent nation. Washington
led the troops that ended the rebellion.

> **Where did the Whiskey Rebellion take place?**
>
> _____

   In the 1790s Americans became politically divided.
Jefferson and Hamilton had different ideas.
Jefferson's followers were called Republicans.
Hamilton's were called Federalists. This led to a **two-
party system** in America. Later, the Republicans
came to be known as **Democratic-Republicans** to
show that they favored democratic government.

CHALLENGE ACTIVITY

Critical Thinking: Drawing Inferences Washington opposed political
parties. Do you think the two-party system has benefited the United States?
Explain your answer in three paragraphs.

Forging the New Republic

MAIN IDEA
The United States faced many challenges during the 1790s. It tried to remain neutral in European wars while dealing with conflicts with Native Americans in the Northwest Territory.

Key Terms and People

Neutrality Proclamation United States would not take sides in foreign wars

Jay's Treaty 1794 treaty between the United States and Britain negotiated by John Jay

Pinckney's Treaty 1795 treaty between the United States and Spain negotiated by Thomas Pinckney

Little Turtle Native American war chief who led the Miamis and Shawnees

Battle of Fallen Timbers 1794 battle between white Americans and Native Americans

Treaty of Greenville 1795 treaty in which Native Americans gave up land in Ohio, Indiana, Illinois, and Michigan

sectionalism loyalty to one's region

XYZ affair incident in which France insulted the United States by sending minor officials to meet with American diplomats

Alien and Sedition Acts laws aimed against French and Irish refugees and outlawing criticism of the government

Virginia and Kentucky Resolutions arguments by Jefferson and Madison that the Alien and Sedition Acts were unconstitutional

nullification the declaration by a state that a federal law is void

Section Summary

REMAINING NEUTRAL

The French Revolution began in 1789. The people overthrew their king. Other European nations declared war on France. Many Americans supported the French people, especially Democratic-Republicans. The Federalists, however, were horrified. Britain and France tried to involve the United States in the war. President Washington recognized the new government in France. He also issued the **Neutrality Proclamation**. It said the United States would not take sides. The British began to seize American ships. They also stirred up trouble with Native Americans. Washington sent Chief Justice John Jay to negotiate. **Jay's Treaty** was signed in 1794. The United States agreed to pay all its debts to Britain. The British

> Which Americans supported the French people?
>
> _____
>
> _____

> What acts did the British commit against the Americans?
>
> _____
>
> _____
>
> _____

agreed to get out of the Northwest Territory. In 1795
Thomas Pinckney negotiated a treaty with Spain.
Pinckney's Treaty settled border and trade disputes.

CONFLICTS IN THE NORTHWEST TERRITORY

Settlers moved into western lands that belonged to
Native Americans. Some Native Americans were
forced to give up their land. The war chief **Little
Turtle** led the Miamis and Shawnees into battle. They
defeated the U.S. Army. However, at the **Battle of
Fallen Timbers** in 1794, the U.S. Army won a big
victory. The 1795 **Treaty of Greenville** forced the
Native Americans to give up land in Ohio, Indiana,
Illinois, and Michigan.

> **Where was the land that the Native Americans gave up in the Treaty of Greenville?**
> _____
> _____

PRESIDENT ADAMS AND THE XYZ AFFAIR

Washington refused a third term as president in 1796.
Sectionalism played a role in the election.
Sectionalism is loyalty to one's region. Jefferson ran
as the Democratic-Republican candidate. The
Federalists chose John Adams. Adams won. The
candidate who came in second was Jefferson. Thus,
Adams's opponent became his vice president.

> **Who was John Adams's vice president?**
> _____

French ships began to seize American merchant
vessels. Adams sent diplomats to France. The French
government sent three minor officials to the meeting.
They demanded bribes and a loan. The incident
became known as the **XYZ affair**. Congress stopped
trade with France. Resentment against foreigners
grew. Congress passed the **Alien and Sedition Acts**.
Some of them were aimed against French and Irish
refugees. Others made it illegal to criticize the
government. Jefferson and Madison drafted the
Virginia and Kentucky Resolutions. They said that
the Alien and Sedition Acts were unconstitutional.
They hoped that state legislatures would declare the
laws void. This is called **nullification**. Instead, the
acts were allowed to expire.

> **Against whom were the Alien and Sedition Acts aimed?**
> _____
> _____
> _____

CHALLENGE ACTIVITY

Critical Thinking: Compare and Contrast Read the Alien and Sedition
Acts. In three paragraphs, compare and contrast them to the USA
PATRIOT Act.

Forging the New Republic

MAIN IDEA
The rise of political parties influenced the election of 1800, bringing Thomas Jefferson and a new outlook to the presidency.

Key Terms and People

Aaron Burr Democratic-Republican candidate who tied Jefferson in the 1800 presidential election

Twelfth Amendment amendment that said that electors must cast separate ballots for president and vice president

Louisiana Purchase purchase of the Louisiana Territory from France for $15 million

Lewis and Clark expedition expedition sent by Jefferson to explore the West

Meriwether Lewis Jefferson's secretary and co-leader of the Lewis and Clark expedition

William Clark experienced frontiersman who was co-leader of the Lewis and Clark expedition

Sacagawea Shoshone woman who helped guide Lewis and Clark

Zebulon M. Pike army lieutenant who explored the West

Judiciary Act of 1801 act that created new judicial positions

judicial review the Supreme Court's right to declare a law unconstitutional

Section Summary

THE ELECTION OF 1800

The election of 1800 was the first time in American history that power passed from one party to another. Democratic-Republican Thomas Jefferson ran against Federalist John Adams. The campaign was vicious. At that time electors cast one ballot for both president and vice president. Jefferson and his Democratic-Republican running mate, **Aaron Burr**, both got the same number of votes. The House of Representatives finally chose Jefferson. Congress then passed the **Twelfth Amendment**. It said that electors must cast separate ballots for president and vice president.

> **What happened for the first time in American history in 1800?**
> _____
> _____

> **Underline what the Twelfth Amendment said.**

JEFFERSON MAKES CHANGES

Jefferson reduced the size and power of the federal government. The administration changed the tax system. Now the government's only revenue came from customs duties and the sale of lands in the West.

Interactive Reader and Study Guide

Jefferson also shrank the size of the army and navy. However, he later began to build up the navy to deal with pirates.

> Why did Jefferson start to build up the navy again?
> _____

THE LOUISIANA PURCHASE

In 1800 Spain returned Louisiana to France. Access to the Mississippi River and New Orleans was important to American business. Jefferson sent James Monroe to France to try to buy New Orleans and West Florida. The French offered to sell the entire Louisiana Territory. This **Louisiana Purchase** cost $15 million. Jefferson sent a number of expeditions to explore the new territory. The most famous was the **Lewis and Clark expedition**. It was led by **Meriwether Lewis**, Jefferson's secretary, and **William Clark**, an experienced frontiersman. They left St. Louis in 1804, heading for the Pacific Ocean. **Sacagawea**, a Shoshone woman, helped guide them. They found many new plants and animals. Another explorer was army lieutenant **Zebulon M. Pike**. He explored the upper Mississippi Valley. He also traveled to the Southwest.

> Circle the name of the Native American woman who helped guide Lewis and Clark.

THE ROLE OF THE SUPREME COURT CHANGES

The Federalists lost control of the presidency and Congress in the 1800 election. Before the inauguration, Federalist legislators passed the **Judiciary Act of 1801**. It created many new judicial positions. However, some new judges did not receive their commissions in time. The Supreme Court decided that the Court did not have the power to force the delivery of the commissions. This case, *Marbury v. Madison*, established the Supreme Court's right to declare that a law violates the Constitution. This power is known as **judicial review**.

> What was the importance of *Marbury* v. *Madison*?
> _____
> _____
> _____

CHALLENGE ACTIVITY

Critical Thinking: Drawing Inferences Presidential electors, known as the Electoral College, still play a pivotal role in politics. Research the 2000 presidential election and report in one page on the Electoral College's role.

Forging the New Republic

> **MAIN IDEA**
> In the early 1800s, Americans unified to face Great Britain in war once again and to battle resistance from Native Americans over attempts to seize their lands.

Key Terms and People

impressment kidnapping men and forcing them to work on ships

Embargo Act law that banned exports to foreign countries

William Henry Harrison governor of the Indiana Territory who forced Native Americans into treaties in which they lost millions of acres of land

Tecumseh Shawnee leader

War Hawks American politicians who hated the British and wanted war

Andrew Jackson Tennessee militia leader who led at the Battle of Horseshoe Bend

Battle of New Orleans battle between the British and the Americans that the Americans won, making Jackson a hero

Treaty of Ghent 1814 treaty that ended the War of 1812

Section Summary

VIOLATING NEUTRALITY

In the early 1800s there were still tensions between the British and the Americans. There were conflicts both on the seas and on the Northwest frontier. On the seas, both France and Britain ignored American neutrality. Americans believed the British were the bigger threat. That was because the British practiced **impressment**. This was kidnapping men and forcing them to work on ships. In response, Congress passed the **Embargo Act**. It banned exports to foreign countries. The ban on trade was a disaster for the American economy. After James Madison won the presidency in 1808, a new law reopened trade with everyone but Britain and France.

> Where did tensions lead to conflict between the United States and Great Britain?
>
> _____
>
> _____

> Which country did Americans believe posed a greater threat, France or Britain?
>
> _____

TECUMSEH RESISTS SETTLERS

Conflict between settlers and Native Americans continued. The British tried to rebuild their old alliances with Native Americans. **William Henry Harrison** was named governor of the Indiana Territory. He was supposed to follow Jefferson's policy. This gave Native Americans the choice to

> Who wanted to make alliances with Native Americans?
>
> _____

Interactive Reader and Study Guide

become part of white society or move west. Harrison
caused the Native Americans to make treaties in
which they lost millions of acres of land. Two
Shawnee brothers tried to unite their people. They
urged their followers to reject white culture. One of
these leaders was known as **Tecumseh**. While he was
away, Harrison attacked his people in the Battle of
Tippecanoe. Both sides suffered heavy losses.

THE WAR OF 1812 BEGINS

Some American politicians hated the British and
wanted war. They were known as **War Hawks**. In
June 1812 the United States declared war on Great
Britain. Much of the war would take place on the
U.S.–Canadian border. The naval war moved into the
Great Lakes. There the United States won the Battle
of Lake Erie. Harrison led an army that defeated
combined British and Native American forces in
Canada. Tecumseh was killed. This ended the alliance
between the British and the Native Americans. In the
South, Tecumseh had organized the Creeks to resist
settlers. **Andrew Jackson** led a militia against them.
At the Battle of Horseshoe Bend, his men massacred
Creek men, women, and children.

> Underline the date when the United States declared war on Great Britain.

> In what battle were Native Americans massacred?
>
> _____
> _____

The British set fire to Washington. They
bombarded Fort McHenry, which protected Baltimore
harbor. That is where Francis Scott Key wrote "The
Star-Spangled Banner." Jackson became a hero after
defeating the British in the **Battle of New Orleans**. In
1814 the **Treaty of Ghent** was signed, ending the
war.

CHALLENGE ACTIVITY

Critical Thinking: Elaborate To fight the Battle of New Orleans, Andrew
Jackson made an alliance with a band of outlaws led by a man named Jean
Lafitte. Do research on the battle and write a one-page report on the
alliance.

From Nationalism to Sectionalism

Chapter Summary

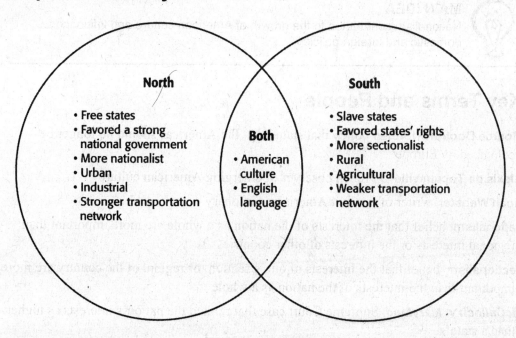

North
- Free states
- Favored a strong national government
- More nationalist
- Urban
- Industrial
- Stronger transportation network

Both
- American culture
- English language

South
- Slave states
- Favored states' rights
- More sectionalist
- Rural
- Agricultural
- Weaker transportation network

COMPREHENSION AND CRITICAL THINKING

Use information from the graphic organizer to answer the following questions.

1. **Identify** Which part of the country was in favor of a strong national government?

   _____

2. **Explain** Which part of the country was agricultural?

   _____

3. **Recall** What two things did both areas of the nation have in common?

   _____

   _____

4. **Predict** If both parts of the country were suddenly required to move troops and equipment long distances, which part of the country would be better prepared?

   _____

   _____

   _____

From Nationalism to Sectionalism

Section 1

MAIN IDEA
Nationalism contributed to the growth of American culture and influenced domestic and foreign policies.

Key Terms and People

Monroe Doctrine foreign policy that stated that the Americas should no longer be colonized by Europe

Alexis de Tocqueville a French observer of emerging American culture

Noah Webster writer of the first American dictionary

nationalism belief that the interests of the nation as a whole are more important than regional interests or the interests of other countries

sectionalism belief that the interests of one's section, or region, of the country are more important than the interests of the nation as a whole

McCulloch v. *Maryland* Supreme Court case that ranked the nation's interests as higher than a state's

James Monroe president from 1817 to 1825

John Quincy Adams secretary of state to Monroe

Adams-Onís Treaty treaty with Spain in which the United States acquired Florida and established the boundary between the Louisiana territory and Spanish land to the west

Missouri Compromise agreement under which Missouri was admitted to the Union as a slave state and Maine was admitted as a free state

Section Summary

A NEW AMERICAN CULTURE

The **Monroe Doctrine** was a bold statement from the young United States. It said that North and South America were no longer to be colonized by Europe. Americans were hard at work building their new nation. As they went about their lives they developed a distinctly American culture. The French philosopher **Alexis de Tocqueville** observed this new culture. He saw that Americans had much energy. He also saw that instead of imitating European cultures they did things their own way. This included original works in art and literature. **Noah Webster** published a dictionary of Americans' unique version of the English language.

> **How did the United States regard European countries setting up colonies in North and South America? Where was this stated?**
>
> _____
> _____
> _____
> _____

From Nationalism to Sectionalism

NATIONALISM INFLUENCES DOMESTIC POLICY

Nationalism is the belief that the interests of the nation as a whole are more important than regional interests or the interests of other countries. In the early 1800s feelings of nationalism swept America. These feelings replaced **sectionalism**. This is the belief that one's own section, or region, of the country is more important than the whole. The feelings of nationalism were reflected in government policies. For example, in the case of *McCulloch* v. *Maryland*, the Supreme Court ruled that the nation's interests ranked higher than any state's interests.

> Underline the definition of sectionalism.

NATIONALISM GUIDES FOREIGN POLICY

In 1816 **James Monroe** was elected president. His secretary of state was **John Quincy Adams**. Adams made an important agreement with Spain. This was the **Adams-Onís Treaty**. In it the United States acquired Florida and fixed the boundary between Louisiana and Spanish lands to the west. The result was the country expanded to the south and east, and the borders in the north and west were defined.

> Underline the details of the Adams-Onís Treaty.

THE MISSOURI COMPROMISE

By 1818 settlers had spread into Missouri. Most came from the South. About 1 of every 6 settlers were enslaved African Americans. When Missouri applied to become a state, it caused a problem. At that time there were an equal number of free states and slave states. Slave and free states had equal representation in the U.S. Senate. If Missouri entered the Union as a slave state, it would upset the balance.

The situation was settled with the **Missouri Compromise**. This agreement stated that Missouri would be admitted as a slave state and that Maine would be admitted as a free state. The balance was preserved. Still, it showed there was sectionalism in the North and South.

> How would Missouri's entrance into the Union have upset the balance in Congress?
> _____
> _____
> _____

> Underline the state that entered the Union with Missouri.

CHALLENGE ACTIVITY

Critical Thinking: Summarize Read a chapter of de Tocqueville's *Democracy in America*. Summarize it in one page.

MAIN IDEA
President Andrew Jackson's bold actions defined a period of American history.

Key Terms and People

Democratic Party political party created by Andrew Jackson and his supporters

Jacksonian Democracy political power held by ordinary Americans

spoils system system in which a politician rewards his supporters with favors

Indian Removal Act law that called for the relocation of five Native American nations to an area west of the Mississippi River

Worcester v. **Georgia** Supreme Court finding that Georgia could not take Cherokee land

Trail of Tears forced march of the Cherokee westward during which many died

Second Bank of the United States a national bank overseen by the federal government

states' rights concept that gave states more power than the federal government

John C. Calhoun vice president under Andrew Jackson

secede to leave the Union

nullification crisis South Carolina's attempt to declare an end to a federal tariff

Section Summary

PATH TO THE PRESIDENCY

Andrew Jackson served in the army in the Revolutionary War. He also fought in the War of 1812. He led the Americans to victory at the Battle of New Orleans. The battle made Jackson famous. In 1824 he ran for president and won the popular vote. However, he did not get the majority of electoral votes. The House of Representatives decided that the winner was John Quincy Adams.

Jackson and his supporters created a new political party. It came to be known as the **Democratic Party**. Four years later Jackson easily defeated Adams. Jackson's supporters were ordinary working Americans. Political power held by ordinary Americans became known as **Jacksonian Democracy**. Jackson replaced many government officials with his supporters. This rewarding of supporters is called the **spoils system**.

> Andrew Jackson won the popular vote in the 1824 presidential election, but he did not become president. Why?
>
> _____
> _____
> _____

> Who holds the power in Jacksonian Democracy?
>
> _____

From Nationalism to Sectionalism

THE INDIAN REMOVAL ACT

In the southeast, Native Americans controlled large amounts of land that white settlers wanted. Congress passed the **Indian Removal Act**. It called for moving the Native Americans to land west of the Mississippi. The U.S. Army forced the Choctaw, Creek, and Chickasaw to march west. About one-fourth died.

Not all Native Americans obeyed the army. The Seminole fought back with raids against U.S. soldiers. Although never officially defeated, about 3,000 Seminole were forced west. The Cherokee fought in court and won. In the case *Worcester* **v.** *Georgia*, the Supreme Court said that Georgia could not take Cherokee land. However, officials found some Cherokee leaders who agreed to sign a treaty. Under the terms of the treaty all the Cherokee were forced on a long, terrible march. It became known as the **Trail of Tears** because so many died on the trail.

Why was the Indian Removal act passed?
_____
_____

What were two tactics used by Native American groups to oppose the Indian Removal Act?
_____
_____
_____
_____

THE NATIONAL BANK

A major issue of the 1832 election was the **Second Bank of the United States**. Jackson wanted to close it. He felt it served the wealthy and that state banks could better help poor farmers. These farmers were Jackson's supporters. Jackson won the election and converted the National Bank into a state bank.

CONFLICT OVER STATES' RIGHTS

States' rights is the concept that the states have more powers than the federal government. Vice president **John C. Calhoun** said that states could reject federal laws if they thought the laws went against the Constitution or did not benefit the state. The discussion arose when new federal tariffs on British goods were welcomed by Northerners but hated by Southerners. South Carolina declared the tariff null and threatened to **secede**, or leave the Union. This was called the **nullification crisis**.

Define states' rights.
_____
_____
_____

CHALLENGE ACTIVITY

Critical Thinking: Compare The Cherokee adopted aspects of American culture. Look for similarities between the U.S. and Cherokee constitutions.

From Nationalism to Sectionalism

MAIN IDEA
The North developed an economy based on industry.

Key Terms and People

Samuel Slater English textile worker who brought secrets of mill design to the United States

Industrial Revolution the birth of modern industry and the social changes that went along with it

Francis Lowell Boston textile merchant for whom the town of Lowell was named

Lowell girls young women who worked in the textile industry in Lowell, Massachusetts

National Road road that stretched from Maryland to Illinois

Erie Canal canal connecting the Great Lakes to the Hudson River and the Atlantic Ocean

Robert Fulton operator of the first successful steamboat service

telegraph device that sent messages through wires using electricity

Samuel F. B. Morse inventor of the telegraph

Section Summary

THE INDUSTRIAL REVOLUTION

In 1789 cloth weaving machines were so new and important to the British economy that it was a crime to give away their design. But **Samuel Slater** secretly came to the United States and helped start the American textile industry. This was the beginning of the **Industrial Revolution**, which went from the mid 1700s to the mid 1800s. It was the birth of modern industry and all the social changes that came with it. For centuries cloth was made by hand at home. Now, a series of inventions used power from running water and steam engines to spin thread and weave cloth.

What was the Industrial Revolution?

_____

_____

_____

THE NORTH INDUSTRIALIZES

The first successful textile mill in the country was the one that Samuel Slater started with his American partner, Moses Brown. The mill spun cotton into thread. The new technology spread quickly throughout New England. The first machines for weaving cloth were used in Lowell, Massachusetts. The city, named

Who started America's first textile mill?

_____

_____

for **Francis Lowell**, a wealthy textile merchant, became the center of textile production. Lowell built mills and employed young women to do the work. These women made good wages but worked 14-hour days, six days a week. They lived in company dormitories and their days were controlled by the ringing of bells. They became known as the **Lowell girls**. As industrialization spread to other industries in the North, more people left farms and moved to cities to take jobs there. In 1820 only 7 percent of Americans lived in cities. Within 30 years the percentage more than doubled.

> Why was Lowell, Massachusetts, important?
> _____
> _____

TRANSPORTATION AND COMMUNICATION

New ways to bring raw materials to factories were needed. With more goods being produced, new ways to deliver these were also needed. The **National Road** was completed in 1841. It stretched 800 miles from Maryland to Illinois. In 1825 the **Erie Canal** opened. It connected the Great Lakes with the Hudson River and the Atlantic Ocean The canal provided a quick and economical way to ship manufactured goods to the West and farm products to the East. Within 15 years there were more than 3,000 miles of canals in the northeast.

Steam power brought the first successful steamboat service in 1807, run by **Robert Fulton**. His success on the Hudson River inspired other services on the Ohio, Mississippi, and other rivers. In 1830 the first steam-powered train in the United States began what would become the most important part of U.S. transportation. By 1840 there were about 3,000 miles of track. Steam-powered printing presses spread information wider than ever before. With trains and steamboats, mail became faster. The greatest advance in communication during this time was the **telegraph**. It sent messages using electricity through wires. **Samuel F. B. Morse** invented it in 1840.

> Fill in the advances made in the following years. There are three important milestones for 1840.
>
> 1807: _____
>
> 1825: _____
>
> 1830: _____
>
> 1840: _____
>
> 1840: _____
>
> 1840: _____
>
> 1841: _____

CHALLENGE ACTIVITY

Critical Thinking: Drawing Inferences The Lowell girls wrote their own newsletter, called *The Lowell Offering*. Find a copy at a library or on the Internet and report to the class about the everyday lives of these workers.

From Nationalism to Sectionalism

Section 4

MAIN IDEA
During the early 1800s, the South developed an economy based on agriculture.

Key Terms and People

Eli Whitney inventor of the cotton gin

cotton gin machine for removing the seeds from cotton

Cotton Belt the region of cotton farms that stretched across the South

King Cotton nickname for the cotton crop

Section Summary

"KING COTTON"

Because of weather conditions in the South, American farmers had to grow a type of cotton that could stand the cold. Unfortunately, the cotton was filled with seeds that were hard to remove. Around 1800 a young man named **Eli Whitney** invented a machine that could clean the seeds out of this cotton. It was called the **cotton gin**. This enabled southern farmers to fill the growing demand for cotton. Mills in the North bought the raw cotton to spin it into thread and weave it into cloth to sell to the growing American population. Great Britain also had a booming textile industry. It needed raw cotton, too. Beginning in the 1820s, the number of acres planted in cotton soared. There were cotton farms in the Carolinas, Tennessee, Georgia, Alabama, Mississippi, and Louisiana. An almost uninterrupted band of cotton farms stretched across the South. This was called the **Cotton Belt**. Many people got rich growing cotton. A senator on the Senate floor pronounced that "Cotton is king." Soon, people were calling the crop **King Cotton**.

> **What did the cotton gin do?**
> _____
> _____

> **Circle the date when the number of acres of cotton began to soar.**

THE SPREAD OF SLAVERY

To farm cotton a lot of workers were needed. The first cotton farms were small. However, wealthy planters soon bought huge tracts of land. They used enslaved African Americans to raise and pick the cotton. The demand for enslaved African Americans increased. In 1808 the United States no longer allowed enslaved

> **Why were enslaved people considered necessary to raising cotton?**
> _____
> _____

people to be brought into the country. However, many were smuggled in. These people and the children of enslaved parents were cruelly bought and sold. In 1810 there were about 1 million enslaved African Americans in the United States. By 1840 the number had more than doubled. Enslaved African Americans accounted for about one-third of the population of the South. Most southerners were not slaveholders. About one-fourth of the South's white families owned slaves.

DIFFERENCES BETWEEN THE NORTH AND THE SOUTH

Besides cotton, farmers in the South grew sugarcane, sugar beets, tobacco, and rice. Agriculture formed the base of the economy of the South. Farming was also important to the North. However, manufacturing and trade formed the base of the North's economy.

> **What was the base of the economy in the South? What was it in the North?**
> _____
> _____

Trade and industry encouraged city living, so the cities in the North grew more than those in the South. Businesses in the North were eager for new technology. Southerners saw little need for labor-saving devices. This was because they had enslaved people to do their work. In the North, people tended to see change as progress. People in the South placed a high value on tradition. The differences between the two areas were heightened by distance. Few people traveled from one region to the other. The greatest difference between North and South, however, concerned slavery. In the South, most white people saw it as a natural situation. They also saw it as necessary. In the North, slavery was illegal. Many people in the North saw slavery as evil.

> **Why did southerners not need labor-saving devices?**
> _____
> _____

CHALLENGE ACTIVITY

Critical Thinking: Elaborate Do research on Eli Whitney's life after his invention of the cotton gin. Make a poster depicting Whitney's impact on agricultural and industrial practices.

A Push for Reform

Chapter Summary

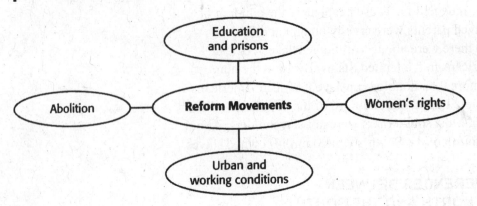

COMPREHENSION AND CRITICAL THINKING

Use information from the graphic organizer to answer the following questions.

1. **Recall** What issues did the reform movements address?

_____

_____

2. **Compare** What might the reform movements have in common?

_____

_____

3. **Make Inferences** Many women were heavily involved in the abolition movement, ending slavery. How do you think this influenced the movement for women's rights?

_____

_____

_____

MAIN IDEA
A revival in religion in the early 1800s helped lead to an era of reform.

Key Terms and People

Charles Grandison Finney the most famous preacher of his time in western New York

Second Great Awakening American religious movement of the 1820s and 1830s

Reform Era time in which many Americans tried to improve American society

temperance movement movement to reduce the use of alcoholic drinks

Horace Mann greatest school reformer of the Reform Era

Dorothea Dix reformer who campaigned for humane treatment of prisoners and the mentally ill

transcendentalist movement movement whose members believed that knowledge could come from reason, intuition, and personal spiritual experiences

Ralph Waldo Emerson leading transcendentalist

Henry David Thoreau major transcendentalist whose essays influenced Mohandas Gandhi and Martin Luther King Jr.

utopian movement movement to build communities that lived up to perfect ideals

Section Summary

RELIGION SPARKS REFORM

In the 1820s and 1830s many Americans were taking a new interest in religion. **Charles Grandison Finney** was one of many preachers who led revivals. A revival is a meeting designed to reawaken religious feelings. So many of these people attended revivals and joined churches that this event is called the **Second Great Awakening**. These people were told that with dedication and hard work, they could create a kind of heaven on earth. This, along with other factors, led to the **Reform Era**. From about 1830 to 1860, many Americans tried to improve U.S. society.

Many reformers wanted to reduce the use of alcoholic drinks. This movement is called the **temperance movement**. They formed clubs and wrote books, plays, and songs about the evils of alcohol. Later they would even raid bars.

> **What is a revival?**
> _____
> _____
> _____

> **What led to the Reform Era?**
> _____
> _____
> _____

A Push for Reform

REFORMING EDUCATION

Many children worked at this time, and the reformers wanted more children to be educated. The greatest school reformer of this era was **Horace Mann**. As secretary of education in Massachusetts, Mann transformed his state's educational system and promoted mandatory school attendance. He also called for special schools to train teachers. William McGuffey was also an education reformer. He wrote children's books that taught reading and moral values.

> **What did William McGuffey write?**
> _____
> _____

REFORMING PRISONS

Dorothea Dix campaigned for humane treatment for prisoners and the mentally ill. Mentally ill people had been kept with violent criminals. Dix and her supporters convinced some states to create separate places to take care of the mentally ill.

> **What did Dorothea Dix campaign for?**
> _____
> _____
> _____

TRANSCENDENTALISM AND UTOPIANISM

The members of the **transcendentalist movement** believed that one could obtain knowledge through reason, intuition, and personal spiritual experiences. The leading transcendentalist was **Ralph Waldo Emerson**. He spoke and wrote essays about his beliefs. He thought that people should be independent and trust their intuition. He also thought they should try to improve society. **Henry David Thoreau** was also a transcendentalist. He wrote that people should act according to their own beliefs, even if it was against the law. His writings influenced Mohandas Gandhi and Martin Luther King Jr.

> **Who did Henry David Thoreau's writings influence?**
> _____
> _____

Some reformers sought to create communities according to perfect ideals. This was known as the **utopian movement**. Most utopian communities were small and lasted for only a short time. The Shakers, a Christian group, were one exception that lasted.

CHALLENGE ACTIVITY

Critical Thinking: Evaluate Read Thoreau's essay *Civil Disobedience.* What do you think of his ideas? Write three paragraphs giving your opinion of his work.

Interactive Reader and Study Guide

A Push for Reform

MAIN IDEA
A wave of Irish and German immigrants entered the United States during a period of urbanization and reform.

Key Terms and People

Great Irish Famine death of about 1 million Irish people due to starvation

push-pull model of immigration a way to describe immigration

nativism opposition to immigration

Know-Nothings anti-immigrant group that later became a political party

tenements poorly made, crowded apartment buildings

wage earners workers who were paid a set amount by business owners

urban working class social class composed of wage earners who lived in cities

labor movement movement by workers trying to improve their situation

Martin Van Buren president who extended a 10-hour workday to many federal employees

Section Summary

IRISH AND GERMAN IMMIGRANTS

Since the 1700s, the poor people of Ireland had relied on potatoes as their major crop. From 1845 to 1849, a disease struck the potato crop. The poor got little help from the ruling British government and many faced starvation. By 1850 about 1 million had died in the **Great Irish Famine**. More than 2 million Irish left the country to save their families. By 1854 about 1.5 million had settled in the United States.

The other major group of immigrants in the 1800s was the Germans. They had not faced famine. They left Germany for many reasons, such as overpopulation and religious persecution.

Immigration can be described using the **push-pull model of immigration**. In this model, the reasons that people leave their homes are called "pushes." The reasons they move to a certain country are called "pulls." Various pushes and pulls in the 1800s led to a record number of immigrants to the United States. By 1860 there were about 3 million Irish and German immigrants in the United States.

> Underline the number of people who died in the Great Irish Famine.

> Underline the number of Irish and German immigrants in the United States in 1860.

A Push for Reform

THE LIVES OF IMMIGRANTS

Most immigrants were poor and struggling. Many Americans resented them because there were so many and because they were poor. Mostly, they were resented for being Roman Catholic. Many Americans believed that the Roman Catholic religion went against democratic principles and that the immigrants would obey the pope and not the president.

Some Americans began to regard immigrants as a threat to their way of life. **Nativism**, or opposition to immigration, grew as the number of Irish immigrants grew. There were many groups opposed to immigration. One such group was called the **Know-Nothings**. The group later became a political party.

German immigrants did not meet with as much hostility as the Irish. Most had more money, and most were Protestants.

> **Why did many Americans resent the Irish for being Roman Catholic?**
>
> _____
> _____
> _____

> **Why did German immigrants not face as much hostility as the Irish?**
>
> _____
> _____

REFORM, URBANIZATION, AND INDUSTRIALIZATION

In the mid-1800s American cities grew, and Irish immigrants greatly contributed to this growth. Most city dwellers lived in **tenements**. These were poorly made, crowded apartment buildings.

The country was industrializing and the number of manufacturing workers increased. These workers were **wage earners**, paid a set amount by their employers. They formed a new social class: the **urban working class**. Most of them were poor and uneducated. Wealthy business owners paid low wages. Workers also experienced long hours in unsafe working conditions. The **labor movement** began as workers campaigned to improve their conditions. The movement faced severe opposition from business owners. President **Martin Van Buren** extended the 10-hour workday to include more federal workers. However, laborers were not able to make significant improvements in their working conditions for many decades.

> **What was true of most of the people in the urban working class?**
>
> _____
> _____

CHALLENGE ACTIVITY

Critical Thinking: Elaborate Create a poster showing some of the contributions of the Irish or the Germans to American culture.

Interactive Reader and Study Guide

A Push for Reform

MAIN IDEA
After leading reform movements to help others, some American women began to work on behalf of themselves.

Key Terms and People

cult of domesticity movement that urged women to stay at home

reform societies groups that organized to promote changes to society

Catharine Beecher educator who worked to establish schools for women

Lucretia Mott prominent abolitionist who helped organize the Seneca Falls Convention

Elizabeth Cady Stanton organizer of the Seneca Falls Convention

Seneca Falls Convention first women's rights convention held in the United States

Section Summary

LIMITS ON WOMEN'S LIVES

In the 1800s American women were denied many of the basic rights of U.S. citizenship. Women could not vote or hold public office. Other than marriage, they could not enter into legal contracts. Married women could not own property, including their own money.

Underline the ways that women were denied equality in the 1800s.

In the early 1800s, many American women took jobs out of their homes for the first time. Still, the wages of a married woman belonged to her husband. Single women were expected to give most of their wages to their families. In addition, the view that women were inferior to men was common. Women were expected to stay home and care for the children, leaving everything else to men. During the Industrial Revolution these expectations grew. This was mostly a response to the belief that industrialization was threatening family life by taking women out of the household to work. Books and magazines praised women who stayed at home. This movement became known as the **cult of domesticity**.

Explain the cult of domesticity.
_____
_____
_____
_____
_____

WOMEN IN THE REFORM ERA

Even though there were limits on their lives, women played leading roles in the reform movement. The Second Great Awakening opened many doors for women. It allowed women to participate more fully in

What opened many doors for women?
_____

Christian religious affairs. Many women's church societies became **reform societies**. These were groups organized to promote changes to society. Members would visit poor neighborhoods, jails, and other places to provide religious instruction and encouragement.

Women also led the movement to reform education. **Catharine Beecher** ran a school for women. She worked to create other schools to train teachers. In 1833 Oberlin College became the first American college to welcome women as well as men.

In addition, women contributed to urban reforms, the labor movement, and the temperance movement.

> **What was the name of the first American college to welcome women as well as men?**
>
> _____

THE SENECA FALLS CONVENTION

Over the years, countless American women had fought for reforms. However, the limits placed on them restricted their influence and success. As a result, many women wanted political power in order to advance the reforms.

Lucretia Mott and **Elizabeth Cady Stanton** organized the **Seneca Falls Convention** in 1848. It was the first women's rights convention held in the United States. Both women were dedicated abolitionists. They had attended the World's Anti-Slavery Convention in London in 1840. Mott was not allowed to speak at that conference because she was a woman. This experience led both women to focus on women's rights.

The Seneca Falls Convention produced the Declaration of Sentiments, written by Stanton. It stated that "all men and women are created equal."

> **When was the Seneca Falls Convention held?**
>
> _____

> **What experience led Mott and Stanton to focus on women's rights?**
>
> _____
>
> _____
>
> _____
>
> _____

CHALLENGE ACTIVITY

Critical Thinking: Elaborate Read a copy of the Declaration of Sentiments that came out of the Seneca Falls Convention. Write three paragraphs telling what you think about it.

A Push for Reform

Section 4

MAIN IDEA
The movement to end slavery dominated the Reform Era.

Key Terms and People

free blacks African Americans who were not enslaved

Nat Turner leader of the deadliest slave revolt in American history

Underground Railroad an informal, constantly changing network of escape routes for slaves

Harriet Tubman escaped slave who became the most famous worker on the Underground Railroad

abolition movement campaign to abolish, or end, slavery

William Lloyd Garrison leading spokesperson for the abolition movement

Frederick Douglass escaped slave who became a prominent abolitionist

Section Summary

THE LIVES OF ENSLAVED AFRICAN AMERICANS

Enslaved African Americans lived in both the North and the South. Slavery was cruel and unjust. Men, women, and children were forced to work almost every day of their lives. Most lived on farms or plantations in the South. Many did hard work in the cotton fields. Others worked in plantation homes. In cities they worked in factories, mills, and mines. There was little shelter provided. Food and clothing were also inadequate. They almost never got medical care.

The law gave slaves no rights at all. They were considered property. Some slaveholders punished their slaves harshly. Slaveholders frequently separated families by selling them to different owners.

African Americans learned to survive. Religion was a source of comfort. Enslaved people also found pleasure in storytelling and songs.

> **In which regions of the country did enslaved African Americans live?**
> _____
> _____

> **How did enslaved people find comfort?**
> _____
> _____

THE ANTISLAVERY MOVEMENT IN THE SOUTH

About 250,000 African Americans in the South were not kept as slaves. They were **free blacks**. Some were former slaves. Others were descendants of freed slaves. They faced harsh legal and social discrimination. Still, they worked to end slavery for all. Many aided people who were escaping. Some bravely spoke out for freedom.

Between 1776 and 1860 there were about 200 slave uprisings and plots in the United States. Most were small. In 1830 **Nat Turner** led the deadliest slave revolt in American history. Turner and others murdered Turner's owner and his family along with dozens more white people. A local militia captured the rebels and executed 20 of them, including Turner.

Thousands of enslaved people tried to escape. No one knows how many succeeded. Over the years an informal, constantly changing network of escape routes developed. This was the **Underground Railroad**. Sympathetic white people and free blacks gave escapees food and hiding places. The most famous worker on the Underground Railroad was **Harriet Tubman**. She was an escaped slave herself.

> **What are two ways that free blacks helped the antislavery movement?**
> _____
> _____
> _____

> **Who gave escapees food and hiding places?**
> _____
> _____

THE ABOLITION MOVEMENT

The **abolition movement** was a campaign to abolish, or end, slavery. It was one of the largest movements of the Reform Era. The abolition movement had deep roots in religion. The Quakers had always condemned slavery. Many religious people in the North saw slavery as a clear moral wrong. One of the most outspoken abolitionists was **William Lloyd Garrison**. Starting in 1831, he published an abolitionist newspaper. In 1833 he started the American Anti-Slavery Society. **Frederick Douglass**, an escaped slave, was an important abolitionist as well. He was highly intelligent and a great speaker. He also published an abolitionist newspaper.

However, there was support for slavery in both the North and the South. Slaveholders viewed the abolition movement as an attack on their livelihood, their way of life, and their religion.

> **Who started the American Anti-Slavery Society?**
> _____
> _____

CHALLENGE ACTIVITY

Critical Thinking: Elaborate Read *The Confessions of Nat Turner*. In an oral presentation, tell your class about Turner's life.

Expansion Leads to Conflict

Chapter Summary

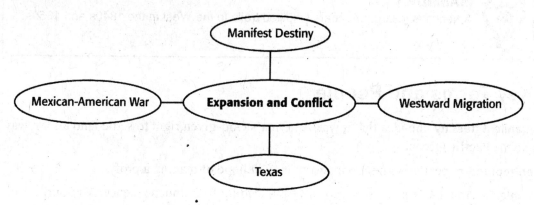

COMPREHENSION AND CRITICAL THINKING

Use information from the graphic organizer to answer the following questions.

1. **Identify** What present-day state was part of the westward migration?

_____

2. **Explain** What do you think manifest destiny means?

_____

_____

3. **Identify** What war was fought for manifest destiny?

_____

_____

4. **Predict** Why do you think the United States and Mexico came to wage war on each other?

_____

_____

_____

Expansion Leads to Conflict

MAIN IDEA
Americans in large numbers followed trails to the West in the 1840s and 1850s.

Key Terms and People

manifest destiny the idea that it was America's God-given right to settle land all the way to the Pacific Ocean

entrepreneur person willing to invest money in hope of making a profit

Santa Fe Trail the first major westward trail, leading from Independence, Missouri, to Santa Fe, New Mexico

Oregon Trail 2,000-mile trail that led from Independence, Missouri, to the Willamette Valley in present-day Oregon

Mormon Trail trail leading to the area around the Great Salt Lake in present-day Utah

James K. Polk president who called attention to the discovery of gold in California; campaigned on the promise to secure Oregon Country for the United States

gold rush mass migration to California of miners looking to find gold and the businesspeople who wanted to make money off them

California Trail trail that branched off the Oregon Trail to lead to California

Butterfield Trail major southern stage line

Pony Express mail service that used young riders on fast horses

Section Summary

AMERICANS HEAD WEST

Hundreds of thousands of Americans migrated west in the 1840s and 1850s. The United States had expanded a great deal after the Revolutionary War. Many Americans believed that this expansion should keep going. They believed in **manifest destiny**. This was the idea that it was America's God-given right to settle land all the way to the Pacific Ocean. Mountain men were the first migrants. They went to trap and trade. Missionaries followed. They wanted to convert the Native Americans to Christianity. Lumberjacks and miners went also. By the 1840s most pioneers were poor farmers who went to farm the rich land they'd heard about. **Entrepreneurs** went with them. These were people who were willing to invest their money to make a profit.

> Underline the name of the belief that Americans had a right to all of North America.

> Circle the names of the groups of people who migrated west.

Interactive Reader and Study Guide

Expansion Leads to Conflict

MAJOR WESTERN TRAILS

Migrants reached the west in wagons pulled by oxen or horses, or by walking. The first major western trail was the **Santa Fe Trail**. It led from Independence, Missouri, to Santa Fe, New Mexico. It began as a trade route. Then migrants began to use it.

The longest trail was the **Oregon Trail**. It was 2,000 miles long. It led from Independence, Missouri, to the Willamette Valley in present-day Oregon. The trail was dangerous, the weather was harsh, and the terrain was difficult. Disease, starvation, and conflict with Native Americans were always possibilities.

In 1830 the Mormon Church was founded. The Mormons faced hostility because their beliefs, such as men being able to have several wives, differed from Protestant Christianity. They migrated to the area around the Great Salt Lake in present-day Utah. The trail they followed was known as the **Mormon Trail**.

> How did the Santa Fe Trail begin?
> _____
> _____
> _____

THE GOLD RUSH

The largest migration west took place in search of gold. In 1848 gold was discovered in California. President **James K. Polk** talked about it in his State of the Union speech. Americans and people from other countries read about it and headed to California. The mass migration of miners and businesspeople who made money off them is known as the **gold rush**. Many Americans got there on the **California Trail**.

> Why did the largest migration west take place?
> _____
> _____

MAJOR EFFECTS OF WESTWARD MIGRATION

The railroad spanned the country by 1869. By then, more than 350,000 migrants had headed west. They communicated with family and friends back East with the **Butterfield Trail**, a private stage coach line that carried mail. For 18 months, the **Pony Express** delivered mail using young riders on fast horses. In 1861 the telegraph linked the East and the West.

> List the ways the East communicated with the West.
> _____
> _____
> _____

CHALLENGE ACTIVITY

Critical Thinking: Drawing Inferences Using a current roadmap, compare present-day highway routes with the trails mentioned in the chapter. Mark places where the highways follow the old trails.

Expansion Leads to Conflict

 MAIN IDEA
American settlers in Texas revolted against the Mexican government and created the independent Republic of Texas.

Key Terms and People

mission system system of small settlements designed to convert Native Americans to Catholicism and make them loyal Spanish subjects

Moses Austin American who approached Spanish officials in Texas with plans to build an American colony there

Stephen F. Austin carried out his father's plans for a colony in Texas

empresarios contractors who were granted land to establish colonies in Texas

Tejanos Texans of Mexican heritage

Antonio López de Santa Anna president and military leader of Mexico when Texas revolted

Texas Revolution revolt of the settlers of Texas against Mexico

Sam Houston leader of the army of Texans who fought the Mexicans

Alamo fort in San Antonio where nearly all the Texan defenders died

William Travis Texan commander at the Alamo

Republic of Texas Texas as a separate nation

Section Summary

THE SPANISH SETTLE TEXAS

The first Europeans to visit Texas were the Spanish. There were already hundreds of groups of Native Americans there. The Spanish attempted to settle Texas with missions. A mission was a small settlement started with the goal to convert Native Americans to Catholicism. Usually there was a fort at the mission. The Spanish thought the **mission system** would make the Native Americans loyal Spanish subjects. It didn't work.

> **Who were the first Europeans to visit Texas?**
> _____

> **Underline the name of the system the Spanish used to try to settle Texas.**

AMERICANS MOVE INTO TEXAS

Moses Austin had a plan to start an American colony in Texas. He proposed his plan to Spanish officials. They said yes to the plan, but Austin died before he

Interactive Reader and Study Guide

Expansion Leads to Conflict

could start his colony. His son, **Stephen F. Austin**, took over. In 1823 he established a colony. By then, Mexico had gotten its independence from Spain. It granted large pieces of land to *empresarios*. These were contractors who agreed to start colonies. By 1830 there were about 30,000 settlers in Texas. About 4,000 of them were **Tejanos**. These were Texans who were of Mexican heritage.

> Circle the name of the man who started the first colony in Texas.

THE TEXAS REVOLUTION

American settlers in Texas had to agree to some things. They had to agree to become citizens of Mexico. They also had to agree to become Catholic. However, most Americans did not do these things. Settlers behaved like Americans who lived in Texas. Mexicans became concerned. They cancelled most of the *empresario* contracts. They put tariffs on trade with the United States. This made the settlers angry. In 1827 the United States offered to buy Texas. Mexico said no to the offer.

> What did Texas settlers have to agree to do?
> _____
> _____
> _____

Texans began to protest. Protests grew bloody. **Antonio López de Santa Anna** became president of Mexico. Texans attacked a Mexican force at Gonzales and won. This began the **Texas Revolution**. Texans met and formed a government. They gave **Sam Houston** the task of raising an army.

Texan forces captured San Antonio. It contained a fort called the **Alamo**. Santa Anna led an army of 6,000 to take back the fort. The Texans' leader was **William Travis**. He had only 200 fighters. Nearly all were killed when the Mexican army attacked. Texans were also defeated at Refugio and Goliad. The Mexican army massacred prisoners at Goliad. Santa Anna followed Houston's forces to San Jacinto. There, the Texans defeated the Mexicans and captured Santa Anna. Santa Anna was forced to sign the Treaties of Velasco. Texas became a separate nation called the **Republic of Texas**.

> Underline the number of Texans and circle the number of Mexican soldiers at the Alamo.

CHALLENGE ACTIVITY

Critical Thinking: Evaluate Watch one of the movies made about the fight at the Alamo. Why do you think Texans used the memory of the Alamo as inspiration? Write three paragraphs to explain.

Expansion Leads to Conflict

MAIN IDEA
Soon after annexing Texas, the United States declared war on Mexico.

Key Terms and People

John Tyler president who signed the 1845 bill adding Texas to the United States

Zachary Taylor American general who led U.S. forces into disputed territory in Texas

Mexican-American War war between the United States and Mexico that began in 1846

Stephen Kearny American general who captured Santa Fe and took control of New Mexico, then went to capture California

Republic of California name given to California for the month when California was an independent country, after Mexican control and before American control

Bear Flag Revolt uprising in California against Mexico

Winfield Scott American general who captured Mexico City

Treaty of Guadalupe Hidalgo treaty that ended the Mexican-American War

Mexican Cession huge area of land that Mexico had to give to the United States

Section Summary

THE ANNEXATION OF TEXAS

Texas had become an independent country. It was called the Republic of Texas. Sam Houston was elected as its first president. The citizens of Texas voted to become part of the United States. Many Texans used to be Americans. They wanted to be Americans again. Joining the United States would mean they could be protected by the American army and navy. Also, the state had economic trouble. Being part of the United States would help the Texas economy. Some Americans were against the annexation, or taking over, of Texas. They did not want to take on Texas' economic troubles. Also, they did not want another slave state in the Union. Texas was a republic for nine years. Then Congress passed a joint resolution annexing Texas. President **John Tyler** signed the annexation bill in 1845.

> Circle the name of the first president of Texas.

> For how many years was Texas an independent country?
>
> _____

Expansion Leads to Conflict

TENSIONS BETWEEN THE UNITED STATES AND MEXICO

The Mexican government believed that Texas had been stolen. The new U.S. president, James K. Polk, wanted to acquire the land between Texas and the Pacific Ocean, now called New Mexico and California. He also wanted to set the boundary of Texas at the Rio Grande. Mexico thought it should be farther north, at the Nueces River. To settle these issues, Polk sent a special messenger to Mexico in 1845. He offered to pay Mexico $30 million for New Mexico and California. No one in Mexico would meet with the messenger.

THE MEXICAN-AMERICAN WAR

President Polk ordered General **Zachary Taylor** to take his troops into the disputed territory. Some of Taylor's soldiers fought a small group of Mexican soldiers. Polk used this as an excuse to ask Congress to declare war on Mexico. On May 13, 1846, the **Mexican-American War** began.

General **Stephen Kearny** led a force that captured Santa Fe and took control of New Mexico. Then he headed west. He wanted to gain control of California. A small group of Californians rebelled against Mexican rule. On June 14, 1846, the Americans declared the independent **Republic of California**. The Californians used a flag with a bear on it. Because of the flag, the uprising was named the **Bear Flag Revolt**. A month later, U.S. forces arrived. They soon took control of California.

General **Winfield Scott** and his troops captured Mexico City. The Mexican government gave in to American demands.

The **Treaty of Guadalupe Hidalgo** ended the war. Under the treaty, Mexico gave a huge area of land to the United States. This land was called the **Mexican Cession**.

> List the names of the three generals on the American side.
>
> _____
> _____
> _____

> For how long was California an independent country?
>
> _____

> Why was the California uprising called the Bear Flag Revolt?
>
> _____
> _____

CHALLENGE ACTIVITY

Critical Thinking: Elaborate Many soldiers who fought in the Mexican-American War went on to fight in the Civil War. Choose a general from this section and report on what he did, or how he impacted the Civil War.

Interactive Reader and Study Guide

The Nation Splits Apart

Chapter Summary

Compromise of 1850
• California enters as a free state
• Popular sovereignty on slavery in rest of Mexican Cession

Kansas-Nebraska Act (1854)
• Popular sovereignty on slavery
• "Bleeding Kansas"

Disputes over the spread of slavery divided the nation

Lincoln-Douglas Debates (1858)
• National attention on slavery dispute
• National attention on Lincon's views

Election of 1860
• Split in Democratic Party
• Antislavery Lincoln elected president
• Lower South secedes

COMPREHENSION AND CRITICAL THINKING

Use information from the graphic organizer to answer the following questions.

1. **Recall** What act made California a free state?

_____

_____

2. **Compare** What provision did the Compromise of 1850 have in common with the Kansas-Nebraska Act of 1854?

_____

_____

3. **Explain** What results did the Lincoln-Douglas debates have on the nation?

_____

_____

4. **Identify Cause and Effect** What was the biggest effect of the election of 1860?

_____

_____

Interactive Reader and Study Guide

MAIN IDEA
The issue of slavery dominated national politics during the 1850s. The federal government forged policies in attempts to satisfy both North and South.

Key Terms and People

radical a person with extreme views

Millard Fillmore president who supported the Compromise of 1850

Compromise of 1850 set of five laws that dealt with slavery issues

Fugitive Slave Act law that made it a federal crime to assist runaway slaves

Harriet Beecher Stowe author of *Uncle Tom's Cabin*

Uncle Tom's Cabin novel about slave life in the South

Stephen Douglas senator from Illinois; led the fight to pass the Compromise of 1850

popular sovereignty the idea of letting residents decide what laws to be governed by; suggested as a way to decide whether slavery should be allowed

Kansas-Nebraska Act law giving popular sovereignty to Kansas and Nebraska

free-soilers people who were against the spread of slavery

Republican Party political party founded in 1854 when members of the Free Soil Party joined forces with northern Whigs and others who opposed slavery

nativism opposition to immigration

Section Summary

SLAVERY IN THE UNITED STATES

By 1850 there had been slavery in America for 200 years. The northern states began to end slavery after the Revolutionary War. By 1790 more than 90 percent of enslaved Americans lived in the South.

By 1850 there were two societies in America. In the North, workers were paid. In the South, huge numbers of workers were enslaved. Many southerners viewed slaves as property. After winning the Mexican-American War in 1848, the United States added 500,000 square miles of new territory. New states would be formed. The question was raised of whether they would allow slavery. In 1850 California applied for statehood. At the time, Congress had the same number of members from free states as from slave states. Adding new states would upset the balance.

> Circle the percent of enslaved Americans who lived in the South by 1790.

> What were the two societies in America in 1850?
>
> _____
>
> _____

> What was going to upset the balance in Congress?
>
> _____
>
> _____

The Nation Splits Apart

Section 1

THE COMPROMISE OF 1850

The Senate held an important debate over the issue. John C. Calhoun said that southern states might secede. Daniel Webster was against slavery. He thought that preserving the Union was more important, however. William Seward was against any compromise on slavery. This made him a **radical**—a person with extreme views. The president, **Millard Fillmore**, favored compromise. Finally Congress passed five laws that became known as the **Compromise of 1850**. California would be admitted as a free state. Residents of the New Mexico and Utah Territories would decide whether to allow slavery. Part of the compromise was the **Fugitive Slave Act**. This act made it a federal crime to help runaway slaves. Many Northerners were angry. One was **Harriet Beecher Stowe**. She wrote a book called *Uncle Tom's Cabin* about slave life in the South.

> **Why was William Seward considered a radical?**
> _____
> _____

THE KANSAS-NEBRASKA ACT

Stephen Douglas was a senator from Illinois. He thought the slavery issue in Kansas and Nebraska should be decided by **popular sovereignty**. This meant that residents should decide whether to allow it. The **Kansas-Nebraska Act** made popular sovereignty the law in these areas in May 1854.

> **What did Douglas propose for Kansas and Nebraska?**
> _____
> _____
> _____

REACTIONS IN NORTH AND SOUTH

Northerners were very angry about the Kansas-Nebraska Act allowing slavery. Many northern Democrats quit the party. The Whig party was also weakened. The Free Soil Party had been formed in 1848. People who opposed slavery were sometimes called **free-soilers**. Northern Whigs and the Free Soil Party joined forces to become the **Republican Party**. They briefly worked with the Know-Nothings, members of the American Party. However, the Know-Nothings favored **nativism**. They were opposed to immigration. Many Americans found this troubling.

CHALLENGE ACTIVITY

Critical Thinking: Drawing Inferences Use current events to develop a platform for a new political party in the United States.

Interactive Reader and Study Guide

The Nation Splits Apart

Section 2

MAIN IDEA
Rising tensions over slavery expanded from political rhetoric into outright violence.

Key Terms and People

"Bleeding Kansas" nickname given to Kansas because there was so much slavery-related violence there

Franklin Pierce president from 1852 to 1856; called Kansas antislavery government rebels

John Brown antislavery leader of the Pottawatomie Massacre

Pottawatomie Massacre killing of five pro-slavery Kansas settlers

guerrilla war fighting marked by sabotage, ambushes, and other surprise attacks

James Buchanan president elected in 1856

John Frémont war hero and California senator; first presidential nominee of the Republican Party in 1852

Dred Scott decision Supreme Court ruling that protected the property rights of people who held slaves

Lecompton Constitution Kansas pro-slavery constitution that was rejected by voters

Section Summary

THE STRUGGLE FOR KANSAS

Many acts of slavery-related violence within the Kansas Territory caused it to be called **"Bleeding Kansas."** Pro- and antislavery and forces struggled for control. Antislavery settlers rushed in. Pro-slavery groups raised money to bring people in. Voters there were to elect a territorial legislature. It would write a constitution that would allow or ban slavery. Then Kansas could become a state. On election day, 1,700 armed men from Missouri came to Kansas and voted. A pro-slavery delegate to Congress was elected.

More voting fraud took place in later elections. In voting for a legislature, more votes were cast than there were voters. A pro-slavery legislature was elected. Antislavery settlers elected their own legislature. By 1856 there were two governments.

In the town of Lawrence, some pro-slavery settlers were shot. Missourians came to attack the town. They turned back when they found antislavery settlers

Why was the Kansas Territory called "Bleeding Kansas"?
_____
_____

Why were there two governments in Kansas?
_____
_____
_____

defending it. President **Franklin Pierce** seemed to be pro-slavery. In January 1856 he called the antislavery government rebels. On May 21, a pro-slavery sheriff and 800 men came to Lawrence. They burned and looted much of the town.

    John Brown was against slavery. He wanted revenge for what happened at Lawrence. He and some followers killed five pro-slavery settlers. This became known as the **Pottawatomie Massacre**. During the next four months, a civil war raged in Kansas. A **guerrilla war** followed. This is fighting marked by sabotage, ambushes, and other surprise attacks. In Congress a pro-slavery congressman beat an antislavery senator nearly to death.

> **Who burned and looted Lawrence?**
> _____
> _____
> _____

THE ELECTION OF 1856

In the presidential election, the Democratic Party nominated **James Buchanan**. The Republican Party nominated **John Frémont**. The Know-Nothings nominated Millard Fillmore. The Democrats won.

BUCHANAN'S PRESIDENCY

Buchanan supported popular sovereignty in the territories. Many Americans thought the crisis was over. Then the Supreme Court handed down the *Dred Scott* decision. The ruling protected property rights of slaveholders. Many people were angry. The ruling further divided northern and southern Democrats. In Kansas, pro-slavery leaders wrote the **Lecompton Constitution**. After three tries, voters overwhelmingly rejected it.

> **Which group, pro-slavery or antislavery, did the *Dred Scott* decision favor?**
> _____

JOHN BROWN'S RAID

John Brown wanted to free slaves by force if necessary. He led a raid on a place where guns were stored at Harpers Ferry, Virginia. Brown was captured by U.S. Marines led by Colonel Robert E. Lee. He was tried and sentenced to death.

> **Circle the name of the leader of the Marines who captured John Brown.**

CHALLENGE ACTIVITY

Critical Thinking: Elaborate Do research on the antislavery (abolitionist) movement. Find out what the goals were and the methods used to further those goals. Write a report to be presented to your classmates.

MAIN IDEA
After gaining national prominence in the late 1850s, Abraham Lincoln became president in 1860.

Key Terms and People

Abraham Lincoln antislavery Republican elected to the presidency in 1860

Lincoln-Douglas debates debates that took place in 1858 when Lincoln opposed Stephen Douglas's bid for a third term in the Senate

Freeport Doctrine position put forth by Douglas during a debate with Lincoln; said that local legislatures could decide whether to allow slavery

platform statement of the principles that a group stands for

John C. Breckinridge southern Democratic candidate for president in 1860 election

John Bell Tennessee senator nominated for president in 1860 by the moderate southern Constitutional Union Party

Section Summary

LINCOLN, POLITICS, AND SLAVERY

Abraham Lincoln was born to poor parents in Kentucky. Lincoln could not remember a time when he was not against slavery. He worked on a boat moving produce from Indiana to New Orleans. There he saw a slave auction. He described it as horrid. As a young man Lincoln moved to Illinois. A year later, he first ran for the state legislature. He lost that election. Two years later he won the first of four terms there.

In 1846 Lincoln ran for Congress. He accused President Polk of starting the Mexican-American War to extend slavery. Lincoln believed that Congress had the right to regulate slavery in the territories and in Washington, D.C. However, he thought that only the states had the right to decide on slavery within their borders. In 1849 Lincoln proposed ending slavery in Washington, D.C., by paying slaveholders to free their slaves. This was called compensated emancipation. It was one solution to many people's belief that private property rights protected slavery. Lincoln resigned from Congress in 1849 and went back to practicing law.

> **What was Lincoln's first job in politics?**
> _____
> _____

> **What rights did Lincoln believe only the states had?**
> _____
> _____
> _____

The Nation Splits Apart

LINCOLN AND DOUGLAS CLASH

Lincoln was upset when Congress passed the Kansas-Nebraska Act. He got back into politics. He was against Stephen Douglas's stand on popular sovereignty. In 1856 Lincoln helped organize the Illinois Republican Party. In 1858 he opposed Douglas's re-election to the U.S. Senate. His speeches made many slaveholders believe that he was against slavery. The **Lincoln-Douglas debates** took place in 1858. In what came to be known as the **Freeport Doctrine**, Douglas said that local legislatures had the power to end slavery. Lincoln spoke of the immorality of slavery. Douglas kept his Senate seat. However, many historians believe Lincoln won the debates. They brought Lincoln national attention. The debates had a direct effect on the presidential election of 1860.

> **How did Lincoln feel about popular sovereignty?**
> _____
> _____

> **What did Lincoln think was immoral?**
> _____

THE ELECTION OF 1860

Both the nation and the Democratic Party were divided in 1860. Southern Democrats wanted to have a **platform** that protected slavery. A platform is a statement of the principles a group stands for. Northern Democrats supported popular sovereignty. The party split. Northern Democrats nominated Douglas. Southern Democrats nominated **John C. Breckinridge**. Southern moderates formed the Constitutional Union Party. They nominated Tennessee senator **John Bell**. The Republican Party platform opposed the spread of slavery. The Republicans nominated Lincoln.

There were actually two sectional elections in the presidential election. Lincoln competed against Douglas in the North. In the South, Bell competed against Breckinridge. Lincoln won nearly every northern state. However, he had less than 40 percent of the total popular vote. This was more than any of the others received. Lincoln was the new president.

> **Circle the name of the person nominated for president by the southern Democrats.**

CHALLENGE ACTIVITY

Critical Thinking: Elaborate Find out about other presidential elections in which candidates from the major parties lost to a third-party candidate or in which a third-party candidate took enough votes to affect the election outcome. Write a one-page essay on how American politics have been affected by third-party candidates in the past.

The Nation Splits Apart

Section 4

MAIN IDEA
The election of Abraham Lincoln led to the secession of the southern states.

Key Terms and People

Jefferson Davis president of the Confederate States of America

provisional temporary

Confederate States of America name the southern states gave to the new nation they formed after leaving the Union

Crittenden Compromise plan to change the Constitution to ban slavery north of the old Missouri Compromise line separating free and slave states, and not interfere with slavery south of that line

Peace Convention meeting of people from the northern states and some southern states that tried to find a way to avoid war

Section Summary

SECESSION!

The United States began breaking apart on November 13, 1860. One week after Lincoln's election, the South Carolina legislature called a meeting to decide whether to leave the Union. In December it issued a resolution. It said South Carolina was dissolving its union with the other states. Mississippi, Florida, and Alabama left in early January 1861. By February 1 Georgia, Louisiana, and Texas had also left. Virginia, North Carolina, Tennessee, and Arkansas warned that they would leave also if the federal government used force against any state. Not everyone in those states was in favor of secession. One-third of Texans opposed it, including Governor Sam Houston. However, even people who were against secession thought that they should unite to resist the U.S. government.

In the North, there were different reactions to secession. Many thought the Union would be better off without the slave states. Others thought the South should be allowed to go in peace. Still others worried about the long-term effects of secession. They pointed out that any minority might decide to secede if it did not get what it wanted.

> **How did Lincoln's election affect South Carolina?**
> _____
> _____

> **How did Northerners react to secession?**
> _____
> _____
> _____
> _____

Although Lincoln had been elected, he would not take office until March. He was afraid that if he made a public statement it would make things worse. President Buchanan did not help. He said that states had no right to secede. However, he also said that the federal government had no power to stop them. Buchanan did refuse to hand over federal property in South Carolina. This included Fort Sumter and Fort Moultrie.

> **What did President Buchanan do about secession?**
>
> _____
> _____
> _____

FORMING THE CONFEDERACY

In February 1861 representatives of the seven seceded states met to form a new nation. In five days they wrote a constitution. They chose **Jefferson Davis** as **provisional**, or temporary, president. Davis had served in the U.S. Senate and as U.S. Secretary of War. The new constitution was based on the U.S. Constitution. However, it specifically recognized and protected slavery. It also recognized the "sovereign and independent" nature of each state. The new nation was similar to the United States under the Articles of Confederation. It was called the **Confederate States of America**. The Confederacy had no money and no way of making any. It got off to a rocky start.

> **How was the Confederacy like the United States under the Articles of Confederation?**
>
> _____
> _____
> _____

COMPROMISE FAILS

To keep the Union together, the U.S. House and Senate came up with several plans for compromise. The **Crittenden Compromise** proposed changing the U.S. Constitution to ban slavery north of the old Missouri Compromise line separating free and slave states. It would also guarantee that slavery would be left alone below the line. Leaders from both North and South opposed the compromise. In 1861 a **Peace Convention** met in Washington, D.C. It came up with no new ideas. Lincoln became president on March 4, 1861. He promised not to interfere with slavery where it already was.

> **Would the Crittenden Compromise have allowed slavery in some of the new territories?**
>
> _____

CHALLENGE ACTIVITY

Critical Thinking: Evaluate If you had been a northerner, how would you have felt about secession? Write three paragraphs explaining your views.

Chapter Summary

The Civil War

Preparing for War	Early Confederate Successes	The Union Gains Advantage	The Final Phase	Results of the War
• Calls for troops • More southern states secede • Holding the border states • The Anaconda Plan • The Union blockade • Cotton diplomacy	• First Battle of Bull Run • The peninsula campaign • Second Battle of Bull Run	• Capture of Fort Henry and Fort Donelson • Battle of Shiloh • The Mississippi River campaign • Battle of Antietam • The Emancipation Proclamation • Siege of Vicksburg • Battle of Gettysburg • Battle of Chickamauga	• Grant's Virginia campaign • Siege of Petersburg • Battle of Atlanta • Election of 1864 • Sherman's march • Surrender at Appomattox	• The end of slavery • Restoration of the Union • Devastation of the South • More than 600,000 deaths

COMPREHENSION AND CRITICAL THINKING

Use information from the graphic organizer to answer the following questions.

1. **Recall** What were some early Confederate successes?

_____

_____

2. **Recall** Name three events that gave the Union the advantage.

_____

_____

3. **Identify** What was one of the last big battles of the Civil War?

_____

_____

4. **Recall** How did the Civil War end?

_____

_____

_____

The Civil War

> **MAIN IDEA**
> The attack on Fort Sumter led both the North and the South to prepare for war in earnest.

Key Terms and People

Robert Anderson Union commander of Fort Sumter

artillery large mounted guns

border states slaveholding states that remained in the Union and formed its border with the Confederacy

martial law rule by military authorities during time of war

Anaconda Plan General Winfield Scott's plan to seal off the South from the rest of the world

cotton diplomacy the use of cotton as a tool of foreign policy

embargo the stopping of trade

Section Summary

THE FALL OF FORT SUMTER

Robert Anderson was the commander of Fort Sumter in South Carolina. When South Carolina seceded, it demanded that he surrender the fort. He refused. Confederate president Jefferson Davis ordered the fort taken. On April 12, 1861, Confederate **artillery**, or large mounted guns, fired on the fort. The Civil War had begun. The next day, Fort Sumter surrendered to the Confederacy.

> Who fired the first shots in the Civil War?
> _____

THE RUSH TO WAR

When Fort Sumter fell, Lincoln called for volunteers to put down the rebellion. Northerners rushed to enlist. The eight slave states in the Union were forced to choose sides. Virginia, Arkansas, Tennessee, and North Carolina seceded.

> Underline the four states that seceded after Lincoln's call for volunteers.

THE BORDER STATES

Delaware, Kentucky, Maryland, and Missouri were **border states**. This meant that they were slaveholding states that remained in the Union and formed its border with the Confederacy. If Maryland seceded,

The Civil War

Washington, D.C., would be surrounded by the Confederacy. Lincoln placed parts of Maryland under **martial law**. This is a type of rule in which military commanders are in control and citizens' rights and freedoms are suspended. The military supervised new elections that brought a pro-Union state legislature into office. Missouri was important because it could control the lower Mississippi River. Those favoring secession were not strong enough to take the state out of the Union. Kentucky at first tried not to choose sides. After a Confederate invasion, it joined the Union.

> **Why was Maryland important to the Union?**
> _____
> _____
> _____

GOALS AND STRATEGIES

Lincoln knew that many northerners would not support the war if it was about slavery. He also knew that making slavery the issue might push border states to secede. So he asked northerners to fight to save the Union. Southerners wanted to be left alone with slavery unchanged. They prepared to defend themselves against invasion. The North was better equipped than the South to fight the war. It had a much larger population. It also had more than 85 percent of the nation's factories.

> **Why did Lincoln ask northerners to fight?**
> _____

The first plan for fighting the war was called the **Anaconda Plan**. It was created by General Winfield Scott. It called for sealing off the South from the rest of the world. It called for a naval blockade and control of the Mississippi River.

One of the South's strengths was its support for the war. It also had good military leadership and much confidence. Also, southerners believed that Great Britain and France would come to their aid. They thought these countries needed the cotton they got from the South. This use of cotton as a tool of foreign policy was called **cotton diplomacy**. Southern planters were told to **embargo**, or totally restrict, exports of cotton to markets overseas. France and Great Britain turned to Egypt and India for cotton.

> **What were the South's strengths coming into the war?**
> _____
> _____
> _____
> _____

CHALLENGE ACTIVITY

Critical Thinking: Design Design a recruiting poster for one of the sides fighting the Civil War.

MAIN IDEA
Widespread fighting occurred during the first two years of the Civil War.

Key Terms and People

First Battle of Bull Run first major battle of the Civil War

Stonewall Jackson nickname for Confederate General Thomas Jackson

infantry foot soldiers

casualties military term for those killed, wounded, or missing in action

George McClellan Union general appointed after the First Battle of Bull Run

cavalry soldiers on horseback

ironclads armored gunboats

Ulysses S. Grant Union general who commanded in the West

Battle of Shiloh Union victory in Tennessee

Battle of Antietam bloodiest day of the Civil War

Section Summary

THE MAJOR BATTLES BEGIN

The first major battle of the Civil War was the **First Battle of Bull Run** in July 1861. The battle was a free-for-all. Some Confederate troops, commanded by General Thomas Jackson, held fast. This earned Jackson the nickname **Stonewall Jackson**. The entire line of southern **infantry**, or foot soldiers, charged. The Union retreated in a stampede. Total **casualties** for both sides were about 5,000. *Casualties* is the military term for those killed, wounded, or missing in action. The battle ended Northern hopes for a short war. Lincoln called for a million more volunteers. He named **George McClellan** as their general. Most of the leadership on both sides had trained in the tactics Napoleon used when he conquered Europe. This included charges by **cavalry**, or soldiers on horseback. However, weapons had come a long way since Napoleon's time. Guns were more accurate and could fire farther and be reloaded faster. The killing power of artillery had increased. Camouflage, the telegraph, and railroads were also used.

> **What was the first major battle of the Civil War?**
> _____

> **What battle ended Northern hopes for a short war?**
> _____

The Civil War

THE FIGHT FOR THE MISSISSIPPI VALLEY

The Union's **ironclads** were successful new weapons. These were armored gunboats. They helped in Union plans to control the Mississippi River. Union gunboats and troops under the command of **Ulysses S. Grant** took Forts Henry and Donelson. Then the Union won the **Battle of Shiloh** in Tennessee. This battle opened the way for the Union to gain complete control of the Mississippi River. New Orleans was captured. The town of Vicksburg, Mississippi, became the last Confederate stronghold on the river.

> **What was the last Confederate stronghold on the Mississippi River?**
>
> _____

THE WAR IN THE EAST

McClellan never seemed ready to fight. He finally attacked Yorktown, Virginia. The Confederates retreated toward Richmond. Suddenly they turned and attacked. Both sides suffered heavy casualties in the Battle of Seven Pines. Robert E. Lee took command of the Confederate army. Then he attacked McClellan in the Seven Days' Battles. McClellan retreated. Lee attacked Union forces at the Second Battle of Bull Run. The Union lost again.

> **Who took command of the Confederate army?**
>
> _____

THE UNION IS INVADED

The defeats in Virginia lowered morale in the North. Lee felt it was time to invade the North. Lee's army crossed the Potomac into western Maryland. Then McClellan discovered Lee's plans. On September 17, 1862, the **Battle of Antietam** took place. It was the bloodiest day of the Civil War. If he had attacked again the next day, McClellan could have destroyed the Confederate army. Instead, the Confederate troops retreated to Virginia. Lincoln replaced McClellan with General Ambrose Burnside. Burnside hoped to surprise Lee at Fredericksburg. His attack resulted in a slaughter of Union troops at the Battle of Fredericksburg.

> **What was the bloodiest day of the Civil War?**
>
> _____
>
> _____

CHALLENGE ACTIVITY

Critical Thinking: Develop Write a newspaper dispatch about one of the battles mentioned in this section.

Interactive Reader and Study Guide

The Civil War

 MAIN IDEA
The Civil War created hardships, challenges, and opportunities for people in the North and the South.

Key Terms and People

Emancipation Proclamation document that freed the slaves in all areas that had rebelled against the United States

emancipation the act of freeing someone from slavery

freedmen emancipated slaves

conscription forced service in the military

Copperheads northerners who were against the war

habeas corpus constitutional right of an arrested person to appear in court and be charged with a crime

Clara Barton nurse who cared for the wounded on the battlefield and later started the American Red Cross

Section Summary

THE EMANCIPATION PROCLAMATION

On Januray 1, 1863, Lincoln issued the **Emancipation Proclamation**. This document freed the slaves in all areas that had rebelled against the United States. **Emancipation** is the act of freeing someone from slavery. Some people worried that freed slaves would compete for jobs. There were riots against black workers. Great Britain thought the proclamation did not go far enough. Lincoln had not freed slaves where he had the power to do so. However, Britain was also unwilling to side with the South, which was a slave power.

> Underline the date when Lincoln issued the Emancipation Proclamation.

> What did Great Britain think of the Emancipation Proclamation?
> _____
> _____

AFRICAN AMERICANS AND THE WAR

Enslaved African Americans made many contributions to the war. They did many of the armies' non-combat jobs. The Emancipation Proclamation urged **freedmen**, or emancipated slaves, to join the Union army and navy. By the end of the war, more than 10 percent of Union soldiers were African American. African Americans fought in some 200 battles.

> Underline the number of battles in which African Americans fought.

LIFE IN THE MILITARY

Most of the troops who died in the war were victims of disease. There were no vaccinations or antibiotics. Civil War doctors did not know about germs. They rarely washed their hands or their instruments. In 1861 Lincoln approved the creation of the United States Sanitary Commission. Most of its volunteers were women. The Sanitary Commission provided nurses and ambulance drivers. Its volunteers also performed many tasks to make life in camp better. On average, soldiers spent 75 percent of their time in camp. They crowded into tents to sleep. Later in the war Confederate soldiers had to sleep in the open. Conditions for prisoners of war were terrible.

> **Why did so many troops die of disease?**
> _____
> _____

LIFE ON THE HOME FRONT

Shortages and high prices made life hard in the South. The Confederate government printed large sums of paper money to pay for the war. As a result, the South suffered inflation. This is a rise in prices due to an increased supply of money. The Confederate Congress enacted the first military draft in American history. This **conscription**, or forced military service, was very unpopular. The Union also had to use the draft. Northerners who were against the war were called **Copperheads**. They called on Union troops to desert. To deal with this threat, Lincoln suspended **habeas corpus**. This is the right of an arrested person to appear in court and be charged with a crime. Women made many contributions to the war. They served as farmers, nurses, and clerks. They worked in factories. Some spied or disguised themselves as men to enlist. **Clara Barton** cared for the wounded on the battlefield. She later started the American Red Cross.

> **Underline the contributions that women made to the war.**

CHALLENGE ACTIVITY

Critical Thinking: Drawing Inferences Create a table that lists arguments for and against the draft if it were to be used today.

The Civil War

MAIN IDEA
Important fighting occurred in all sections of the country as well as at sea.

Key Terms and People

***Trent* affair** the taking of a British ship by a U.S. warship in order to capture two Confederate leaders

Battle of Glorieta Pass Union victory in northern New Mexico

Battle of Pea Ridge Arkansas battle in which Native Americans took part

Stand Watie Native American Confederate general

Battle of Chancellorsville Robert E. Lee's greatest victory

Battle of Gettysburg three-day battle that ended Lee's invasion of the North

George Meade Union general at Gettysburg

James Longstreet Lee's most trusted commander after Stonewall Jackson died

Pickett's Charge Confederate charge at Gettysburg from which half the 15,000 soldiers did not return

Battle of Chickamauga battle in northwest Georgia that ended in a Confederate victory

Section Summary

THE CIVIL WAR AT SEA

The Civil War was a world event. It affected trade. It also affected relations with other nations. In the ***Trent* affair,** two Confederate leaders were trying to get to Great Britain to seek aid for the South. A Union naval captain boarded the British ship they were on and seized them. After Britain sent troops to Canada, Lincoln released the two men.

The Union blockaded the South. To export its cotton and get supplies, ships called blockade runners were built. However, the South was still short of supplies. The Confederates built an ironclad ship from a captured Union ship, the *Merrimack*. The Union built an ironclad, the *Monitor*, which fought the *Merrimack*. The battle had no clear winner. The Confederacy also bought raider ships in Europe. These ships attacked Union merchant ships on the world's oceans.

> **What was the *Trent* affair?**
> _____
> _____
> _____

> **What were the names of the two ironclad ships that fought each other?**
> _____
> _____

Interactive Reader and Study Guide

THE WAR IN THE WEST

About 90 Civil War battles were fought west of the Mississippi. Confederates from Texas tried to invade western Union territories in 1862. Volunteers from California, Kansas, and Colorado helped stop them in the **Battle of Glorieta Pass**. More than 10,000 Native Americans took part in the war on both sides. Some took part in the **Battle of Pea Ridge**, the biggest battle west of the Mississippi. Native Americans under Cherokee leader **Stand Watie** fought for the Confederacy. Watie was the only Native American to hold the rank of general. He was also the last Confederate general to surrender when the war ended.

> Circle the number of Civil War engagements that were fought west of the Mississippi.

THREE MAJOR BATTLES

The **Battle of Chancellorsville** lasted three days. The South won, but Stonewall Jackson was killed. The battle was Lee's greatest victory. The South had defeated a force nearly twice its size. In June 1863 Lee marched his army into Pennsylvania. The two sides fought for three days in the **Battle of Gettysburg**. The Union army was now under the command of **George Meade**. **James Longstreet** was Lee's most trusted commander after Jackson's death. He tried to talk Lee into retreating. On the third day, Lee called on one of his officers to lead an attack. In **Pickett's Charge**, 15,000 men marched across an open field into the line of fire. Only about half of the soldiers returned. Lee was forced to retreat back to Virginia. There, news reached him that Grant had captured Vicksburg.

> What battle is considered to be Lee's greatest victory?
> _____

THE CHATTANOOGA CAMPAIGN

The Confederate army won a major victory at the **Battle of Chickamauga** in northwest Georgia. However, the Union army was still able to capture Chattanooga, which was its main purpose. Union troops were trapped there until Grant ended the Confederate siege. Victories in this area opened the way for the Union to invade Georgia.

> What opened the way for the Union to invade Georgia?
> _____
> _____

CHALLENGE ACTIVITY

Critical Thinking: Elaborate Do research on the Battle of Chancellorsville and plot its progress on a map.

MAIN IDEA
Southerners continued to hope for victory in 1864, but military and political events caused those hopes to fade.

Key Terms and People

William Tecumseh Sherman Union general who replaced Grant in the West

Battle of the Wilderness battle where the South tried to stop Grant's push to Richmond

Battle of Spotsylvania 11-day series of clashes that failed to stop Grant's push to Richmond

Battle of Cold Harbor battle fought as Union soldiers pushed to Richmond

Battle of Atlanta battle that led to the capture of Atlanta by Sherman's troops

Thirteenth Amendment constitutional amendment ending slavery in the United States

Section Summary

GRANT VERSUS LEE

In March 1864 Lincoln gave Ulysses S. Grant the command of all Union armies. Grant named **William Tecumseh Sherman** to replace him as commander on the western front. It was the year of a presidential election. Lee hoped that if the South could hold out until the November election, northerners might get tired of the war. They might reject Lincoln and a different president might accept southern independence. Grant hoped to end the war before November. He moved the Union army toward Richmond. The North and the South fought in the two-day **Battle of the Wilderness**. Grant's losses were nearly twice Lee's. Still he pushed on. The armies then fought for 11 days in what became known as the **Battle of Spotsylvania**. Grant continued to push toward Richmond. The armies fought again at the **Battle of Cold Harbor**. In the first 30 minutes, there were 7,000 Union casualties. Then Grant started a siege of Richmond. Meanwhile, Sherman set out from Chattanooga on his invasion of Georgia. Atlanta was an important manufacturing and transportation center in the South. General John Hood tried to stop Sherman in the **Battle of Atlanta**. Sherman laid siege to the city. On September 2 the Union army marched into the city.

Circle the name of the man who took over for Grant in the West.

Underline the names of the battles that took place on Grant's way to Richmond.

Why was Atlanta valuable to the Confederacy?

_____

_____

CONFEDERATE HOPES FADE

The Democrats chose General George McClellan as
their candidate for the upcoming presidential election.
They wanted an end to the war. To get more support,
Republicans placed Andrew Johnson on the ticket
with Lincoln. Johnson was a pro-Union Democrat
from Tennessee. Still, Lincoln was afraid that he
would lose the election unless there was a change in
the war. Sherman's capture of Atlanta was the change
he needed. Lincoln was easily reelected. His victory
allowed Congress to pass the **Thirteenth
Amendment**. The amendment ended slavery in the
United States.

> **How did Republicans try to get more support in the election of 1864?**
> _____
> _____

THE WAR COMES TO AN END

After the election Sherman began to march across
Georgia. His army destroyed everything they could
along the way. Their path of destruction was 300
miles long and 50 to 60 miles wide. Sherman wanted
to punish the South and show them that further
resistance was hopeless. On December 21 Sherman
entered Savannah. Then he turned north into South
Carolina. Again, he left a path of destruction. Sherman
then headed north to join Grant.

On April 3, 1865, Grant and his army marched into
Richmond. The Confederate army retreated. Grant
chased the army and finally surrounded them at the
town of Appomattox Court House, Virginia. Lee
decided to surrender. Grant gave the Confederates
generous terms. They had only to lay down their
weapons and leave. Then Grant offered food for Lee's
starving troops. The last of the Confederate forces did
not surrender until May 26, 1865. Lincoln, however,
did not live to see the end of the war.

> **Where did Lee's army finally surrender?**
> _____
> _____

CHALLENGE ACTIVITY

Critical Thinking: Evaluate The terms of surrender that Grant offered
Lee were very generous. Write two paragraphs explaining why you agree
or disagree with his actions.

Reconstruction

Chapter Summary

Presidential Reconstruction
- Freedmen's Bureau
- Lincoln's Ten Percent Plan
- Johnson's plans and actions

Congressional Reconstruction
- Civil Rights Act
- Fourteenth and Fifteenth Amendments
- Reconstruction Acts
- Enforcement Acts

Reconstruction Government
- Republican rule
- Scalawags and carpetbaggers
- African American elected officials
- Republican improvement programs

The Reconstruction Era

Resistance to Reconstruction
- Black Codes
- Violence against freedmen
- Violence against Republican rule
- Democratic Redeemers

Reconstruction Economics
- Labor contracts and wage-labor system
- Sharecropping and tenant farming
- Continued dependence on cotton
- African American land ownership

Reconstruction Ends
- Reconstruction's failures
- Declining support
- Liberal Republicans
- Compromise of 1877

COMPREHENSION AND CRITICAL THINKING

Use information from the graphic organizer to answer the following questions.

1. **Recall** What was Lincoln's plan for Reconstruction called?

_____

2. **Identify** What amendments to the Constitution were passed during Reconstruction?

_____

3. **Identify** On what crop was the South dependent during Reconstruction?

_____

4. **Make Inferences** How do you think some southerners reacted to Reconstruction? How did you arrive at that inference?

_____

_____

_____

Reconstruction

> **MAIN IDEA**
> Northern leaders had differing ideas for dealing with the many issues and
> challenges of restoring the southern states to the Union.

Key Terms and People

Freedmen's Bureau government organization aimed at helping black and white
southerners who had lost their homes in the fighting

Ten Percent Plan Lincoln's plan for readmitting southern states to the Union

Thaddeus Stevens Republican leader opposed to the Ten Percent Plan

Wade-Davis Bill Congressional plan for Reconstruction that Lincoln refused to sign

pocket veto when the president prevents a bill's passage by ignoring it

John Wilkes Booth a southerner who shot and killed Abraham Lincoln

Andrew Johnson vice president under Lincoln; later president

Section Summary

THE SOUTH AFTER THE WAR

After the Civil War many southern cities were in
ruins. Farms and plantations were destroyed or
neglected. Farm buildings, machinery, work animals,
and other livestock were gone. More than one-fifth of
the South's white male population had died. Railroad
lines were useless. Although free, nearly 4 million
African Americans faced an unknown future. Most
had no money or education. They did not have jobs. In
addition, there were many legal and political questions
to be answered. Should Confederates be forgiven?
What place would African Americans have in political
life in the South?

> **What problems did freed
> slaves in the South face?**
>
> _____
> _____
> _____
> _____

WARTIME RECONSTRUCTION

In 1865 Congress created the **Freedmen's Bureau**. Its
purpose was to help black and white southerners who
had lost their homes in the war. Even during the war,
people had tried different ways to help freed African
Americans. In some places former slaves were hired
to work land. They could keep or sell the crops they
raised. In South Carolina and Georgia more than
40,000 freedmen were farming by the end of the war.

Reconstruction

Some northerners wanted to punish the South. Lincoln hoped to treat the South with mercy. In 1863 Lincoln issued a Proclamation of Amnesty and Reconstruction. It offered forgiveness to all southerners (except top Confederate leaders) who signed an oath of loyalty to the Union and supported emancipation. If 10 percent of state's voters took the oath, they could organize a new state government. This was known as the **Ten Percent Plan**. Before the war ended, Lincoln accepted three states back into the Union on these terms. However, Congress wanted to be in charge of Reconstruction. Some in Congress thought that the Ten Percent Plan was too easy. Republican leader **Thaddeus Stevens** spoke against Lincoln's plan. Congress passed its own Reconstruction plan. It was called the **Wade-Davis Bill**. Instead of 10 percent, it required a majority of a state's white male citizens to pledge loyalty. However, Lincoln used the **pocket veto** and killed the bill by ignoring it and not signing it.

> **How did Lincoln want to treat the South?**
> _____
> _____

> **What did members of Congress think of the Ten Percent Plan?**
> _____
> _____

LINCOLN'S ASSASSINATION

On April 14, 1865, **John Wilkes Booth** shot President Lincoln. Booth was a supporter of secession and the Confederacy. The nation grieved deeply for Lincoln. **Andrew Johnson**, the vice president, was sworn in as president a few hours after Lincoln's death.

> **Circle the date when Lincoln was shot.**

JOHNSON AND CONGRESS DIFFER OVER RECONSTRUCTION

Andrew Johnson wanted to reunite North and South but not give Congress control of Reconstruction. While Congress was in recess, Johnson called for southern states to rejoin the Union by repealing secession, abolishing slavery, and refusing to pay Confederate debts. When Congress returned, all the southern states except Texas were back in the Union.

> **What happened while Congress was in recess?**
> _____
> _____
> _____

CHALLENGE ACTIVITY

Critical Thinking: Evaluate How do you think the South should have been treated after the war? Explain your opinion in one page.

Interactive Reader and Study Guide

Reconstruction

 MAIN IDEA
Congress took control of Reconstruction as a new, radical branch of the Republican Party was emerging.

Key Terms and People

Black Codes laws passed in the South to keep freedmen in a slavelike condition

Ku Klux Klan group of white southerners who terrorized African Americans and whites who were loyal to the U.S. government

Radical Republicans members of Congress who favored strict Reconstruction programs

Civil Rights Act made African Americans citizens; gave them the benefits whites had

Fourteenth Amendment amendment that wrote the Civil Rights Act into the Constitution

Reconstruction Acts stricter laws passed by Radical Republicans

impeachment process for charging a federal official with a crime

Fifteenth Amendment amendment saying people cannot be denied the right to vote because of their race

Section Summary

RECONSTRUCTION UNDER PRESIDENT JOHNSON

White southerners welcomed Johnson's approach to Reconstruction. His plan let them form new state governments on their own terms. Johnson pardoned nearly every planter and former Confederate leader who applied. Generally, the states restored their pre-war governments. In order to make sure that blacks and whites remained unequal, southern states passed laws called the **Black Codes**. These laws kept freedmen in a slavelike condition. To discourage freedmen from starting businesses, the Black Codes did not allow them to rent property in towns or cities. Freedmen who left a job could be arrested for being jobless. A few states taxed guns and dogs so that freedmen could not even hunt for food.

Some white southerners formed groups like the **Ku Klux Klan**. These groups terrorized African Americans and whites who were loyal to the U.S. government. Local officials did not often prosecute whites who used violence against African Americans.

> How did white southerners feel about Johnson's approach to Reconstruction?
>
> _____

> Underline some of the things that Black Codes required or outlawed.

Interactive Reader and Study Guide

Reconstruction

CONGRESS TAKES CONTROL OF RECONSTRUCTION

Northerners felt that if southern states could abuse freedmen the North's victory was meaningless. A congressional group called the **Radical Republicans** wanted Reconstruction to be tougher on the South. They wanted freed slaves to have the same rights as white citizens. Congress passed the **Civil Rights Act**, which gave citizenship to African Americans. Anyone who denied freedmen their rights would be tried in federal court. When Johnson vetoed the bill, Congress passed the bill over his veto.

> **Underline what the Radical Republicans wanted.**

RADICAL RECONSTRUCTION

Worried that the Civil Rights Act might be weakened, Republicans passed the **Fourteenth Amendment**, writing the Civil Rights Act into the Constitution. Then in the election of 1866, Republicans were victorious over candidates favored by Johnson. This allowed radicals in Congress to take control of Reconstruction.

> **What did the Fourteenth Amendment give to African Americans?**
> _____

Congress passed four **Reconstruction Acts** dividing the South into five military districts. States had to ratify the Fourteenth Amendment and guarantee freedmen the right to vote. They had to form new governments elected by all male citizens including African Americans. Johnson was against these policies. When the secretary of war supported Congress, Johnson fired him. The House of Representatives voted to **impeach** the president, or remove him from office. The Senate fell one vote short, leaving Johnson in office. Although Johnson lost control of Reconstruction, he continued to issue pardons to Confederate leaders.

> **What did the Reconstruction Acts require the states to do?**
> _____
> _____
> _____
> _____
> _____
> _____

In 1868 the Republicans nominated Ulysses Grant for president. He won. The Republicans passed the **Fifteenth Amendment**. This stated that people could not be denied the right to vote because of their race.

CHALLENGE ACTIVITY

Critical Thinking: Compare and Contrast Do research on Johnson's impeachment and that of President Clinton. Write about how they are similar and how they are different. Use one page.

Reconstruction

Section 3

MAIN IDEA
Republican Reconstruction had a significant impact on life in the South.

Key Terms and People

scalawag a southerner who supported Reconstruction

carpetbagger a northerner who came south to take part in the region's political and economic rebirth

Hiram Revels first African American to serve in the U.S. Senate

Southern Homestead Act law that set aside 45 million acres of government-owned land in several southern states to provide free farms for African Americans

sharecropping farming system where the farmer was an employee of the landowner and received a share of the crop

tenant farming farming system where the farmer rents the land

Section Summary

REPUBLICAN GOVERNMENT BRINGS CHANGE TO THE SOUTH

To former Confederates, a **scalawag** was a southerner who supported Reconstruction. Many scalawags were farmers who had never owned slaves and had been against the war. They became allied with notherners who came south for Reconstruction. These northerners were called **carpetbaggers**. They wanted to be a part of the political and economic rebirth in the South. These two groups were joined by the freedmen.

African Americans were the largest group of Republican voters in the South. Nearly 700 African Americans served in southern state legislatures during Reconstruction. Sixteen African Americans served in Congress. **Hiram Revels** was the first African American to serve in the U.S. Senate. The Republican governments created the region's first public school systems. They built hospitals and orphanages. The property requirements for voting and holding office were eliminated. The Black Codes were repealed. Also, to help the South grow, Republicans built thousands of miles of railroads.

> How had many scalawags felt about the Civil War?
> _____
> _____

> Circle the numbers of African Americans who served in state legislatures and in Congress.

> Underline the things that the new Republican governments did during Reconstruction.

LIFE AFTER SLAVERY FOR AFRICAN AMERICANS

Some freedmen were able to search for family members who had been sold. Some looked for jobs. Others moved to cities in the north or west. However, most stayed in the rural South. African Americans started new businesses or worked as miners, soldiers, or cowboys. Freed slaves were eager to have education. They built schools. They also started their own churches. Some of the black colleges were started by churches. Freedmen started debating clubs, drama societies, and trade associations. They started fire companies and mutual aid societies, and collected money to create orphanages and soup kitchens. African Americans started employment agencies and raised funds to aid the poor.

> Underline the types of organizations formed by African Americans.

RECONSTRUCTION AND LAND OWNERSHIP

President Johnson gave southern land back to its original owners. This left freedmen without land. Congress passed the **Southern Homestead Act** in 1866. This law set aside 45 million acres of government-owned land for African Americans. However, most freedmen could not afford to buy seed, animals, and supplies. Only about 4,000 families were able to take advantage of the offer.

Freedmen struggled to buy land in other places. Many white landowners did not want to sell to them. A system called **sharecropping** came to be used. In this system, the employer provided the land, the seed, and tools. The farmer got a share of the crop. Some also used a system called **tenant farming**. Tenant farmers rented their land. They could choose what crops to grow. A nationwide depression, however, caused cotton prices to fall. Farmers were then deeper in debt. Even industrial growth in the South did not benefit African Americans.

> Why were many freedmen not able to take advantage of the Southern Homestead Act?
>
> _____
> _____
> _____
> _____

CHALLENGE ACTIVITY

Critical Thinking: Drawing Inferences Draw a political cartoon that expresses your opinion or makes a statement about what happened to many African Americans during Reconstruction.

Reconstruction

MAIN IDEA
A variety of events and forces led to the end of Reconstruction, which left a mixed legacy for the nation.

Key Terms and People

Enforcement Acts laws with heavy penalties for anyone who tried to prevent a qualified citizen from voting

Liberal Republicans Republicans who broke with the party over the Enforcement Acts and the scandals in the Grant administration

Redeemers Democrats who controlled southern states

Rutherford B. Hayes Republican candidate for president in the 1876 election

Compromise of 1877 agreement that gave the presidency to Rutherford B. Hayes in exchange for removal of federal troops from the South

New South the South after Reconstruction because of its industrialization and economic change

Solid South name used for the South because it was so solidly Democratic until the 1970s

Section Summary

PROBLEMS WITH RECONSTRUCTION

Reconstruction also brought violence by southerners who were against it. The Ku Klux Klan was a group that terrorized people. There were other terrorist groups similar to the Klan. All of these groups wanted to undo the new structure of the South.

The groups targeted African Americans. Some whites were their victims, too. They threatened people and burned their homes. Thousands were murdered. State governments could not stop the violence. They needed help from the federal government. Congress passed the **Enforcement Acts**. These were laws with heavy penalties for anyone who tried to stop a qualified citizen from voting. The laws also banned using disguises to take away another person's rights. These acts broke the Klan's power, but the other groups were still around.

The acts caused support for Reconstruction to decrease in the North. Many northerners were upset that the army was still needed to control the South.

> How many people were murdered by white southern terrorists?
> _____

> Why did Congress pass the Enforcement Acts?
> _____
> _____

Even southern Republicans lost faith in Reconstruction. African Americans were unhappy about widespread poverty. They were upset about the lack of land reform.

The railroad building programs raised charges of government corruption. The **Liberal Republicans** broke with the party. They were upset by the Enforcement Acts and the scandals in the Grant administration. Grant was reelected in 1872. However, the Democrats got control of the House of Representatives in 1874.

> **Why did African Americans lose faith in Reconstruction?**
> _____
> _____
> _____

THE END OF RECONSTRUCTION

In 1873 the Supreme Court ruled that most civil rights and freedoms were under state control. Therefore, they were not protected under the Fourteenth Amendment. Other things also weakened Reconstruction. Southern Democrats got stronger. Terrorism grew. Grant refused to send military help to quiet the terrorism.

By 1876 all but three states were under Democratic control. Southern Democrats called themselves **Redeemers** because they won back their states. Many former Confederate leaders were back in power. **Rutherford B. Hayes** was the Republican candidate for president in 1876. The results of the election, however, were not clear. The **Compromise of 1877** gave Hayes the presidency in exchange for removing federal troops from the South. Reconstruction was over.

> **How did the Supreme Court affect Reconstruction?**
> _____
> _____
> _____

RECONSTRUCTION'S LEGACY

It was a time of industrialization and economic change in the South. So much changed that some southerners called it the **New South**.

Many southerners hated the federal government. They voted for Democrats in such numbers that the region was called the **Solid South**.

> **Why was the South sometimes called the New South?**
> _____
> _____

CHALLENGE ACTIVITY

Critical Thinking: Elaborate Write a letter to the editor of a newspaper in the North. In it, give your opinion on the success of Reconstruction.

The American West

Chapter Summary

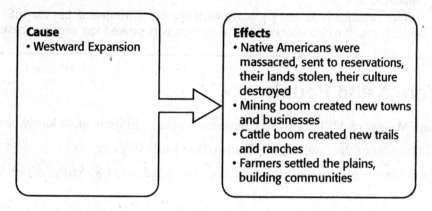

Cause
• Westward Expansion

Effects
• Native Americans were massacred, sent to reservations, their lands stolen, their culture destroyed
• Mining boom created new towns and businesses
• Cattle boom created new trails and ranches
• Farmers settled the plains, building communities

COMPREHENSION AND CRITICAL THINKING

Use information from the graphic organizer to answer the following questions.

1. **Recall** Where did farmers settle as Americans moved west?

_____

_____

2. **Identify Cause and Effect** Besides farming, what other food industry impacted the Plains?

_____

_____

3. **Identify Cause and Effect** How did changes in the location of mining change the West?

_____

_____

4. **Evaluate** What did the Native Americans lose when white settlers moved west?

_____

_____

_____

MAIN IDEA
Native Americans fought the movement of settlers westward, but the U.S. military and the persistence of American settlers proved too strong to resist.

Key Terms and People

Sand Creek Massacre killing of 150 Cheyenne women, children, and elderly people

Sitting Bull leader of the Sioux at the Battle of the Little Bighorn

Battle of the Little Bighorn battle between the Sioux and the U.S. Army, which the Sioux won

George Armstrong Custer U.S. Army colonel in charge at the Battle of the Little Bighorn

Wounded Knee Massacre killing of about 300 Sioux men, women, and children

Chief Joseph Nez Percé leader during their forced move from the Pacific Northwest

Americanization changing Native Americans' cultures and traditions

Bureau of Indian Affairs agency that managed Native American reservations

Dawes Act law breaking up reservations into individual plots of land

Section Summary

STAGE SET FOR CONFLICT

Many different Native American nations made up the Plains Indians. The buffalo was their source of food, clothing, shoes, and tepees. They moved from place to place following the buffalo herds. They did not settle down on the land, and they did not believe it could be owned. American settlers wanted to own it.

Until the 1850s the U.S. government simply moved Native Americans farther west. From the 1850s on, the government began taking their lands and sending them to reservations. The goal was to destroy the power of the Plains Indians and allow settlers on their land. One way to do this was to kill the buffalo.

> **How did the Plains Indians use the buffalo?**
> _____
> _____
> _____

> **Why did the U.S. government want to destroy the buffalo herds?**
> _____
> _____
> _____

THE INDIAN WARS

As settlers moved onto the Plains, there were more and more conflicts with the Plains Indians. In 1864 a group of Cheyenne raided nearby ranches. The U.S. Army first got the trust of the Cheyenne, then, in a surprise attack called the **Sand Creek Massacre**, killed about 150 Cheyenne women, children, and elderly people. This attack led the Cheyenne and other Native Americans to step up attacks on white settlers.

Thousands of Native Americans led by **Sitting Bull** fought the Army at the **Battle of the Little Bighorn**. The Army commander was **George Armstrong Custer**. He and his troops were killed. The U.S. government became even more determined to put down the Indian threat to settlers.

A Native American religious movement called the Ghost Dance gave hope to its believers. Some whites thought it meant an Indian uprising was coming. The Army went to arrest Sitting Bull, who had joined the movement. Fighting broke out and Sitting Bull was killed. The survivors were led to a camp. There, in the **Wounded Knee Massacre**, Colonel James Forsyth led his soldiers in killing about 300 Sioux men, women, and children.

> What did the Ghost Dance give its believers that the U.S. Army might fear? Why?
>
> _____
> _____
> _____
> _____

RESISTANCE ENDS IN THE WEST

In the Pacific Northwest, **Chief Joseph** led the Nez Percé. In 1863 the U.S. government took back most of their reservation land. Some Nez Percé fled to Canada, pursued by the army. Less than 40 miles from the Canadian border, the Nez Percé were forced to surrender. In the Southwest, Apache leader Geronimo led raids along the Arizona-Mexico border until he and his followers were caught a few years later.

> Why did the Nez Percé have to leave their reservation in the Pacific Northwest?
>
> _____
> _____
> _____

LIFE ON THE RESERVATIONS

In order to end the Native American's way of life and beliefs, the government began a policy of **Americanization**. The **Bureau of Indian Affairs** ran the reservations. It sent Native American children to far-away schools where they could only speak English and could not wear traditional clothing. The **Dawes Act** divided reservations into smaller plots. The best lands were sold, and the Native Americans got the poor lands. They could not farm the land because they could not afford the animals and supplies they needed.

> Why were Native Americans not successful at farming after the Dawes Act?
>
> _____
> _____
> _____

CHALLENGE ACTIVITY

Critical Thinking: Elaborate Prepare a report on reservations today.

MAIN IDEA
Many people sought fortunes during the mining and cattle booms of the American West.

Key Terms and People

Comstock Lode area in Nevada that was rich in silver

placer mining the finding of precious metals in loose sand or gravel

hydraulic mining using water under high pressure to blast away dirt and expose the minerals beneath

hard-rock mining cutting deep shafts in solid rock to reach and extract minerals

Chisholm Trail important trail for cattle drives; began in San Antonio and ended in Kansas

Section Summary

STRIKING GOLD AND SILVER

In 1859 prospectors found silver in Nevada. This was called the **Comstock Lode**. It produced about $500 million worth of silver. A huge gold strike was made in 1897 along the Klondike River in Canada's Yukon Territory. Soon gold was discovered across the border in Alaska. Nearly 100,000 Americans went to search for gold in the Klondike. Most were disappointed. Almost all miners were men. They lived in rough camps. The camps had no law enforcement. There was much violence. Some mining camps developed into towns and slowly grew as more families arrived.

> Underline the amount of silver that was taken out of the Comstock Lode.

MINING AS BIG BUSINESS

Individual miners often practiced **placer mining**. They looked for minerals in loose sand or gravel. When supplies of minerals on the Earth's surface wore out, new methods were developed. **Hydraulic mining** used water under high pressure to blast away dirt. This exposed the minerals beneath the surface. The dirt that was washed away clogged rivers and caused floods. **Hard-rock mining** meant cutting deep shafts into solid rock to get at the minerals. Because this was expensive to do, hard-rock mining was done

> Why did hydraulic mining come to be used?
>
> _____
>
> _____

The American West

by big companies. Miners became employees of the mining company rather than lone prospectors. Mining was dangerous work. Some miners began to form unions in order to get better working conditions and pay. However, the mine owners resisted these unions. In Colorado in 1903 gun battles broke out between union members and people who backed the mining companies. Over 30 people were killed.

> **Why did miners become employees?**
> _____
> _____
> _____

THE CATTLE BOOM

The first ranchers in the West were the Spanish. They and later the Mexicans learned to raise cattle under dry and difficult conditions. These ranchers developed a new breed of cattle called the longhorn. Longhorns could travel long distances without much water. They could live on grass alone. They were also immune to Texas fever, a disease that killed other breeds. The Spanish also introduced sheep ranching. Conflict often arose between cattle ranchers and sheep ranchers. Cattle ranchers believed that sheep ruined the grass.

> **Underline the reasons why longhorns were so well-suited to the Plains.**

As the population grew in the East, so did the demand for beef. Ranchers hired cowboys to drive the cattle to towns with railroads. One of the most important trails was the **Chisholm Trail**. It began in San Antonio and ended in Kansas. The long drive north usually lasted three months.

Joseph Glidden invented barbed wire. This was fencing material made of short, sharp pieces of wire wrapped around a long, single strand of wire. It helped Plains ranchers fence in their land and keep track of their cattle. In just four years more than 400 cattle corporations sprang up. In the 1880s large cattle companies backed by eastern and European investors turned ranching into big business. The severe winters of 1885–1886 and 1886–1887 brought huge losses to the industry.

> **How did barbed wire affect ranches?**
> _____
> _____

CHALLENGE ACTIVITY

Critical Thinking: Make Inferences Do research on placer mining and develop a list of supplies that a miner would need to work and survive in the gold or silver fields.

The American West

MAIN IDEA
The government promoted the settlement of the West, offering free or cheap land to those willing to put in the hard work of turning the land into productive farms.

Key Terms and People

Homestead Act law that allowed any head of household over the age of 21 to claim 160 acres of land

Pacific Railway Act law giving land to the railroad companies in order to help build railroads and telegraph lines

Morrill Act law that gave land to states to start agricultural and mechanical arts colleges

Frederick Jackson Turner historian who believed that American history was based on settling the West

Benjamin "Pap" Singleton community builder and former slave who urged African Americans to move West

Exoduster name for an African American who migrated to Kansas

dugout shelter dug out of the sides of hills

sod house home made of turf and soil squares used like bricks

James Oliver inventor of a plow that made farming the Plains easier

bonanza farm farm operated like a factory

Section Summary

INCENTIVES FOR SETTLEMENT

A visitor to the Great Plains called the region "the Great American Desert." The U.S. government encouraged people to go there to farm. The 1862 **Homestead Act** allowed any head of household over 21 to claim 160 acres of land. Homesteaders had to build a home and farm the land for five years. Then the land became theirs. In 1862 the **Pacific Railway Act** gave land to railroad companies. This was done to help build railroads and telegraph lines. The **Morrill Act** in 1862 gave land to the states for agricultural colleges. It was the first federal aid to higher education.

Railroad companies made money not only by selling tickets, but also by selling to the settlers the land the government gave them. They encouraged ✿

How did homesteaders get ownership of their land?

_____

_____

_____

What did the Morrill Act do?

_____

_____

settlers to come west. Railroad companies placed ads in eastern newspapers and in Europe.

In 1879 a Cherokee activist found that 2 million acres had not been assigned to any Native American nation. Ten years later, in the Oklahoma Land Run, thousands of settlers lined up to rush in and claim land. The U.S. Census Bureau considered land to be frontier if there were fewer than two people living in each square mile. In 1890 it said that the frontier was closed. Historian **Frederick Jackson Turner** said the history of America was the story of settling the frontier. Other historians disagree.

> **What was the Oklahoma Land Run?**
> _____
> _____
> _____

MIGRATING WEST

Most people moving west belonged to one of three groups: white Americans from the East, African Americans from the South, and immigrants. In the 1870s many African Americans were inspired by **Benjamin "Pap" Singleton**. He was a community builder and former slave. He urged African Americans to build their own communities in the West. Some 15,000 of them moved to Kansas in one year. They were known as **Exodusters**. Many Scandinavians and Germans came to the West. Chinese immigrants helped start California's fruit industry. However, laws prevented the Chinese from owning land.

> **Underline the three groups that made up the majority of settlers in the West.**

NEW WAYS OF FARMING

Farmers faced challenges. The climate was harsh. Water and lumber were scarce. Some settlers lived in **dugouts** or shelters dug out of the sides of hills. Others built **sod houses** made from blocks of grass, roots, and earth cut out of the prairie ground. **James Oliver** invented a new plow that made plowing easier. New farming machines such as combine harvesters were expensive. Giant **bonanza farms**, owned by large companies, were run like factories. However, by the 1890s most bonanza farms had been broken up.

> **How did farmers deal with the lack of lumber?** .
> _____
> _____
> _____

CHALLENGE ACTIVITY

Critical Thinking: Design With the information you have about the Plains, design a newspaper advertisement to lure settlers. Be sure to include the government's incentives in your ad.

The Second Industrial Revolution

Chapter Summary

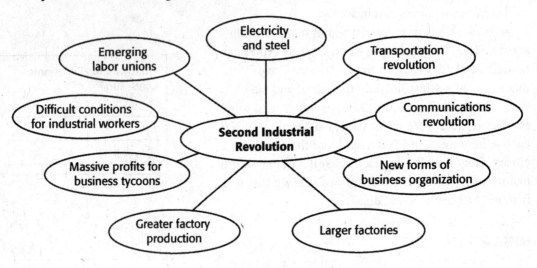

COMPREHENSION AND CRITICAL THINKING
Use information from the graphic organizer to answer the following questions.

1. **Recall** What happened to factories and factory production during the Second Industrial Revolution?

_____

_____

2. **Identify** What kind of profits did business tycoons make during the Second Industrial Revolution?

_____

_____

3. **Recall** What happened to business organization during the Second Industrial Revolution?

_____

_____

4. **Identify Cause and Effect** What working conditions caused industrial workers to create labor unions?

_____

_____

_____

The Second Industrial Revolution

MAIN IDEA
During the late 1800s, new technology led to rapid industrial growth and the expansion of railroads.

Key Terms and People

Bessemer process a steel-making process that was quicker and cheaper than earlier methods

Edwin L. Drake person who drilled the first commercial oil well

wildcatter oil prospector

transcontinental railroad railroad that crossed the entire country

Section Summary

NEW INDUSTRIES EMERGE

The Industrial Revolution took place in the early 1800s. By the late 1800s, new technologies such as electricity helped industries grow even more. Electrical power replaced steam and water power. Factories became larger. People developed faster transportation. Industrial growth was so dramatic in the late 1800s that the period is sometimes called the Second Industrial Revolution. In the 1850s Henry Bessemer invented the **Bessemer process**. This was an inexpensive way to make steel from iron. Many new uses for steel were discovered. Steel could be used to build bigger bridges and taller buildings. By 1910 the United States became the world's top steel producer.

In the late 1800s oil also became an important source of power. Oil refined into kerosene fueled lamps. **Edwin L. Drake** drilled the first commercial oil well. It was in Pennsylvania. Other oil prospectors, called **wildcatters**, soon drilled more wells. At Spindletop, in Texas, a huge new oil field was found. This started an oil boom in Texas. Many of the world's leading oil companies got their start at Spindletop. These include Exxon Mobil, Gulf Oil, and Texaco. They refined oil into kerosene and gasoline. These new products became major sources of energy. They fueled a revolution in transportation and industry.

> **What kind of power replaced steam and water power?**
> _____

> **Where was there an oil boom?**
> _____

The Second Industrial Revolution

RAILROADS EXPAND

Railroads grew quickly in the late 1800s. The federal government helped the growth by giving thousands of acres of land to railroad companies. Railroad companies used some of the land for new routes and sold some of it to pay for new materials to build the new routes. Cheap steel also helped the railroads to grow. On May 10, 1869, the first **transcontinental railroad** was completed. It went across the entire country. Laying track westward from Omaha, Nebraska, were Irish, German, English, African American, and Native American workers. Those who laid the track eastward from Sacramento, California, were mostly Chinese workers. The tracks met at Promontory Summit in Utah Territory.

The first transcontinental railroad was soon followed by others. Regional railroads grew too. This helped to unite the country.

Railroads helped the economy grow. They made trade easier. They also provided jobs. They used rails, which helped the steel industry grow. The need for railcars gave a boost to train manufacturers. The railroads brought settlers to the West and promoted Western settlement. They cut the time of the journey west from months to a few days. Wherever railroads were built, new towns sprang up, and existing towns grew into bigger cities.

Railroads also led to the use of standard time. Earlier, people kept time based on the position of the sun. Some states had more than 20 different local times. However, running a railroad required accurate timekeeping. New York school principal C. F. Dowd was the first to propose dividing the earth into time zones. All places within the zone would set their clocks to the same time. Railroad officials liked the idea. In 1918 Congress adopted standard time for the nation as a whole.

> How did the federal government help the railroads to grow?
>
> _____
>
> _____

> Underline the ways that the railroads helped the economy grow.

CHALLENGE ACTIVITY

Critical Thinking: Elaborate Find out what time zone you live in. Choose a time. Then figure out what time it is in all four time zones of the country.

Interactive Reader and Study Guide

The Second Industrial Revolution

MAIN IDEA
Corporations run by powerful business leaders became a dominant force in the American economy.

Key Terms and People

entrepreneur risk-taker who uses personal money and talents to launch a new business

capitalism an economic system in which private businesses run most industries; competition determines prices and wages

laissez-faire type of capitalism that lets companies conduct business without government intervention

social Darwinism belief that "survival of the fittest" benefits society

monopoly an industry in which one corporation has complete control

John D. Rockefeller oil tycoon; founder of Standard Oil

vertical integration owning the companies that supply a business

horizontal integration owning companies that produce the same thing

Andrew Carnegie steel tycoon; gave away $350 million to charity

Cornelius Vanderbilt railroad tycoon

Section Summary

A FAVORABLE CLIMATE FOR BUSINESS

Many people in the late 1800s believed that people's hard work would make them successful. America liked **entrepreneurs**. These were risk takers who used their money and talents to start new businesses. The American system is called **capitalism**. This means that private businesses run most industries. Prices and wages are determined by competition. In the late 1800s most business leaders believed in **laissez-faire** capitalism. This meant business without government intervention. People knew there were inequalities that happened under this system. Many believed in **social Darwinism**. This means that they thought that survival of the fittest was good for society.

> **How are prices and wages determined under capitalism?**
>
> _____
>
> _____

BUSINESS STRUCTURES CHANGE

At the end of the Civil War, most businesses were small. Most were run by individual owners. These were called proprietorships. Some were run by

Interactive Reader and Study Guide

The Second Industrial Revolution

Section 2

partners. In both of these, the owners were personally responsible for the debts of the business. In the late 1800s large businesses began organizing as corporations. This is a business with the legal status of an individual. It is owned by stockholders. These are people who buy stocks, or shares, of the company. Major decisions are made by a board of directors. Corporate officers are hired to run the business. Some companies formed trusts. These were competing companies that joined together and were then run as one company. Some companies became so large that they controlled entire industries. An industry run by only one company is called a **monopoly**. A monopoly has no competition from other firms.

> **Who owns a corporation? How do they own it?**
> _____
> _____
> _____
> _____

INDUSTRIAL TYCOONS

Some businessmen got very rich. **John D. Rockefeller** was in the oil business. To increase profits, he used **vertical integration**. This meant he bought all the companies that supplied his company. He also used **horizontal integration**. This meant he bought out his competitors. **Andrew Carnegie** got very rich in the steel business. He gave away almost $350 million, mostly to support education. **Cornelius Vanderbilt** got rich in railroads. Critics said these men profited unfairly, others said they made the economy stronger.

> **Underline the names of three businessmen who got very rich in the late 1800s.**

MASS MARKETING

As stores carried more and more goods, department stores were developed. These were large stores that sold many different kinds of products under one roof. For people who didn't live anywhere near the stores, the stores printed and mailed catalogs. These were sent out by mail-order companies like Sears, Roebuck. People's purchases arrived by mail.

> **How did people who didn't live in the city shop without going to the store?**
> _____
> _____

CHALLENGE ACTIVITY

Critical Thinking: Analyze At home or in the library, find an example of a catalog. Explain in two paragraphs how a catalog creates more business for the merchant.

The Second Industrial Revolution

MAIN IDEA
Grim working conditions in many industries led workers to form unions and stage labor strikes.

Key Terms and People

Sherman Antitrust Act law that made it illegal to form trusts that interfered with free trade

sweatshop workshop set up in a tenement

Knights of Labor labor union founded in 1869

Terence V. Powderly leader of the Knights of Labor

xenophobia fear of foreigners

blacklist list of workers thought to be troublemakers

Samuel Gompers founder of the American Federation of Labor

American Federation of Labor labor union of skilled workers founded in 1886

Eugene V. Debs leader of the American Railway Union

Grover Cleveland president of the United States from 1885 to 1889

Section Summary

GOVERNMENT AND BUSINESS

In the late 1800s government did not regulate business. As corporations grew larger, some of them began to run entire industries. Some people began to worry about their power. Congress passed the **Sherman Antitrust Act**. This act made it illegal to form trusts that interfered with free trade. The act was not very well enforced, however. The government also paid little attention to workers. Inequality in income was growing. The rich were getting extremely rich, while the poor stayed very poor.

> What was happening to inequality of income during the late 1800s?
>
> _____
> _____
> _____

INDUSTRIAL WORKERS

Most factory workers were immigrants. The best jobs went to native-born whites or European immigrants. Lesser jobs went to African Americans. Many workers were children, some as young as five years old. Most unskilled workers worked 10 hours per day, six days a week. They had no vacations, no sick leave, and no help if they were injured on the job. Many

> Underline how long workers worked per day.

Interactive Reader and Study Guide

worked in **sweatshops**. These were workshops set up in a tenements.

WORKERS SEEK CHANGES

By the late 1800s working conditions were so bad that workers began to join together to make their demands heard. Early unions had remained small and local. After the Civil War, unions began to grow. The **Knights of Labor** was founded in 1869. It was led by **Terence V. Powderly**. By 1886 the group had more than 700,000 members. They demanded an eight-hour workday, an end to child labor, and equal pay for equal work. The first major U.S. rail strike happened in 1877. Railroad workers walked off the job and blocked trains from moving. Most freight traffic was stopped for more than a week. State militias were called out, and the U.S. Army finally put down the strike. More than 100 people were killed. Chicago's Haymarket Riot occurred when crowds of striking workers gathered in Haymarket Square to protest police violence. Someone threw a bomb into the crowd. Then there was gunfire. Eleven people died.

Many people had **xenophobia**, or fear of foreigners. They blamed foreigners for the violence. Some employers forced their workers to sign papers agreeing not to join unions. Often employers would share a **blacklist**. This was a list of workers thought to be troublemakers. Blacklisted workers were not hired.

In 1886 **Samuel Gompers** led a group of skilled workers to form the **American Federation of Labor**. They used strikes and other tactics to get wage increases and shorter work weeks. The steelworkers' union held a strike that was put down by the state militia. **Eugene V. Debs** led the American Railway Union in the Pullman strike. This time, President **Grover Cleveland** sent federal troops to bring it to an end.

> **Why did workers begin to form unions?**
> _____
> _____

> **What was the Haymarket Riot?**
> _____
> _____
> _____

> **Underline the definition of xenophobia.**

CHALLENGE ACTIVITY

Critical Thinking: Evaluate If you had been a worker in the late 1800s, would you have joined a union? How would you have wanted the U.S. government to handle unions and their tactics? Write three paragraphs explaining your views.

The Second Industrial Revolution

MAIN IDEA
Important innovations in transportation and communication occurred during the Second Industrial Revolution.

Key Terms and People

mass transit public transportation systems that carry large numbers of people and make regular stops along established routes

Orville and Wilbur Wright inventors and pilots who made the first successful airplane flight

telegraph machine for sending messages over wires with electricity

Alexander Graham Bell inventor of the telephone

Thomas Alva Edison creator of hundreds of inventions, including the light bulb and the first research laboratory

Section Summary

ADVANCES IN TRANSPORTATION

As cities grew, they became too big for people to walk everywhere. People needed ways to travel locally. Cities developed **mass transit**. This was public transportation that could carry large numbers of people. It made regular stops along established routes. The first cable car line was built in San Francisco in 1873. Cable cars were able to go uphill by connecting to a moving cable in a slot under the street. A steam engine in a central station kept the cable moving. By 1900 most cable cars were replaced by streetcars. These were powered by overhead electrical wires. Soon the streets became crowded and traffic became a problem. Boston and New York built subways. These were underground trains powered by electricity.

Other kinds of transportation were also invented in the Second Industrial Revolution. Early automobiles were hand-built and very expensive. Some inventors were working on air travel. **Orville and Wilbur Wright** built an airplane. They made the first flight on December 17, 1903, at Kitty Hawk, North Carolina.

> **Why did cities develop mass transit?**
> _____
> _____

> **Underline the place where the first airplane flight took place.**

COMMUNICATIONS REVOLUTION

In 1837 Samuel F. B. Morse patented the **telegraph**. The telegraph sent messages over wires with electricity. Operators tapped out patterns of long and short signals that stood for letters of the alphabet. This system was called Morse code. After the Civil War, telegraph wires were strung alongside railroads.

Alexander Graham Bell developed a device that could transmit voices using electricity. This was a telephone. Bell's design was patented in 1876. By 1900 more than a million telephones had been installed in offices and homes around the country.

In 1867 the first practical typewriter was developed. The inventor then developed the QWERTY keyboard. He put the most-used letters of the alphabet far apart so the keys of the typewriter would not jam. This keyboard is still used on computers today.

> What is Morse code?
> _____
> _____
> _____
> _____

> Why are the letters arranged as they are on the QWERTY keyboard?
> _____
> _____

THOMAS EDISON

Thomas Alva Edison was an amazing inventor. He opened his own research laboratory in Menlo Park, New Jersey, in 1876. He and his team of workers invented the first phonograph. He invented the first incandescent light bulb. He then designed and produced all the parts needed for an electricity network to power the light bulbs. In 1882 Edison put in a lighting system in New York near Wall Street. Electric power plants soon were built all over the country. Edison invented the motion picture camera and projector. By the time of his death, he had more than 1,000 U.S. patents.

> Underline the names of Edison's inventions.

CHALLENGE ACTIVITY

Critical Thinking: Design If you could ask Thomas Alva Edison to invent something today, what would it be? Design something that you think would help people today. How would it work and how would it help people?

Life at the Turn of the 20th Century

Chapter Summary

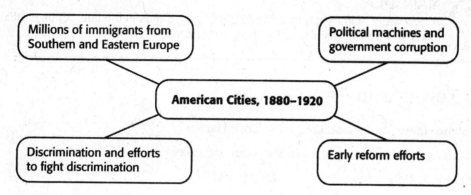

Millions of immigrants from Southern and Eastern Europe

Political machines and government corruption

American Cities, 1880–1920

Discrimination and efforts to fight discrimination

Early reform efforts

COMPREHENSION AND CRITICAL THINKING

Use information from the graphic organizer to answer the following questions.

1. **Identify** From what parts of Europe did immigrants come during this period?

   _____

   _____

2. **Explain** What words described government and politics during this time?

   _____

   _____

3. **Recall** How did some people respond to discrimination?

   _____

   _____

4. **Recall** How were cities' problems being dealt with during this period?

   _____

   _____

Life at the Turn of the 20th Century

Section 1

MAIN IDEA
A new wave of immigrants came to the United States in the late 1800s, settling in cities and troubling some native-born Americans.

Key Terms and People

Ellis Island immigration station in New York Harbor

Angel Island immigration station in San Francisco Bay

benevolent society group that helps immigrants

Denis Kearney Irish immigrant who led the Workingman's Party, which was against Chinese immigration

Chinese Exclusion Act 1882 law that did not allow Chinese immigration for 10 years

Gentlemen's Agreement 1907 agreement between President Theodore Roosevelt and Japan to prevent unskilled Japanese workers from coming to the United States

literacy test an exam to determine whether immigrants could read English

Section Summary

CHANGING PATTERNS OF IMMIGRATION

Between 1800 and 1880 more than 10 million immigrants came to the United States. Most came from Northern and Western Europe. Most were Protestant. Most came in search of economic opportunity. The huge supply of land in the United States drew people. Some immigrants came from China after the gold rush. From 1880 to 1910, about 18 million more immigrants came. These new immigrants came from Southern and Eastern Europe. Many were Roman Catholics, Jews, or Orthodox Christians. Some Japanese immigrants also came.

> Underline the religious backgrounds of the immigrants who came to the United States between 1880 and 1910.

COMING TO AMERICA

Most of these immigrants came to America for a better life. Some came to escape persecution, prejudice, or poverty. The journey to America was long and hard. Sometimes it took a long time just to get to a seaport. Immigrants had to give information to authorities before they were allowed to board the ship. Doctors also checked them. On the ship, most immigrants traveled in steerage. This meant they were in the bottom of the ship. It was crowded and dirty.

> Underline the reasons why immigrants came to America.

Life at the Turn of the 20th Century

Ellis Island was an immigration station in New York Harbor. Immigrants had to pass inspection there. Doctors checked them. If they had a serious disease or disability, they were sent home. **Angel Island** was an immigration station in San Francisco Bay. Asian immigrants were examined there. Many Chinese people were held in prisonlike conditions for weeks.

Most immigrants settled in crowded cities. They settled near others from their homeland. They started churches and synagogues. They also started **benevolent societies**. These organizations helped immigrants get jobs, health care, and education. The government did not help poor people, but benevolent societies did.

> **Where did most immigrants settle?**
> _____
> _____

NATIVISTS RESPOND

Immigrants helped make the U.S. economy strong, but some native-born Americans saw them as a threat. Americans who opposed immigration were called nativists. They thought that immigrants lowered everyone's wages. Many Americans especially blamed Chinese immigrants for taking away jobs. **Denis Kearney** was an Irish immigrant. He led the Workingman's Party, which was against Chinese immigration. In 1882 Congress passed the **Chinese Exclusion Act**. This law did not allow Chinese immigration for 10 years. It also said that the Chinese already in America could not become citizens. Nativists on the West Coast also disliked Japanese immigrants. They made Japanese children go to separate schools. The Japanese government complained. President Theodore Roosevelt negotiated the **Gentlemen's Agreement**. Japan agreed to stop unskilled Japanese workers from coming to the United States. Nativists also called for immigrants to take a **literacy test**. This was an exam to find out if immigrants could read English. Not all native-born Americans were against immigration. Some wanted to help immigrants become citizens.

> **What effect did immigrants have on the U.S. economy?**
> _____
> _____

> **What did nativists on the West Coast do to Japanese children?**
> _____
> _____
> _____

CHALLENGE ACTIVITY

Critical Thinking: Elaborate Ellis Island is now a museum. After doing research on it, make a travel poster advertising the museum.

Life at the Turn of the 20th Century

> **MAIN IDEA**
> In cities in the late 1800s, people in the upper, middle, and lower classes lived
> different kinds of lives because of their different economic situations.

Key Terms and People

Elisha Otis inventor of the safety elevator

Frederick Law Olmsted landscape architect who designed many city parks

settlement house place where volunteers provided services to people in need

Jane Addams co-founder of Chicago's Hull House, one of the first settlement houses in
the United States

Lillian Wald founder of the Henry Street Settlement in New York City

Social Gospel idea that religious faith should be shown through good works

Section Summary

AMERICAN CITIES CHANGE

Before industrialization, cities were compact. Few
buildings were taller than four stories. In the late
1800s cities began to run out of space. They began to
build upwards. To do this, architects used strong steel
frames. **Elisha Otis** invented the safety elevator. This
made taller buildings practical. Urban planners began
to plan cities. They included green spaces. **Frederick
Law Olmsted** was a landscape architect. He designed
many city parks. Some of them were in New York
City and Boston.

> What invention allowed
> buildings to become taller?
> _____

> In what cities did Olmsted
> build parks?
> _____

CLASS DIFFERENCES

In the late 1800s the richest Americans did not come
from families that had money. They made their money
in industry and business. They used their wealth to
show how successful they were. They spent large
amounts of money on houses and vacation homes. To
the upper classes, a woman's place was in the home.

The middle class grew. More and more people
became accountants, clerks, and managers. There was
a growing need for teachers, engineers, lawyers, and
doctors. During the 1870s and 1880s schools began to
set standards for these professions. Few professions
accepted women. Women did become salesclerks,

> How did the upper classes
> get their money?
> _____
> _____
> _____
> _____

Life at the Turn of the 20th Century

secretaries, and typists. When young, middle-class women married, they usually stopped working outside the home. Managing a household took less work than in earlier times. Women took part in reform movements, reading clubs, and other social groups.

Many people in the cities, however, lived in terrible poverty. They crowded into tenements. These were run-down apartment buildings. They were usually close to factories and stockyards. At home and at work the poor had to put up with filth and pollution. Tenements did not have good lighting or fresh air. There was no indoor plumbing. This made housekeeping hard work. Many working-class women also worked in low-paying jobs outside the house.

> **What was the economic condition of many people in the cities?**
> _____
> _____

THE SETTLEMENT HOUSE MOVEMENT

In Britain, reformers started **settlement houses**. These were places where volunteers provided services to people in need. They taught immigrants English. They also offered job training. There were social activities such as clubs and sports. In 1889 **Jane Addams** co-founded Hull House in Chicago. It was one of the first settlement houses in America. **Lillian Wald** started the Henry Street Settlement in New York City.

Most settlement house workers were college-educated women. They lived among the people they served. Most believed in the **Social Gospel**. This was the idea that religious faith should be shown through good works. Social Darwinists criticized the Social Gospel movement. They saw life as a struggle. They thought people were poor because they were not as good as others. For this reason, they thought social services could not help the poor.

> **Underline the educational and other activities available at settlement houses.**

CHALLENGE ACTIVITY

Critical Thinking: Elaborate Read a biography of Jane Addams and write a two-page book report.

Interactive Reader and Study Guide

Life at the Turn of the 20th Century

MAIN IDEA
Political corruption was common in the late 1800s, but reformers began fighting for changes to make government more honest.

Key Terms and People

William Marcy Tweed corrupt political boss of Tammany Hall in New York

Thomas Nast political cartoonist who attacked corruption

James A. Garfield Republican, elected president in 1880

Chester A. Arthur vice president who became president after Garfield was assassinated

National Grange first major farmer's organization

Populist Party political party started in 1892 by farmers, labor leaders, and reformers

William McKinley Republican, elected president in 1896

Section Summary

POLITICAL MACHINES

After the Civil War, groups of professional politicians began to manage cities. These groups were called political machines. They built loyalty by doing favors for people. They often used illegal methods to keep control. Machine bosses used jobs and favors to buy votes. Sometimes they hired men to vote several times in an election. Machine bosses demanded bribes and payoffs in exchange for contracts and jobs. Tammany Hall was a famous political machine. This group ran the Democratic Party in New York City. In 1863 **William Marcy Tweed**, called Boss Tweed, became its head. He got very rich by stealing money from the city. **Thomas Nast** was a political cartoonist. He attacked this corruption. In 1873 Tweed was convicted for fraud and obtaining money unlawfully.

> Underline the ways that machine bosses were corrupt.

> Circle the name of the man who attacked corruption through cartoons.

FEDERAL CORRUPTION

Ulysses S. Grant became president in 1869. There were several scandals in his administration. One of the worst was the Crédit Mobilier scandal. Crédit Mobilier was a company set up to build part of the transcontinental railroad. It charged taxpayers about $23 million more than the railroad actually cost. Many people wanted reform.

Republican Rutherford B. Hayes became president in 1877. He made some reforms. In 1880 the Republicans nominated **James A. Garfield**. He won, but was assassinated soon after taking office. His vice president, **Chester A. Arthur**, became president. Arthur helped pass the Pendleton Civil Service Act. It required government officials to be promoted only on their merits. It was a first step in cutting down on government corruption.

> How did promoting people based on their merits help cut down on government corruption?
>
> _____
> _____
> _____

THE POPULIST MOVEMENT

In the late 1800s farmers were in a desperate situation. It seemed that everyone else was making money off them. The railroads in particular made money by charging farmers high rates. Farmers organized into a group called the **National Grange**. It fought the railroads and the banks. It got several states to regulate railroad rates. At first the Supreme Court supported these regulations. Nine years later the Court said only the federal government could control traffic that went across state lines. This led to the passing of the Interstate Commerce Act. It was the first time the federal government regulated an industry. Farmers started other organizations in Texas and New York.

> How did the railroads make money unfairly off the farmers?
>
> _____
> _____

The Farmer's Alliance wanted to expand the money supply. The United States' economy was based on the gold standard. This meant that currency could be exchanged for its value in gold. The amount of money in circulation could not be greater than the amount of gold held by the government. Farmers wanted money to be backed by silver as well. They thought that this would raise prices for their products. Farmers, labor leaders, and reformers started the **Populist Party**. They supported backing money by silver in the 1896 election. They lost. Republican **William McKinley** won the election. He supported the gold standard and thought it was the key to the country's prosperity.

> What had to happen in order for the money supply to grow while the nation was on the gold standard?
>
> _____
> _____

CHALLENGE ACTIVITY

Critical Thinking: Elaborate *The Wizard of Oz* may have been written as a Populist fable about the gold standard. Do research on the story and see if can find evidence that supports this theory.

Interactive Reader and Study Guide

Life at the Turn of the 20th Century

MAIN IDEA
The United States in the late 1800s was a place of great change—and a place in need of even greater change.

Key Terms and People

poll tax fee people were charged to vote, intended to keep African Americans from voting

grandfather clause law that said that a man could vote if he, his father, or his grandfather had been able to vote before 1867

Jim Crow law law that discriminated against African Americans

Plessy v. *Ferguson* case in which the Supreme Court ruled that segregation was legal

racial etiquette strict rules of behavior that governed the social and business relations between whites and African Americans

lynching murder of an individual by a group or a mob

Booker T. Washington African American leader who thought African Americans should accept segregation for the moment and focus on getting farming and job skills

W. E. B. Du Bois civil rights leader who thought African Americans should fight for full rights immediately

NAACP National Association for the Advancement of Colored People; civil rights organization started by W. E. B. Du Bois

debt peonage system that tied workers to their jobs until they could pay off debts they owed their employer

Section Summary

LEGALIZED DISCRIMINATION

After Reconstruction, southerners passed many laws that limited the rights of African Americans. They made voters pay a **poll tax**. Most African Americans were too poor to pay the poll tax. Voters had to pass a literacy test. Many African Americans had been denied the education they needed to pass the literacy test. White southerners did not have to pay the tax or pass the test. Many southern states also passed **grandfather clauses**. These laws said that a man could vote if he, his father, or his grandfather had been able to vote before 1867. Before 1867, of course, only white men could vote. **Jim Crow laws** were passed. These laws created and enforced segregation.

> Underline the tactics southerners used to keep African Americans from voting.

> Why was the date of 1867 important to the grandfather clause?
>
> _____
> _____
> _____

Interactive Reader and Study Guide

Life at the Turn of the 20th Century

In *Plessy* v. *Ferguson*, the Supreme Court ruled that segregation was legal.

> Underline the case in which the Supreme Court allowed segregation.

INFORMAL DISCRIMINATION

There were strict rules of behavior called **racial etiquette**. These rules guided the social and business relations between whites and African Americans. African Americans were supposed to "know their place." They were supposed to show respect to white people. If they did not, there might be a **lynching**. This is the murder of an individual by a group or a mob, usually by hanging. Between 1882 and 1892 lynch mobs killed nearly 900 African Americans.

> What might happen to African Americans who did not follow racial etiquette?
> _____
> _____
> _____

PROMINENT BLACK LEADERS

Booker T. Washington was an African American leader. He thought African Americans should accept segregation for the moment. He wanted them to focus on improving their farming and job skills. He founded the Tuskegee Institute to teach African Americans practical skills. **W. E. B. Du Bois** believed otherwise. He thought that African Americans should fight for total equality and full rights immediately. He helped start the **NAACP** (National Association for the Advancement of Colored People), an organization that worked to end discrimination.

OTHERS SUFFER DISCRIMINATION

Mexican Americans, Asian Americans, and Native Americans all experienced discrimination. Most Mexican Americans worked on farms. Many were trapped in their jobs by **debt peonage**. In this system, people were tied to their jobs until they paid off debts they owed their employers. Asian Americans faced segregation. Native Americans were not even considered to be American citizens until 1924. They had no opportunity for economic advancement. The government tried for years to destroy their cultures.

> Circle the date when Native Americans were finally allowed to become citizens.

CHALLENGE ACTIVITY

Critical Thinking: Contrast Use the Internet to do research on Booker T. Washington and W. E. B. Du Bois. Write a one-page report giving present-day African Americans' opinions of the two men.

Chapter Summary

The Progressives

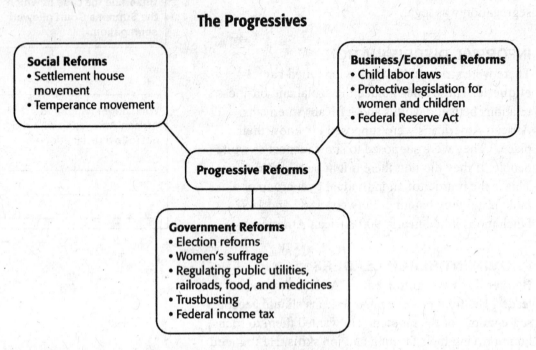

Social Reforms
• Settlement house movement
• Temperance movement

Business/Economic Reforms
• Child labor laws
• Protective legislation for women and children
• Federal Reserve Act

Progressive Reforms

Government Reforms
• Election reforms
• Women's suffrage
• Regulating public utilities, railroads, food, and medicines
• Trustbusting
• Federal income tax

COMPREHENSION AND CRITICAL THINKING

Use information from the graphic organizer to answer the following questions.

1. **Recall** What were two reform movements that were part of the Progressive movement?

_____

_____

2. **Describe** What were three economic reforms associated with Progressivism?

_____

_____

The Progressives

MAIN IDEA
Progressives focused on three areas of reform: easing the suffering of the urban poor, improving unfair and dangerous working conditions, and reforming government at the national, state, and local levels.

Key Terms and People

progressivism a reform movement

muckrakers journalists who exposed the problem areas of society

Ida Tarbell journalist who exposed corrupt business practices

Lincoln Steffens journalist who exposed corrupt city governments

Jacob Riis reformer who focused people's attention on the problems of the urban poor

Robert M. La Follette progressive Wisconsin governor whose agenda of reforms was known as the Wisconsin Idea

Seventeenth Amendment gave voters the power to elect their senators directly

initiative gave voters the power to put a proposed law on the ballot for public approval

referendum allowed voters to approve or veto a recently passed law

recall enabled voters to remove an elected official from office by special election

Section Summary

WHAT WAS PROGRESSIVISM?

Industrialization brought problems such as dangerous working conditions and extreme poverty. There was also a great deal of government and business corruption. The movement that fought these ills was called **progressivism**. Journalists known as **muckrakers** helped expose the problems. **Ida Tarbell** wrote about corrupt business practices. **Lincoln Steffens** wrote about the corruption of city governments.

> Underline the problems that came with industrialization.

> Name three people who focused attention on the problems in American society.
> _____
> _____
> _____

REFORMING SOCIETY

Reformers like **Jacob Riis** called people's attention to the problems of the urban poor. In New York, the Tenement Act of 1901 brought some improvement to urban life. The NAACP (National Association for the Advancement of Colored People) was formed by a group of black and white activists in 1909. It was formed to fight for civil rights for African Americans. In 1913 the Anti-Defamation League (ADL) was

Interactive Reader and Study Guide

The Progressives

founded to fight anti-Semitism, or hostility toward Jews.

REFORMING THE WORKPLACE

Florence Kelley worked for laws to stop child labor and limit the hours women could work. Business owners fought such labor laws in court. In 1911 a terrible fire at the Triangle Shirtwaist Company inspired the New York legislature to pass fire safety laws. Many workers joined unions to fight for better pay. The International Ladies' Garment Workers Union (ILGWU) won a shorter workweek and higher wages when tens of thousands of members struck.

> **What inspired New York to pass fire safety laws?**
> _____

REFORMING GOVERNMENT

Progressives worked to make government less corrupt and more efficient. **Robert M. La Follette**, in Wisconsin, pushed for direct primary elections and regulation of railroads and utilities. Progressives pushed for the **Seventeenth Amendment**. This gave voters the power to elect senators directly. Progressives also fought for three other reforms: The **initiative** gives voters the power to put a proposed law on the ballot for public approval. The **referendum** allows them to approve or veto a recently passed law by voting on it. The **recall** enables voters to remove an elected official from office by special election.

> **What did the Seventeenth Amendment allow?**
> _____
> _____

CHALLENGE ACTIVITY

Critical Thinking: Summarize Make a list of the reforms that were passed during the Progressive period. Write two paragraphs telling which of these still affect our lives today.

Interactive Reader and Study Guide

The Progressives

MAIN IDEA
Women during the Progressive Era actively campaigned for reforms in
education, children's welfare, temperance, and suffrage.

Key Terms and People

Prohibition movement to ban making, selling, and transporting alcoholic drinks

Woman's Christian Temperance Union national organization which supported
Prohibition

Frances Willard 1879–1898 leader of the Woman's Christian Temperance Union

Carry Nation evangelist who smashed saloons and gave speeches supporting Prohibition

Eighteenth Amendment amendment to the Constitution that outlawed the manufacture,
sale, and distribution of alcohol

National Association of Colored Women organization formed to fight against
discrimination and for women's rights

Susan B. Anthony co-founder of National Woman Suffrage Association

National American Woman Suffrage Association pro-suffrage organization formed by
the joining of the National Woman Suffrage Association and the American Woman
Suffrage Association

Section Summary

OPPORTUNITIES FOR WOMEN

By the late 1800s there were more chances for women
to gain education and employment. As they looked to
the world beyond their own homes, they began
working to better society.

Women began to go to college in larger numbers.
By 1870 only about 20 percent of college students
were women. By 1900 this increased to more than 33
percent. Women also began to work in offices and
industry. They were almost always paid less than men.

> What new opportunities did
> the late 1800s bring for
> women?
>
> _____
>
> _____

GAINING POLITICAL EXPERIENCE

As women began to work for political causes, one of
their first concerns was children's health and welfare.
They succeeded in getting the Federal Children's
Bureau opened in 1912.

Women also worked for **Prohibition**, the
movement calling for a ban on making, selling, and

The Progressives

transporting alcoholic drinks. They believed alcohol caused crime, poverty, and violence. The **Woman's Christian Temperance Union** (WCTU), a national organization dedicated to Prohibition, was led by **Frances Willard** from 1879 to 1898. Evangelist **Carry Nation** spread the message of Prohibition by smashing up saloons and making fiery speeches. In 1919 the states ratified the **Eighteenth Amendment**. This amendment barred the manufacture, sale, and distribution of alcohol. The amendment was unpopular and hard to enforce.

> Why did Prohibitionists want to do away with alcoholic drinks?
> _____
> _____

Women also worked for civil rights. In 1896 African American women formed the **National Association of Colored Women**. They campaigned to fight poverty, segregation, and lynching. They also campaigned against Jim Crow laws and alcohol abuse and for women's suffrage.

> For what political causes did women campaign?
> _____
> _____
> _____
> _____

RISE OF THE WOMEN'S SUFFRAGE MOVEMENT

After the Civil War, the Fifteenth Amendment gave African American men the right to vote but denied it to all women. Suffragists worked to change the laws. Many people, businesses, and churches were against them. In 1869 Elizabeth Cady Stanton and **Susan B. Anthony** formed the National Woman Suffrage Association (NWSA). This organization campaigned for a constitutional amendment. In 1872 it supported the first woman to run for president, Victoria Woodhull. Meanwhile, the American Woman Suffrage Association (AWSA) focused on changing laws state-by-state. They won in several western territories and states.

> The two national suffrage associations used different approaches to gain women the right to vote. What were they?
>
> NWSA: _____
>
> _____
>
> AWSA: _____
>
> _____

In 1890 the two organizations merged and formed the **National American Woman Suffrage Association** (NAWSA), first led by Elizabeth Cady Stanton and then Susan B. Anthony. Women finally won the right to vote in 1920.

CHALLENGE ACTIVITY

Critical Thinking: Predict Write three paragraphs describing what the nation would be like today if women had not won the right to vote.

Interactive Reader and Study Guide

Section 3

> **MAIN IDEA**
> Theodore Roosevelt used the power of the presidency to push for progressive reforms in business and in environmental policy.

Key Terms and People

Theodore Roosevelt progressive reformer who became president when President McKinley was shot

bully pulpit use of the presidency to publicize and get support for important issues

Square Deal Theodore Roosevelt's belief that the needs of workers, business, and consumers should be balanced

Elkins Act 1903 law that forced railroads charge the same prices to all their customers

Hepburn Act 1906 law that authorized the Interstate Commerce Commission to set maximum railroad rates

Upton Sinclair writer who exposed filthy conditions in the meat packing industry

Meat Inspection Act law that required the federal government to inspect meat shipped across state lines

Pure Food and Drug Act law that outlawed the manufacture, sale, or transportation of food and medicine containing harmful ingredients

John Muir naturalist who helped get government protection of Yosemite

Newlands Reclamation Act 1902 law that allowed the federal government to build irrigation projects to make dry land productive

Gifford Pinchot conservationist; first head of the U.S. Forest Service

Section Summary

ROOSEVELT'S VIEW OF THE PRESIDENCY

Theodore Roosevelt was a progressive reformer. Political bosses thought they could silence him by making him vice president. However, when President William McKinley was shot, Roosevelt became president. Roosevelt used the presidency as a **bully pulpit**. This meant that he used it to publicize and get support for important issues. In 1902 coal miners in Pennsylvania struck for higher wages, shorter hours, and recognition of their union. Roosevelt became involved and forced both sides to accept arbitration. This meant allowing a third person, who would not take sides, to act as judge and settle the dispute. The result was a compromise. Roosevelt called the results

> **Why would political bosses want to silence Roosevelt?**
>
> _____
> _____

> **Underline the definition of a bully pulpit.**

The Progressives

Section 3

a **Square Deal**. This expression became Roosevelt's campaign promise and belief. It meant that the needs of workers, business, and consumers should be balanced. The popular Roosevelt easily won the election of 1904.

What was Roosevelt's Square Deal?
_____
_____
_____

REGULATING BIG BUSINESS

Roosevelt wanted businesses to act responsibly. He used the Sherman Antitrust Act to sue a railroad for forming a monopoly and won. He then launched a trustbusting campaign. He went after trusts and monopolies that sold bad products, competed unfairly, or corrupted public officials. In 1903 Congress passed the **Elkins Act**, which forced the railroads to charge the same prices to all their customers. The **Hepburn Act** of 1906 authorized the Interstate Commerce Commission to set maximum railroad rates.

Which trusts and monopolies did Roosevelt go after?
_____
_____
_____

In 1906 writer **Upton Sinclair** wrote a book about the filthy conditions in the meat packing industry. Roosevelt acted to protect the consumer. The **Meat Inspection Act** required federal government to inspect meat shipped across state lines. The **Pure Food and Drug Act** outlawed making, selling, or transporting food and medicine with harmful ingredients.

ENVIRONMENTAL CONSERVATION

Roosevelt signed laws creating many national monuments and parks. Naturalist **John Muir**, who convinced the government to protect Yosemite, thought all wilderness should be kept natural. Roosevelt thought some lands should be protected but others should be put to use. Accordingly, the **Newlands Reclamation Act** allowed the government to build irrigation projects to make dry land productive. Conservationist **Gifford Pinchot**, who first used the word *conservation*, supported Roosevelt. He became the first head of the U.S. Forest Service.

How was Roosevelt's view of conservation different from John Muir's?
_____
_____
_____
_____

CHALLENGE ACTIVITY

Critical Thinking: Evaluate Write a short summary of the achievements of Theodore Roosevelt's presidency.

Interactive Reader and Study Guide

The Progressives

MAIN IDEA
Progressive reforms continued during the Taft and Wilson presidencies, focusing on business, banking, and women's suffrage.

Key Terms and People

William Howard Taft Republican winner of the 1908 presidential election

Sixteenth Amendment amendment allowing Congress to collect taxes based on an individual's income

Hiram W. Johnson California governor who ran with Roosevelt against Taft in 1912

Woodrow Wilson Democratic winner of 1912 presidential election

New Freedom reform plan proposed by Woodrow Wilson

Federal Reserve Act law meant to prevent bank collapse during financial panics

Clayton Antitrust Act law that clarified and extended the Sherman Antitrust Act

Alice Paul co-founder of the Congressional Union for Woman Suffrage

Nineteenth Amendment amendment that gave women the right to vote

Brownsville incident unjust discharging of African American soldiers who were falsely accused of a shooting spree

Section Summary

PROGRESSIVISM UNDER TAFT

Theodore Roosevelt's friend and adviser **William Howard Taft** became president in 1908. Taft did not seek new reforms. He did support increasing the nation's forest reserves and creating a Department of Labor to enforce labor laws. He also passed the **Sixteenth Amendment**, which allowed Congress to collect taxes based on an individual's income.

Taft eventually lost the support of the Progressives. This began with a bill meant to lower tariffs but which actually did the opposite. Conservationists turned against Taft when it came out that his secretary of the interior, Richard Ballinger, allowed the illegal purchase of protected land in Alaska. When Gifford Pinchot accused Ballinger of sabotaging government conservation efforts, Taft fired Pinchot.

By the 1912 election, many Progressive Republicans had formed the new Progressive Party. Their candidates for president and vice president were

> **What were some of President Taft's reforms?**
> _____
> _____
> _____

> **Why did conservationists stop trusting Taft?**
> _____
> _____
> _____

Interactive Reader and Study Guide

The Progressives

Theodore Roosevelt and the popular California governor **Hiram W. Johnson**. With the Republicans split, the Democrats won.

WILSON'S NEW FREEDOM

Woodrow Wilson became president. He proposed a reform program called the **New Freedom**. It called for lower tariffs, banking reform, and stronger antitrust laws. In 1913 tariffs were lowered. To make up for the loss in income, a graduated income tax was introduced. This meant that people paid taxes according to their income level. Another of Wilson's reforms was the **Federal Reserve Act**, which was meant to prevent bank collapse during financial panics. The **Clayton Antitrust Act**, which clarified antitrust laws, finally made strikes, boycotts, and peaceful picketing by workers legal.

> **What is a graduated income tax?**
> _____
> _____
> _____

WOMEN GAIN THE VOTE

Alice Paul and Lucy Burns formed the Congressional Union for Woman Suffrage in 1914. These activists picketed the White House, chained themselves to railings, and went on hunger strikes. By patriotically supporting U.S. troops in World War I, women won more support. Wilson, too, supported women's suffrage. Ratified in 1920, the **Nineteenth Amendment** finally gave women the vote.

> **Beginning in 1914, what new tactics did the woman suffragists use?**
> _____
> _____
> _____

PROGRESSIVISM AND THE RIGHTS OF AFRICAN AMERICANS

The Progressives had a mixed record on civil rights. In 1906 African American soldiers were falsely accused of a shooting spree. Their entire regiment was discharged. The injustice of what became known as the **Brownsville incident** was not corrected until 1972. With people devoting energy to the war and not the reform movement, progressivism came to an end.

CHALLENGE ACTIVITY

Critical Thinking: Develop Choose one reform that, in your opinion, our nation needs today. Plan a campaign for getting it enacted.

Interactive Reader and Study Guide

Chapter Summary

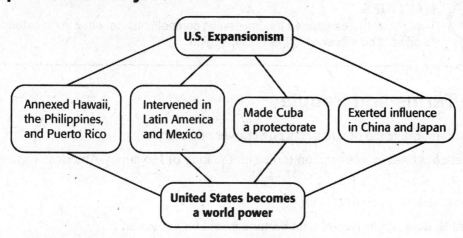

COMPREHENSION AND CRITICAL THINKING

Use information from the graphic organizer to answer the following questions.

1. **Recall** In which three regions did the United States annex territory?

   _____

   _____

2. **Rank** In your opinion, which region was most important to U.S. expansionism?

   _____

3. **Evaluate** How do you think U.S. expansionism helped the country become a world power?

   _____

   _____

Entering the World Stage

MAIN IDEA
The United States entered the imperialist competition late, but it soon extended its power and influence in the Pacific region.

Key Terms and People

imperialism extension of a nation's power over other lands

bayonet constitution constitution forced on the king of Hawaii by American business leaders

Liliuokalani last queen of Hawaii

Sanford B. Dole sugar tycoon who became president of Hawaii

sphere of influence geographic area where an outside nation has special political or economic control

Open Door Policy policy that would give all nations equal trading rights in China

Boxer Rebellion rebellion by anti-imperialist Chinese group

Russo-Japanese War war between Russia and Japan over control of Korea and Manchuria

Section Summary

IMPERIALIST ACTIVITY

From the 1870s to the 1910s, the industrialized nations of Great Britain, France, Belgium, Germany, Japan, and the United States competed for land in Africa, Asia, and Latin America. This competition was known as **imperialism**. Industrialized nations were looking for new customers and sources of raw materials. Their navies needed bases for refueling and repairs. The imperialists had a strong sense of nationalism. They thought that their cultures were superior to others. They wanted to civilize less developed countries and spread Christianity.

> Underline the names of the countries that were imperialistic.

TAKING CONTROL OF HAWAII

Hawaii was an ideal place for coaling stations and naval bases for ships traveling to and from Asia. American traders and missionaries came. They brought diseases that severely reduced the number of number of native Hawaiians. Some Americans became rich sugar planters and brought in workers from Asia. American businessmen formed the

> Why was Hawaii attractive to the Americans?
> _____
> _____
> _____

Entering the World Stage

Hawaiian League to take over Hawaii. They forced King Kalakaua to sign a new constitution at gunpoint. It was called the **bayonet constitution**. It gave Pearl Harbor to the United States. When Kalakaua died, his sister **Liliuokalani** became queen. The American minister to Hawaii ordered U.S. marines ashore and forced Queen Liliuokalani to surrender. **Sanford B. Dole** became the president of the Republic of Hawaii. An investigation by President Cleveland condemned the revolt. However, Dole refused to step down. In 1898 President McKinley annexed Hawaii. It became the 50th state in 1959. In 1993 Congress apologized for the U.S. role in overthrowing Liliuokalani.

> **What action was ordered by the American minister to Hawaii?**
> _____
> _____
> _____

> **Circle the date when Congress apologized to Hawaii.**

INFLUENCE IN CHINA

In 1895 Japan seized China's Liaotung Peninsula and the island of Taiwan. Russia, France, Germany, and Great Britain carved out **spheres of influence**. These were geographic areas where an outside nation had special political or economic influence. In 1899 the United States proposed the **Open Door Policy**. This would give all nations equal trading rights with China. Many Chinese were unhappy with the foreign influence. This led to the **Boxer Rebellion**, during which a group of Chinese rebels laid siege to the city of Beijing. Western nations put down the rebellion and forced China to sign a humbling settlement.

> **What caused the Boxer Rebellion?**
> _____
> _____
> _____

INFLUENCE IN JAPAN

Japan became industrialized after the United States forced it to open to trade. Japan and Russia both wanted control of Korea and Manchuria. This led to the **Russo-Japanese War**. President Roosevelt helped negotiate a peace treaty. With this victory, Japan became the strongest power in East Asia. It rivaled the United States for influence in China and the Pacific.

> **What was the result of the Russo-Japanese War?**
> _____
> _____
> _____

CHALLENGE ACTIVITY

Critical Thinking: Drawing Inferences How do you think that imperialism contributed to later events such as World War II? Write two paragraphs to explain.

Interactive Reader and Study Guide

MAIN IDEA
A quick victory in the Spanish-American War gave the United States a new role as a world power.

Key Terms and People

José Martí leader in Cuba's struggle for independence

William Randolph Hearst *New York Journal* publisher, known for yellow journalism

Joseph Pulitzer *New York World* publisher, also known for yellow journalism

yellow journalism exaggerated style of reporting news

de Lôme letter letter ridiculing President McKinley written by Spain's minister to the United States

George Dewey commander of the U.S. Navy's Asiatic Squadron during the Spanish-American War

Emilio Aguinaldo leader of a rebel army of Philippine patriots

Rough Riders volunteer cavalry regiment in the Spanish-American War led by Theodore Roosevelt

Battle of San Juan Hill battle for control of a ridge above Santiago, Cuba

Section Summary

SIMMERING UNREST IN CUBA

By the 1890s Spain's only colonies in the Western Hemisphere were Puerto Rico and Cuba. Since 1868 Cuba had struggled for independence from Spain. **José Martí** was one of the leaders of the Cuban independence movement. He was exiled, but continued to promote independence. Martí became one of Cuba's greatest heroes and was killed in battle. Spain's ruthless treatment of Cuban civilians shocked Americans.

> Underline the name of one of Cuba's greatest heroes.

AMERICANS GET WAR FEVER

Many Americans felt sympathy for the Cubans. The media fed this sympathy in order to sell papers. New York newspaper publishers **William Randolph Hearst** and **Joseph Pulitzer** competed for readers. They used an exaggerated style of reporting called **yellow journalism**. Hearst's newspaper, the *Journal*, published a letter from the Spanish minister to the

> How did Hearst and Pulitzer compete for readers?
> _____
> _____
> _____

United States. The **de Lôme letter**, named for its writer, ridiculed President McKinley. Then the *Maine*, a U.S. battleship, mysteriously blew up in Havana Harbor. Americans blamed Spain. On April 25, 1898, Congress declared war on Spain.

> Underline the name of the U.S. battleship that blew up in Cuba.

THE COURSE OF THE WAR

The war lasted about four months. Commodore **George Dewey** had orders to move the U.S. Navy's Asiatic Squadron to the Philippines if war was declared. They attacked and destroyed the entire Spanish fleet. Philippine rebels led by **Emilio Aguinaldo** supported the Americans. Spanish forces in the Philippines surrendered on August 14, 1898.

In Cuba, many soldiers were volunteers. The most famous volunteers were the **Rough Riders**. This was a cavalry regiment led by Theodore Roosevelt. African American soldiers of the Ninth and Tenth Cavalries, known as Buffalo Soldiers, also fought in Cuba. In the **Battle of San Juan Hill** the Buffalo Soldiers led the attack, supported by the Rough Riders. They captured the ridge above the city of Santiago. Two days later the U.S. Navy sank the entire Spanish fleet off Cuba. Spain signed a peace treaty giving up all claims to Cuba. It also gave Puerto Rico and Guam to the United States. The United States paid $20 million for the Philippines.

> What were the results of the Spanish-American War?
> _____
> _____
> _____
> _____
> _____

ANNEXING THE PHILIPPINES

Some people wanted the United States to annex the Philippines. Other people thought that annexation would be against American ideals. The United States did annex the Philippines, infuriating the Filipinos. For three years Filipino fighters fought the United States. Americans won the war in 1901. The United States said its goal was to prepare the islands for independence. The Philippines finally became independent in 1946.

> How did the Filipinos feel about being annexed by the United States?
> _____
> _____

CHALLENGE ACTIVITY

Critical Thinking: Interpret Yellow journalism did not end with the Spanish-American War. Make a list of current publications that engage in yellow journalism. List the types of subjects they report on.

Entering the World Stage

MAIN IDEA
The United States began to exert its influence over Latin America in the wake of the Spanish-American War.

Key Terms and People

Platt Amendment amendment to Cuba's constitution giving the United States the right to intervene in Cuba's affairs and acquire naval bases and fueling stations

protectorate a country under the control and protection of another country

Foraker Act law that allowed the United States to appoint Puerto Rico's governor and legislature

Roosevelt Corollary addition to the Monroe Doctrine pledging that the United States would use force to keep Europe out of Latin America

dollar diplomacy reliance on economic power instead of military force

Section Summary

CUBA AND PUERTO RICO

To restore order after the Spanish-American War, President McKinley set up military governments in Cuba and Puerto Rico. Yellow fever was a serious problem in Cuba. U.S. Army doctors proved that mosquitoes caused it. They got rid of breeding places for mosquitoes. To keep other nations from taking over Cuba, the United States forced Cuba to include the **Platt Amendment** in its constitution. This amendment made Cuba a U.S. **protectorate**. It gave the United States the right to intervene in Cuba's affairs. It also required Cuba to sell or lease land to the United States for naval bases. This was how the United States acquired the base at Guantánamo Bay. The **Foraker Act** allowed the United States to appoint the upper house of Puerto Rico's legislature as well as its governor. In 1952 Puerto Rico became a self-governing commonwealth.

> **How did U.S. Army doctors help Cuba?**
> _____
> _____
> _____

> **What gave the United States the right to intervene in Cuban affairs?**
> _____

THE PANAMA CANAL

The French were the first to try to build a canal across Panama. This would allow ships to go to Asia without sailing around South America. The United States took over the project. Colombia, which ruled Panama, would not allow the United States to build a canal.

> **Who ruled Panama before the Panamanians rebelled?**
> _____

Entering the World Stage

The United States supported Panamanian rebels in their struggle to break away from Colombia. When the rebels won, they gave the United States control over a 10-mile-wide Canal Zone. Work on the canal began in 1904. Building the canal posed great technical problems. In addition, malaria slowed construction. Sanitation workers had to drain swamps and clear vegetation to get rid of the mosquitoes that caused malaria. The canal finally opened in 1914.

THE ROOSEVELT COROLLARY

The Monroe Doctrine had said that the Western Hemisphere was off limits to European nations. However, the United States did not back this up. Europeans and Americans made large loans to Latin America. Latin American countries had a hard time paying these off. President Roosevelt issued the **Roosevelt Corollary**. This said that the United States would use military force to keep Europe from seizing Latin American territory for payment of debts. Later the United States used the Roosevelt Corollary to justify other intervention in Latin American affairs.

> What was the Monroe Doctrine?
> _____
> _____
> _____

RESHAPING U.S. DIPLOMACY

President William H. Taft believed in **dollar diplomacy**. This was a policy that relied on economic power instead of military force. Taft suggested that Americans buy out European loans to Latin America. Some Latin American countries disliked this policy. After American banks made loans to Nicaragua, U.S. leaders had to send troops to stop a revolt. President Woodrow Wilson disagreed with dollar diplomacy. He preferred to protect U.S. interests by strengthening constitutional governments.

> How did dollar diplomacy affect Nicaragua?
> _____
> _____
> _____

CHALLENGE ACTIVITY

Critical Thinking: Identify Cause and Effect Cuba and the United States have been on opposing sides of many issues since Castro took power. What causes for this situation can you find in this chapter? Write two paragraphs explaining your answer.

Entering the World Stage

MAIN IDEA
American intervention in Mexico's revolution caused strained relations between the two neighbors.

Key Terms and People

Porfirio Díaz dictator of Mexico between 1877 and 1910

Francisco Madero Díaz opponent who became president of Mexico after Díaz's overthrow

Emiliano Zapata rebel leader of an army of mostly Native American peasants

Francisco "Pancho" Villa rebel leader in northern Mexico

Victoriano Huerta military officer who overthrew Madero

Tampico incident arrest of nine American sailors in the port city of Tampico

Battle of Veracruz battle between the U.S. Marines and Mexican civilians for control of the port city of Veracruz

Mexican Revolution uprisings against Díaz's government

John J. Pershing leader of American invasion of Mexico to capture Pancho Villa

Section Summary

DICTATORSHIP SPARKS A REVOLUTION

Between 1877 and 1910, Mexico was ruled by the dictator **Porfirio Díaz**. Díaz jailed his opponents. He did not permit freedom of the press. He used the army to maintain order. Díaz used money from foreign investors to modernize Mexico. However, the only ones who benefited were the very wealthy. In the 1910 election, **Francisco Madero** ran against Díaz. Madero was a wealthy landowner who supported reforms. Díaz jailed Madero and claimed to have won the election. Uprisings against Díaz started in different parts of Mexico. In the south, **Emiliano Zapata** led an army of mostly Native Americans. In northern Mexico, **Francisco "Pancho" Villa** led a large-scale revolt. In May 1911, Díaz resigned and Madero became president. In 1913 the commander of government forces, **Victoriano Huerta**, overthrew him. Four armies immediately rose up to fight Huerta.

> Underline the years when Porfirio Díaz ruled Mexico. How long did he rule?
>
> _____

> Who became president after Díaz resigned?
>
> _____

Entering the World Stage

Section 4

THE UNITED STATES INTERVENES

Many European governments recognized Huerta's
government. The United States did not. President
Wilson supported Huerta's enemies. On April 9, 1914,
nine American sailors were arrested in the city of
Tampico. They were quickly released, and Mexico
apologized. The United States, however, demanded a
21-gun salute to the American flag. Mexico refused
the humiliating demand. Wilson used the **Tampico
incident** as an excuse to ask Congress to allow the use
of armed force against Mexico. Before Congress
agreed, Wilson learned that a German ship with
weapons for the Huerta government was headed for
Mexico. He ordered the U.S. Navy to seize the port of
Veracruz. The U.S. forces stopped the German ship.
Huerta's forces had withdrawn from Veracruz. Only
civilians and local authorities were left behind. After
the **Battle of Veracruz**, the United States took the
city. Six months later, Huerta resigned.

How did President Wilson react to Huerta's takeover?
_____
_____

What city did the United States seize?
_____

THE REVOLUTION CONCLUDES

Venustiano Carranza declared himself leader of the
revolution in August 1914. By then, the **Mexican
Revolution** was a struggle between two groups. One
group supported Carranza. The other group supported
Pancho Villa and Emiliano Zapata. The United States
recognized Carranza. Villa led troops across the U.S.
border on a raid. It was the first armed invasion of the
United States since the War of 1812. President Wilson
ordered a military expedition into Mexico to capture
Villa. General **John J. Pershing** led the expedition.
They searched for 11 months but were never able to
find him. The Mexicans resented the American
presence in their country. In 1917 Wilson withdrew
U.S. troops because of the war in Europe. Also in that
year, a new Mexican constitution went into effect. It
included the ideas of all the revolutionary groups. It
protected the liberties and rights of citizens. However,
fighting went on until 1920.

Who did the U.S support in the later years of the Mexican Revolution?
_____
_____
_____

CHALLENGE ACTIVITY

Critical Thinking: Evaluate Do you think the United States was justified
in invading Mexico? Write two paragraphs explaining your position.

Chapter Summary

The First World War

European rivalries lead to the outbreak of war in 1914.	The United States enters the war in 1917 and helps turn the tide for an Allied victory.	With the Treaty of Versailles, the Allies determine the terms for peace in the postwar world.
• Nationalism • Militarism • Imperialism • Alliances	• Won victory in the Battle of Chateau-Thierry • Stopped German advance at Belleau Wood • Defeated Germans' last offensive in the Second Battle of the Marne	• Forced Germany to pay massive reparations • Created the League of Nations • Treaty not ratified by U.S. Senate • United States did not join the League of Nations

COMPREHENSION AND CRITICAL THINKING

Use information from the graphic organizer to answer the following questions.

1. **Recall** What led to the outbreak of war in 1914?

_____

_____

2. **Identify Cause and Effect** What helped turn the tide for an Allied victory and when?

_____

_____

3. **Make Judgments** Why did the Allies get to make the terms for postwar peace?

_____

_____

The First World War

MAIN IDEA
Rivalries among European nations led to the outbreak of war in 1914.

Key Terms and People

Archduke Franz Ferdinand archduke of Austria whose assassination triggered World War I

Kaiser Wilhelm II German emperor during World War I

militarism policy of military preparedness and building up weapons

Triple Alliance alliance between Germany, Austria-Hungary, and Italy

Triple Entente alliance between Great Britain, France, and Russia

balance of power situation in which nations or alliances have equal strength

Central Powers Germany, Austria-Hungary, and the Ottoman Empire

Allied Powers Great Britain, France, and Russia

trench warfare fighting from trenches

Section Summary

CAUSES OF WORLD WAR I

In 1914 a Serbian terrorist assassinated **Archduke Franz Ferdinand** of Austria-Hungary while he was visiting Sarajevo. Nationalism had caused intense competition among European nations. They all wanted greater power and control of overseas colonies. **Kaiser Wilhelm II**, emperor of Germany, knew that Germany needed a stronger military to compete. **Militarism** is a policy of military preparedness and building up weapons. Germany began building up its military. Other nations began to worry about Germany's intentions. They built up their militaries to be prepared. Nations also formed alliances, or partnerships. Germany formed the **Triple Alliance** with Austria-Hungary and Italy. Great Britain, France, and Russia formed the **Triple Entente**, another alliance. Many leaders thought the alliances provided a **balance of power**. They thought that if alliances had equal strength, it would decrease the chances of war. However, when the archduke was killed, these alliances led Europe into war.

> Where was the archduke visiting when he was killed?
> _____

> Underline the members of the Triple Alliance.

Section 1

WAR BREAKS OUT

The Serbian government had provided the assassins with bombs and weapons. Austria-Hungary blamed Serbia and declared war. Russia had promised to protect Serbia, so it declared war on Austria-Hungary. Austria-Hungary's ally, Germany, declared war on Russia, and then on France, Russia's ally. To catch France by surprise, Germany invaded Belgium in August 1914. This drew Belgium's ally, Great Britain, into the war. Germany, Austria-Hungary, and the Ottoman Empire fought as the **Central Powers**. Britain, France, and Russia fought together as the **Allied Powers**. By the time the war ended, 30 other nations had been drawn into it.

The German attack on Belgium was fierce. The Germans burned anything in their path. Civilians were executed. The Germans were armed with machine guns. The French came to help Belgium. They were armed only with rifles. The Germans soon moved into France. The French stopped them at the First Battle of the Marne. In five days, 250,000 lives were lost. However, the Germans were slowed down. This gave the Russians a chance to mobilize. Then Germany had to pull some of their troops out of France. They were needed on the Eastern Front to fight the Russians.

> Why did Austria-Hungary blame Serbia for the assassination of Archduke Ferdinand?
> _____
> _____
> _____

> Which country did the Germans invade first?
> _____

THE WAR REACHES A STALEMATE

Both the French and the Germans dug miles of trenches. In **trench warfare**, soldiers fought in the trenches. Opposing forces used machine guns, grenades, and artillery. Anyone who went over the top was shot at. The war bogged down. Then the German military started using poison gas. The Allies soon used it as well. Soldiers began to carry gas masks for protection. These prevented the gas from working. Armored tanks were developed. Airplanes were used at first to spy. Then machine guns were mounted on planes and planes began to carry bombs.

> What happened to anyone who went over the top of the trenches?
> _____
> _____

CHALLENGE ACTIVITY

Critical Thinking: Drawing Inferences Write a three-paragraph journal entry about the life of a soldier fighting in the trenches in World War I. Describe the rain, the mud, the rats, the poison gas, and an attack.

The First World War

> **MAIN IDEA**
> The United States helped turn the tide for an Allied victory.

Key Terms and People

isolationism a policy of not being involved in the affairs of other nations

U-boats small German submarines

Lusitania passenger ship sunk by German U-boats during World War I

Sussex **pledge** Germany's promise not to sink merchant ships without warning and without saving lives

Zimmerman Note German telegram proposing an alliance between Germany and Mexico

Selective Service Act U.S. law requiring young men to register for the military draft

convoy system strategy of surrounding troop-transport ships with destroyers or cruisers for protection

Communists people who seek the equal distribution of wealth and the end of all private property

Section Summary

UNITED STATES STAYS NEUTRAL

Most Americans thought World War I did not concern them. They favored **isolationism**. This was a policy of not being involved in the affairs of other nations. However, U.S. businesses sold many war goods to the Allies. They could not sell to Germany because of a British blockade. Germany used **U-boats** to wage naval warfare. These were small submarines. In 1915 they sank the passenger ship *Lusitania*. This violated the laws of neutrality. Many American lives were lost. Tensions rose between the United States and Germany.

> Why couldn't American businesses sell war goods to the Germans?
>
> _____
>
> _____

HEADING TOWARD WAR

The German government agreed to attack only supply ships. However, in 1916 they attacked the French passenger ship *Sussex*. President Wilson threatened to end diplomatic ties with Germany. The Germans issued the *Sussex* **pledge**. They promised not to sink merchant vessels without warning or saving lives.

Interactive Reader and Study Guide

The First World War

Germany went back to unrestricted submarine warfare in 1917. The United States ended diplomatic relations with Germany. The Germans sent a telegram called the **Zimmerman Note** to Mexico. Germany wanted Mexico as an ally against the United States. The Americans got copies of the note and called for war. A revolution in Russia removed Czar Nicholas II from power. Now Americans supported the Allies even more. When Germany sank three American merchant ships, America declared war.

> **Why did the United States end diplomatic relations with Germany?**
>
> _____
>
> _____
>
> _____

AMERICANS IN EUROPE

In order to raise an army, Congress passed the **Selective Service Act**. This required young men to register to be drafted into the armed forces. Most young men went willingly. Almost nothing was ready for the new recruits. Still, training for the soldiers was intense. General John J. Pershing led the American Expeditionary Force that sailed to Europe. To transport the troops, a **convoy system** was used. This called for surrounding troop-transport ships with cruisers and destroyers for protection.

> **Underline the name of the leader of the American troops.**

Meanwhile, **Communists** took over Russia. They believed there should be an equal distribution of wealth and no private property. They pulled Russia out of the war. The Germans pushed the Allies back to the Marne River. American troops were a major factor in the war. They helped stop the German advance.

THE WAR ENDS

The Germans launched a last attack at the Second Battle of the Marne. They lost, and the Allies pushed them back into Belgium. In the Battle of the Argonne Forest, the Americans suffered 120,000 casualties. However, the Central Powers lost the will to keep fighting. On November 11, 1918, a truce, or armistice, went into effect.

> **Where did the Germans launch their last attack?**
>
> _____

CHALLENGE ACTIVITY

Critical Thinking: Elaborate Before the United States entered the war, many Americans went to Canada and volunteered to fight on the side of the Allies. Write two paragraphs telling whether you might have done this or not, and why.

Interactive Reader and Study Guide

MAIN IDEA
The United States mobilized a variety of resources to wage World War I.

Key Terms and People

Liberty bonds a form of loan to the government to pay for the war

Bernard Baruch head of the War Industries Board during World War I

National War Labor Board organization to settle disputes between workers and management during the war

Committee on Public Information organization to promote American support for the war

George Creel head of the Committee on Public Opinion

propaganda posters, newspaper stories, and other materials designed to influence people's opinions

Schenck v. United States Supreme Court decision explaining limits of free speech

Section Summary

MOBILIZING THE ECONOMY

Going to war was a huge and expensive thing to do. Congress passed the War Revenue Act to pay for the war. The act established very high taxes. The government also borrowed money. Much of the money was borrowed from Americans who bought **Liberty Bonds**. The War Industries Board was formed to regulate all materials needed for the war effort. **Bernard Baruch** headed the board. American industrial production increased 20 percent.

The Food Administration was formed to manage and increase food production. Americans planted vegetables in "victory gardens." There were "meatless Mondays" and "wheatless Wednesdays." Since alcohol used up grain, people were encouraged not to drink it. In 1918 the Eighteenth Amendment banned the manufacture, sale, or transportation of alcoholic beverages. The Fuel Administration made sure that military needs for fuel would be met. Supplies from America were vital to the struggling Allies. The power of manufacturing and farming gave a needed boost to the American economy as well.

> What were two ways the government raised money to pay for the war?
>
> _____
>
> _____

> How did the Eighteenth Amendment help the war effort?
>
> _____
>
> _____
>
> _____

MOBILIZING WORKERS

Profits of many corporations rose sharply during the war. Prices went up. Workers' wages did not go up enough to make up for the higher prices. Workers had to work longer hours, sometimes in dangerous conditions. These conditions led many workers to join labor unions. The **National War Labor Board** was formed to help prevent strikes. The Board judged disputes between workers and management. It also set policies to improve working conditions. Many women took jobs that men had left to go into the military. They made great contributions to the war effort.

In 1918 and 1919 there was a severe flu epidemic. About half of the American troops who died in the war died from influenza. The disease killed 600,000 Americans.

> Why did many workers join labor unions during the war?
>
> _____
>
> _____

INFLUENCING PUBLIC OPINION

Wilson had to change the minds of those Americans who had been against the war. He created the **Committee on Public Information**. It was headed by **George Creel**, a former reporter. Creel used **propaganda** to promote American support of the war. Propaganda is material designed to influence people's opinions. Movie stars and artists encouraged people to support the war.

Americans began to distrust anything that was German. Anti-German feelings grew after German secret agents planted a bomb in New York. Congress passed laws that limited Americans' freedom. They punished people for speaking out against the war or refusing military duty. Charles Schenck was one of many people jailed for violating the new laws. In *Schenck* v. *United States*, the Supreme Court ruled that freedom of speech could be limited if it caused danger for the country.

> Why did Wilson form the Committee on Public Information?
>
> _____
>
> _____

> What was the result of *Schenck* v. *United States*?
>
> _____
>
> _____
>
> _____

CHALLENGE ACTIVITY

Critical Thinking: Contrast As a result of the terrorist attacks on September 11, 2001, the USA PATRIOT Act was passed. It limits certain freedoms in order to allow the government to investigate suspected terrorists. Write two paragraphs contrasting this act with the laws limiting freedom of speech during World War I.

The First World War

MAIN IDEA
The Allies determined the terms for peace in the postwar world.

Key Terms and People

Fourteen Points President Wilson's plan for peace following World War I

self-determination the right of people to decide their own political status

League of Nations organization of nations that would work together to settle disputes, protect democracy, and prevent future wars

David Lloyd George British prime minister at the Paris Peace Conference

Georges Clemenceau French premier at the Paris Peace Conference

Big Four leaders of the United States, Britain, France, and Italy at the Paris Peace Conference

Treaty of Versailles treaty ending World War I

reparations payments for damages and expenses caused by the war

Henry Cabot Lodge head of the Senate Foreign Relations committee and leader of the group who wanted changes in the Treaty of Versailles

Section Summary

THE FOURTEEN POINTS

World War I caused a shocking loss of life and property. President Wilson wanted "a just and lasting peace." He wanted to ensure that such a war would never happen again. He outlined his vision to Congress. His plan was called the **Fourteen Points**. The first four points called for open diplomacy, freedom of the seas, free trade, and reduction of the military. The fifth point proposed a system to resolve disputes over colonies. The next eight points dealt with **self-determination**. This was the right of people to decide their own political status. The fourteenth point called for creating a **League of Nations**. It would be an organization of nations working together for peace. Wilson wanted a new philosophy for U.S. foreign policy. The Fourteen Points applied the principles of progressivism. Most importantly, they stated that the foreign policy of a democratic nation should be based on morality, not just on what was best for that nation.

> **Why did Wilson want "a just and lasting peace"?**
> _____
> _____
> _____

> **What did the fourteenth point call for?**
> _____
> _____

The First World War

PARIS PEACE CONFERENCE

President Wilson attended the peace conference in
Paris in 1919. Some people back home criticized him
for leaving the country. But Wilson wanted to make
his dream a reality. The Allied leaders at the
conference were President Wilson, Prime Minister
David Lloyd George of Great Britain, Premier
Georges Clemenceau of France, and Prime Minister
Vittorio Orlando of Italy. They were known as the
Big Four. Many delegates wanted to punish Germany.
Some wanted to build new nations, such as
Czechoslovakia. The **Treaty of Versailles** was the
result. It was much harsher than Wilson wanted. It
forced Germany to disarm. It also forced Germany to
pay war **reparations**. These were payments for
damages and expenses of the war. The amount assessed
was much greater than Germany could afford to pay.
However, the treaty did create the League of Nations.

> **How did the Treaty of Versailles deal with Germany?**
> _____
> _____
> _____
> _____

THE FIGHT OVER THE TREATY

Wilson presented the treaty to Congress. Some
Democrats were in favor of the treaty. Some senators
wanted to reject the treaty outright. Others were partly
in favor, but wanted changes. In this group was
Senator **Henry Cabot Lodge**. Wilson refused to
compromise. He traveled 8,000 miles in 22 days to
speak directly to the American people. Then he
suffered a stroke. Lodge presented the treaty to the
Senate with a list of proposed changes. Wilson refused
to budge. The treaty was rejected.

> **What did Wilson do instead of compromising?**
> _____
> _____
> _____

THE IMPACT OF WORLD WAR I

In all, the war, disease, and starvation killed more than
14 million people. It left 7 million men disabled. It
cost more than $300 billion. The war led to the
overthrow of monarchies in Russia, Austria-Hungary,
and Germany. It devastated European economies. The
United States became the world's leading economic
power.

> **Underline how many people were killed and disabled. Circle how much the war cost.**

CHALLENGE ACTIVITY

Critical Thinking: Evaluate Write two paragraphs explaining how you
would have voted on the Treaty of Versailles.

From War to Peace

Chapter Summary

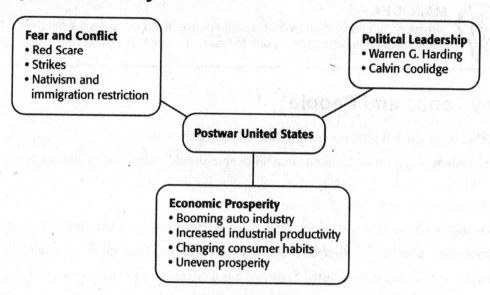

Fear and Conflict
- Red Scare
- Strikes
- Nativism and immigration restriction

Political Leadership
- Warren G. Harding
- Calvin Coolidge

Postwar United States

Economic Prosperity
- Booming auto industry
- Increased industrial productivity
- Changing consumer habits
- Uneven prosperity

COMPREHENSION AND CRITICAL THINKING

Use information from the graphic organizer to answer the following questions.

1. **Recall** What were two things that caused Americans to be fearful after World War I ended?

_____

_____

2. **Identify cause and effect** What contributed to the booming auto industry?

_____

_____

3. **Predict** Why might consumer habits be changing?

_____

_____

From War to Peace

MAIN IDEA
Although the end of World War I brought peace, it did not ease the minds of many Americans, who found much to fear in the postwar years.

Key Terms and People

Bolshevik group that took power after the Russian Revolution

communism a system which holds that all people should share equally in society's wealth

Red Scare widespread fear of communism

A. Mitchell Palmer Attorney General who used wartime laws to attack suspected radicals

Palmer raids attacks on suspected radicals, led by Attorney General A. Mitchell Palmer

alien a person living in the United States who is a citizen of another country

deportation being sent back to one's country of origin

anarchist a person who believes in the destruction of government

Section Summary

THE FIRST RED SCARE

After World War I ended, many people lost their jobs in the United States, and a deadly flu epidemic spread across the world. It became a time of fear.

Wartime hatred of Germans led to a postwar movement called 100 Percent Americanism. The movement supported all things American and opposed or attacked ideas or people it viewed as foreign or anti-American. In Russia the Red Army of the **Bolsheviks**, led by Vladimir I. Lenin, took control and later created the Soviet Union. This caused fear in Americans because the Bolsheviks believed in worldwide **communism**. Communists think that all people should share equally in society's wealth. The Soviet Union wanted to replace capitalism with communism.

Although capitalism was the foundation of American life, Communist parties formed here, too. Newspaper stories spread fear of "reds," as Communists were called, across the nation. This caused the 1919 **Red Scare**.

The government began an anti-Communist campaign. Attorney General **A. Mitchell Palmer**

What was it about communism that Americans feared?

_____
_____
_____
_____

From War to Peace

rounded up suspected radicals in **Palmer raids**. Many radicals were **aliens**. These were people who lived in the United States but were foreign citizens. Many were faced with **deportation**, being sent back to one's country of origin.

LABOR STRIFE GROWS

Many people suspected unions of being Communist. In 1919 some 4 million workers took part in over 3,000 strikes. They almost always lost. Job seekers were plentiful, and striking workers could easily be replaced. In Boston, Governor Calvin Coolidge put down a police strike and suddenly became a national hero. A miners' strike won wage increases but not a five-day work week or safer working conditions. The mine workers' union leader, John L. Lewis, knew that their demands would have to wait.

LIMITING IMMIGRATION

The Red Scare and lack of jobs led to nativism, the distrust of anything foreign. Both nativists and labor leaders wanted to limit immigration. In 1921 new federal laws reduced the number of immigrants allowed. In 1924 the numbers were set for specific countries, favoring immigrants from some places over others. Nativism helped revive the Ku Klux Klan, a hate group from the South. It also led to the unfair trial—for armed robbery and murder—of Nicola Sacco and Bartolomeo Vanzetti. The two Italian immigrants were **anarchists**, people who want to destroy government. The trial focused on their backgrounds and political beliefs. Although the evidence against them was weak, they were convicted and, in 1927, executed.

CHALLENGE ACTIVITY

Critical Thinking: Compare Write a paragraph explaining how 100 Percent Americanism and nativism were similar.

> **Why were many aliens deported in 1919 and afterwards?**
>
> _____
> _____
> _____

> **What was one result of nativism?**
>
> _____
> _____

> ### MAIN IDEA
>
> New products, new industries, and new ways of doing business expanded the economy in the 1920s, although not everyone shared in the prosperity.

Key Terms and People

Henry Ford first automaker to build inexpensive cars by using assembly lines

assembly line system of making products in which the product moves forward through many work stations as workers at each station perform specific tasks

productivity the amount of products made by workers or machines

welfare capitalism the practice of companies giving workers extra benefits to keep them happy and loyal so they will not want to join unions or demand higher pay

suburb a smaller town located outside a larger city

installment buying paying for an item with a series of small payments over time

credit borrowing money

Section Summary

FORD REVOLUTIONIZES INDUSTRY

The first cars were made by hand. Only the wealthy could afford them. **Henry Ford** began making cars that most people could afford. He did this by making car manufacturing simpler and cheaper. He used an **assembly line**, in which the car would pass through many work stations as workers at each station performed specific tasks. Ford also paid his workers well. This allowed the workers to buy the cars.

Other automakers and industries learned from Ford. They began using assembly lines. This raised worker **productivity**, the amount of products a worker or machine can produce. Businesses boomed in the 1920s and began **welfare capitalism**. They gave their workers extra benefits such as retirement pensions and recreation programs. They wanted to keep workers out of unions and away from higher pay demands.

> What was Henry Ford's contribution to American industry?
>
> _____
> _____
> _____
> _____
> _____

INDUSTRY CHANGES SOCIETY

The automobile industry led to the growth of spinoff industries. These were businesses that made the materials and parts for the cars such as glass, steel, and rubber.

Ford and other carmakers were located around Detroit, Michigan. Their success led to Detroit's growth. Between 1910 and 1930 Detroit's population tripled. Other cities in the Midwest also grew, especially those with automotive spinoff industries. Akron, Ohio, for example, boomed because it was the center for tire manufacturing.

Because of cars, **suburbs** grew. These were smaller towns outside of cities. Cars allowed people to drive to work from a distance. People also began using their cars to visit parts of the country they had never been to before. In Florida this led to a land boom.

> Why did suburbs grow in the 1920s?
> _____
> _____
> _____
> _____

THE NEW CONSUMER

The business boom of the 1920s was fueled by consumers. New electrical products such as refrigerators, vacuum cleaners, and radios appealed to people. The advertising industry persuaded people to buy more. **Installment buying** was introduced. Consumers paid for an item over time in small payments. This is also called **credit**, which is borrowing money.

Listening to the radio connected people to the world. A new form of public transportation, the passenger airline, also connected people.

> How did new electrical products and advertising lead to the rise of buying on credit?
> _____
> _____
> _____
> _____
> _____

WEAKNESSES IN THE ECONOMY

Not everyone in the United States was prosperous. Farmers had done well during the war, when there was not much competition from Europe. After the war, prices fell. Prices only rose when the government passed a tariff on farm products.

Nature also affected business. Cotton farmers faced boll weevils that destroyed their crops. Florida was hit by a severe hurricane, and the Mississippi River flooded, causing about a thousand deaths.

> Underline two reasons why farmers did not do well during this time.

CHALLENGE ACTIVITY

Critical Thinking: Sequence Make a time line, but instead of dates and events, use it to represent an assembly line building a car or other product. Fill in all the tasks you can think of and the order in which they are done.

From War to Peace

Section 3

MAIN IDEA
The nation's desire for normalcy and its support for American business was reflected in two successive presidents it chose—Warren G. Harding and Calvin Coolidge.

Key Terms and People

Warren G. Harding Republican president who helped business and suffered scandals

Teapot Dome piece of federally owned land that became the center of a scandal

Calvin Coolidge Republican vice president who took over when Harding died

reparation payments to make up for the damages of war

arms race competition between nations to build more and more weapons

Charles Evans Hughes Secretary of State under Calvin Coolidge

Kellogg-Briand Pact treaty signed by 60 countries agreeing not to go to war

Billy Mitchell U.S. brigadier general who pushed for building up air power

Section Summary

THE HARDING PRESIDENCY

Warren G. Harding was elected president in 1920. He promised a return to normalcy. People understood this as a return to what the country was like before the war. Harding avoided taking a stand on the League of Nations. He favored business and the wealthy because he thought wealthy people started and expanded businesses and that would improve the economy. The one thing he did to help struggling farmers, signing the 1921 tariff on European farm products, only helped for a short time.

Harding chose some highly skilled people for his Cabinet. Other choices were not so good. Some in his administration were dishonest. There were many scandals. In the worst one, the secretary of the interior went to jail for accepting bribes to allow oil companies to drill on federally owned land. The land was called **Teapot Dome**. In 1923, as rumors of the scandals grew, Harding died suddenly. **Calvin Coolidge**, his vice president, took office.

Why did Harding support business and the wealthy?
_____
_____
_____

What was the Teapot Dome scandal?
_____
_____

Section 3

THE COOLIDGE PRESIDENCY

Coolidge had become nationally known for putting down the Boston Police Strike in 1918. Now his reputation for honesty helped him get rid of the corrupt officials from the Harding administration. His success helped him win the election of 1924.

Coolidge believed that businesses would help the economy. He thought that business, not government, should support the arts and sciences, and fund charities. Coolidge felt the role of government should be limited. He worked to reduce taxes and the federal budget. He stopped government plans to help farmers. He said the government should not provide bonuses to World War I veterans. In 1928, although popular, Coolidge chose not to run for re-election.

> **Name two ways Coolidge limited the role of government.**
>
> _____
> _____
> _____
> _____

THE LINGERING EFFECTS OF WORLD WAR I

During the war the United States had loaned European nations $10 billion dollars. The war-torn nations had difficulty paying it back, especially after the U.S. tariffs of 1921. To pay their debts, they turned to Germany's **reparations**, or payments to make up for the damage of war. Germany was unable to pay and had to borrow money from the United States.

Many Americans wanted the government to save money and reduce the threat of war by cutting the armed forces. Great Britain and Japan were heading for a naval **arms race**, a competition by nations to build more and more weapons. In 1921, the United States called the Washington Naval Conference. Major naval powers, including the United States, agreed to reduce their navies. Secretary of State **Charles Evans Hughes** said it was a great step towards keeping peace.

Another move for peace was the **Kellogg-Briand Pact**, in which 60 countries promised not to use warfare to settle their problems. Meanwhile, Brigadier General **Billy Mitchell** was trying to convince the U.S. military to build up its air power. He was not successful.

> **Some people say that the United States paid for World War I twice. What do you think they mean?**
>
> _____
> _____
> _____
> _____
> _____

CHALLENGE ACTIVITY

Critical Thinking: Make Judgments Write two paragraphs explaining what you think about President Coolidge's beliefs about business.

The Roaring Twenties

Chapter Summary

Social Developments
- Changing roles for women
- Growing urbanization
- Cultural and religious conflict
- Prohibition

The Roaring Twenties was a time of great cultural upheaval

A New Popular Culture
- Mass entertainment—radio and movies
- An era of heroes—movie stars, sports figures, Lindbergh and Earhart
- Literature and art

The Harlem Renaissance
- Great Migration—movement of African Americans from South to North
- Harlem—focal point of major African American literary and cultural movement

COMPREHENSION AND CRITICAL THINKING

Use information from the graphic organizer to answer the following questions.

1. **Recall** How did American society change in the 1920s?

_____

_____

2. **Draw Conclusions** How did the Great Migration affect the Harlem Renaissance?

_____

_____

3. **Predict** How did new forms of mass entertainment affect society?

_____

_____

MAIN IDEA
The United States experienced many social changes during the 1920s.

Key Terms and People

flapper young woman who behaved in nontraditional ways

values key ideas and beliefs

fundamentalism religious beliefs based on a strict interpretation of the Bible

Billy Sunday popular fundamentalist preacher

Aimee Semple McPherson popular fundamentalist preacher

evolution theory saying current life on Earth is the result of millions of years of change and development

Clarence Darrow attorney for the defense in the Scopes trial

William Jennings Bryan prosecutor in the Scopes trial

bootlegger smuggler of illegal liquor

speakeasy illegal bar where liquor was sold during Prohibition

Section Summary

NEW ROLES FOR WOMEN

In 1920 women finally won the right to vote. A number of women were soon elected to state and local offices. However, women as voters did not cause great changes in the nation. Other new roles did.

Many women took low-paying jobs during the booming 1920s. As the rules for proper female behavior began changing, some women looked for more equality in their relationships with men. The **flapper** became the symbol of the 1920s. Flappers defied tradition by cutting their hair, wearing makeup, and promoting a lifestyle of independence and freedom.

> What changes came with women voting?
> _____
> _____
> _____

EFFECTS OF URBANIZATION

The 1920s' prosperity did not include farmers. Many people left farms for cities. For the first time in history, more Americans lived in urban areas than in rural areas. The automobile allowed rural people to spend more time in urban areas. As the population

> Why did people leave farms in the 1920s?
> _____
> _____
> _____

shifted to the cities, states began requiring that children attend school. As industry grew, people earned more and could afford to send their children to high school and college.

CONFLICTS OVER VALUES

The population shift to the cities produced a change in values. **Values** are the key ideas and beliefs a person holds. The values of urban Americans differed from the values of rural dwellers. Many people felt rural values represented traditional America: hard-working, self-reliant, religious, and independent. Some felt that cities represented change that threatened those values. Uncertainty led to **fundamentalism**, or a strict interpretation of the Bible. Tough-talking **Billy Sunday** and glamorous **Aimee Semple McPherson** were well-known fundamentalist preachers.

In Tennessee, fundamentalists outlawed the teaching of **evolution**, the theory that populations change over time and new species arise. A science teacher, John Scopes, was put on trial for violating the law. Criminal lawyer **Clarence Darrow** represented Scopes and stated the case was about freedom of speech. **William Jennings Bryan**, a champion of rural values, called it a contest between Christianity and evolution. Scopes was convicted and fined $100.

> Circle the belief system that calls for a strict interpretation of the Bible.

PROHIBITION

In 1920, the Volstead Act became law. It enforced the recently passed Eighteenth Amendment, which outlawed making, transporting, or selling alcohol. The ban was known as Prohibition. Many people believed this would have a good effect on society. However, liquor smugglers, or **bootleggers**, snuck alcohol through the ports and borders. Many people continued to drink, sometimes in illegal bars called **speakeasies**. Law-enforcement agents could not keep up with the smugglers. The illegal liquor business funded the criminal activities of gangsters such as Al Capone.

> What did the Eighteenth Amendment ban and what was the ban called?
>
> _____
>
> _____
>
> _____
>
> _____

CHALLENGE ACTIVITY

Critical Thinking: Make inferences Write a paragraph explaining how flappers, the Scopes trial, and Prohibition illustrate conflict over values.

The Roaring Twenties

MAIN IDEA
Transformations in the African American community contributed to a blossoming of black culture centered in Harlem, New York.

Key Terms and People

Great Migration movement of thousands of African Americans from the rural South to northern cities

Marcus Garvey African American leader who wanted his people to return to Africa

Harlem Renaissance African American cultural flowering based in Harlem, New York

Zora Neale Hurston scholar and writer who was part of the Harlem Renaissance

James Weldon Johnson writer, publisher, and NAACP leader

Langston Hughes celebrated African American poet

Paul Robeson actor and singer who proved that African Americans could perform serious stage roles

Louis Armstrong prominent jazz musician

jazz music that blends different music forms and is often composed on the spot

Bessie Smith legendary blues singer

Section Summary

THE GREAT MIGRATION

In the early 1900s, life was still hard for African Americans in the South. There was much poverty and racial violence. During World War I many jobs opened up in the North. African Americans moved North by the thousands. This became known as the **Great Migration**. After the war, racial violence grew with the lack of jobs.

> **What was the Great Migration?**
> _____
> _____

LIFE IN HARLEM

Harlem is a neighborhood in New York City. Thousands of African Americans lived there in the 1920s. It became a center for African American culture and activism. In 1909 W.E.B. Du Bois helped found the National Association for the Advancement of Colored People (NAACP), which worked to end discrimination and mistreatment of African Americans. He also edited a magazine, *The Crisis*, for black writers and poets. This helped make Harlem a center for literature.

Marcus Garvey founded the Universal Negro Improvement Association, or UNIA. He believed in blacks helping other blacks, without the help of whites. He also wanted to build up African American economic success in order to support the idea that African Americans should move to Africa and there create a new empire. This went against the ideas of Du Bois and the NAACP. Each organization criticized the other. In 1925 Garvey was sent to jail for mail fraud. When he was released, two years later, he was forced to leave the country, and UNIA collapsed.

> **Why did the NAACP and the UNIA not agree on how to help African Americans?**
>
> _____
>
> _____
>
> _____

A RENAISSANCE IN HARLEM

Many talented African American writers, thinkers, musicians, and artists came to live in Harlem and sparked the **Harlem Renaissance**, a cultural rebirth. **Zora Neale Hurston** was already an accomplished writer when she moved there in the 1920s. She wrote on many topics, including African American folklore. **James Weldon Johnson**, a journalist, teacher, and lawyer, wrote songs and poetry, and published other poets' work, too. **Langston Hughes** was an important poet who wrote of black pride and hope.

Besides literature, Harlem became a center of the performing arts. Actor and singer **Paul Robeson** won fame for serious roles on the stage. **Louis Armstrong** was a leading jazz performer. **Jazz** blended several musical forms from the South and was often composed on the spot. White fans traveled to Harlem to hear such great musicians as Armstrong, Cab Calloway, and **Bessie Smith**, one of the great blues singers.

> **Underline the great thinkers and writers of the Harlem Renaissance. Draw a circle around the performers and musicians.**

CHALLENGE ACTIVITY

Critical Thinking: Make Judgments Write three paragraphs, each one explaining and giving examples of different reasons why a cultural flowering such as the Harlem Renaissance is important to the progress of a people.

MAIN IDEA
New technologies helped produce a new mass culture in the 1920s.

Key Terms and People

D. W. Griffith first moviemaker to use advanced techniques

Charlie Chaplin silent movie actor who created the character of a tramp

transatlantic across the Atlantic Ocean

Charles A. Lindbergh first man to fly solo nonstop across the Atlantic Ocean

Amelia Earhart first woman to fly across the Atlantic

F. Scott Fitzgerald American writer who is closely linked with the 1920s

George Gershwin composer of popular songs

Section Summary

MASS ENTERTAINMENT IN THE 1920S

In the 1920s Americans invented new ways to learn about the world and enjoy themselves. The radio was invented in the late 1800s. During the 1920s radio became widely popular. By 1922 there were 570 radio stations in the United States. The invention of the vacuum tube improved the quality of radio sound. Soon people were listening to music, news, religious services, sports, and stories. The radio helped bring rural people and urban people closer together by giving them the same programs to listen to. They also heard the same ads and bought the same products.

> How did radio bring rural people and city people closer?
> _____
> _____
> _____
> _____

Movies were another form of mass entertainment that became popular in the 1920s. During World War I, moviemaker **D. W. Griffith** had used advanced techniques to show that movies could be a form of art. Up until 1927, movies were silent. Words on the screen described the story as music was played in the theater. In 1927 the first movie with sound came out and swept the country. The following year the first animated star was born: Mickey Mouse.

> Why was 1927 an important year for movies?
> _____
> _____
> _____

AN ERA OF HEROES

In the 1920s a new kind of celebrity was born: the movie star. One of the first silent film stars was

Charlie Chaplin. People laughed at his signature character, the tramp. Fan magazines followed romantic movie stars like Rudolph Valentino and Clara Bow, and Hollywood, California, became the center of the motion picture industry.

Not all heroes came from the screen. When he made the first solo, nonstop **transatlantic** (across the Atlantic Ocean) flight, **Charles A. Lindbergh** became a hero to millions. A little more than a year later, **Amelia Earhart** became the first woman to do the same thing. Earhart also set other records.

Radio brought sporting events to people, too. Sports heroes such as baseball's Babe Ruth and tennis's Helen Wills became some of the most famous and wealthy people in the world.

> **What was Charles Lindbergh's major accomplishment?**
> _____
> _____

ARTS OF THE 1920S

The economic and social changes of the 1920s gave authors much to write about. **F. Scott Fitzgerald** is closely linked to the 1920s. His books drew detailed pictures of life at that time, often including glamorous characters. Sinclair Lewis wrote about the empty lives of the middle class of the time and the cost of success. Women such as poet Edna St. Vincent Millay and novelists Willa Cather and Edith Wharton had much to say. Some writers had been deeply affected by World War I. Ernest Hemingway and John Dos Passos wrote about their war experiences, among other things. Many of them chose to live in Paris and came to be called the Lost Generation. **George Gershwin** wrote music. He is remembered for *Rhapsody in Blue*. This piece, written for an orchestra, showed the powerful impact of jazz music. Gershwin also wrote popular songs with his brother, Ira.

> **What are some themes that authors wrote about in the 1920s?**
> _____
> _____
> _____
> _____

CHALLENGE ACTIVITY

Critical Thinking: Summarize Do some research into the movies of the 1920s. If you can, watch one silent film and one sound film from that time. Then create a list of articles that might appear in a fan magazine at the beginning of 1928. Who were the stars? What were the issues facing moviemakers? How might animation and sound impact silent film stars? Choose one topic and write a full article.

The Great Depression Begins

Chapter Summary

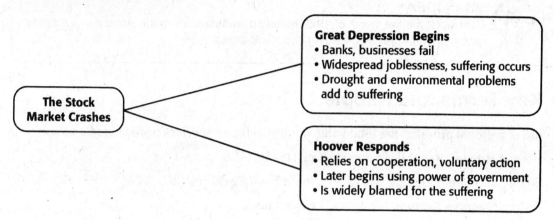

The Stock Market Crashes

Great Depression Begins
• Banks, businesses fail
• Widespread joblessness, suffering occurs
• Drought and environmental problems add to suffering

Hoover Responds
• Relies on cooperation, voluntary action
• Later begins using power of government
• Is widely blamed for the suffering

COMPREHENSION AND CRITICAL THINKING

Use information from the graphic organizer to answer the following questions.

1. **Identify** What happened to banks and businesses after the stock market crashed?

_____

_____

2. **Describe** What caused the suffering of the Great Depression?

_____

_____

3. **Explain** How did President Hoover respond to the Great Depression?

_____

_____

_____

The Great Depression Begins

 MAIN IDEA
The stock market crash of 1929 revealed weaknesses in the American economy and helped trigger a spreading economic crisis.

Key Terms and People

gross national product the total value of all goods and services produced in a nation

Herbert Hoover Republican president elected in 1928

buying on margin buying stocks with loans from stockbrokers

Federal Reserve System the nation's central bank

Black Tuesday October 29, 1929—the worst day of the stock market crash

Section Summary

AN APPEARANCE OF PROSPERITY

Between 1922 and 1928 business boomed, and the U.S. **gross national product** grew quickly. Gross national product is the value of goods and services produced in the nation. Unemployment was low, and many people now felt wealthy. However, farmers and certain other workers did not prosper.

Stocks are bought and sold in the stock market. A share of stock is a share of ownership in a company. As business boomed, the stock market rose sharply. The value of the stocks sold on the stock market increased by four times between 1920 and 1929. Ordinary Americans began to buy stocks.

Republican presidents Harding and Coolidge both favored business growth, and most Americans agreed with this policy. Coolidge decided not to run in the 1928 elections. His replacement, former secretary of commerce **Herbert Hoover**, won easily.

> **Which groups did not prosper during the 1920s?**
> _____
> _____

> **What is a share of stock?**
> _____
> _____

ECONOMIC WEAKNESSES

In spite of the boom, there were still problems in the economy. The wealthiest people saw their incomes grow sharply, but the average worker saw only small gains. Rising prices wiped out increases in wages, especially for farmers and coal miners. By 1929 70 percent of the nation's families did not earn enough for a good standard of living.

> **Circle the percent of people who did not earn enough to have a good standard of living in 1929.**

Interactive Reader and Study Guide

The Great Depression Begins

Many new goods were introduced in the 1920s, and people often bought them on credit. By the end of the 1920s, people had used up their credit. Spending dropped sharply, and warehouses filled with products that no one could afford to buy.

Stockbrokers loaned people money to buy stocks. This was called **buying on margin**. This was very risky. If the value of the stock dropped, people could not pay back their loans and lost the money they had put in. The **Federal Reserve System** is our nation's central bank. It took steps to reduce buying on margin but was only partly successful.

> **What caused spending to drop sharply at the end of the 1920s?**
> _____
> _____

THE STOCK MARKET CRASHES

Rumors started that big investors were going to pull their money out of the stock market. This caused many to sell their stock. There were many sellers and not many buyers, so stock prices fell. Some leading bankers bought stocks, trying to prop up the market. On October 29, 1929, the market collapsed. This day became known as **Black Tuesday**.

> **Why did stock prices fall?**
> _____
> _____
> _____
> _____

THE EFFECTS OF THE CRASH

Many investors were ruined. Those who had bought on margin could not pay back their loans. Many banks also lost money that they had loaned to businesses and to stockbrokers. Frightened people rushed to take their money out of the banks. Businesses were forced to lay off workers. With no income, people could not buy things, so spending and sales dropped further.

The trouble spread to Europe because America had been Europe's banker. World trade dropped, which made everything worse.

CHALLENGE ACTIVITY

Critical Thinking: Evaluate Write two paragraphs evaluating how the two weaknesses of overuse of credit and buying on margin caused the stock market crash to weaken the entire economy.

The Great Depression Begins

Section 2

MAIN IDEA
The Great Depression and the natural disaster known as the Dust Bowl produced economic suffering on a scale the nation had never seen before.

Key Terms and People

Great Depression the most severe economic downturn in the history of the United States

foreclosure a lender taking over ownership of a property from an owner who has not made loan payments

hobo person who travels, usually by train, in search of a job

Hooverville shantytown where homeless people lived during the Great Depression

drought a period of below average rainfall

Dust Bowl areas where severe dust storms destroyed topsoil, homes, and farm equipment

Okie a person who left the Dust Bowl to move to California

Woody Guthrie singer and songwriter who wrote songs about the Great Depression

Section Summary

THE DEVELOPMENT OF THE GREAT DEPRESSION

The **Great Depression** was the worst economic downturn in the history of the United States. It was triggered by the stock market crash. However, the downturn spread through the whole economy. Many banks failed as a result of the crash. People who had money in the banks lost it. (Today, there is insurance to protect against this.) By 1933, more than $140 billion in savings had been lost.

Farmers were already facing hard times. When people lost their jobs, there was no money for food. Food prices fell. This made farmers worse off than before. Many Americans went hungry. By 1933 food prices were about half what they had been in 1929. Farmers often borrowed money from banks. When prices fell, they could not make their loan payments.

By 1935, 750,000 farms had gone bankrupt or been foreclosed. **Foreclosure** means that a lender has taken possession of a property because the owner could not make loan payments.

> Circle how much savings had been lost by 1933.

> How did food prices in 1933 compare to those of 1929?
> _____

> Circle how many farms had gone bankrupt or been foreclosed by 1935.

The Great Depression Begins

By 1933 gross national product had dropped by 40 percent. Unemployment reached 25 percent. In some places it was even worse than that.

THE HUMAN IMPACT OF THE GREAT DEPRESSION

Millions of people were out of work. To survive, many begged. Many went from town to town in search of a job. These people were called **hoboes**. Many people lost their homes. They made shelters of whatever they could find. Sometimes they used cardboard boxes. The shantytowns they built were called **Hoovervilles**.

Americans felt deep shame at their poverty. There was a rise in suicide rates.

What were Hoovervilles?

_____

_____

_____

DEVASTATION IN THE DUST BOWL

Nature helped make the Great Depression worse. There was a severe drought in the Great Plains region. A **drought** is a time when there is not enough rainfall. Before the drought, careless farming practices left the topsoil with no plants to anchor it. When storms came, they blew the soil away. Huge dust storms developed. This occurred in parts of Oklahoma, Kansas, Colorado, New Mexico, and Texas. It was called the **Dust Bowl**. Farms and machinery were destroyed. Many people had no way to earn a living and moved away. Dust Bowl farmers tried moving to California. They were called **Okies,** even though they were from other states besides Oklahoma.

Writers and artists such as John Steinbeck and **Woody Guthrie**, a folksinger, wrote about the Dust Bowl and the Okies.

How did nature make the Great Depression worse?

_____

_____

_____

_____

CHALLENGE ACTIVITY

Critical Thinking: Design The Okies took with them only what they could pack in a truck or a car. What items do you think they might take with them? Trace their route on a map.

 MAIN IDEA
Herbert Hoover came to office with a clear philosophy of government, but the events of the Great Depression overwhelmed his responses.

Key Terms and People

associative state Hoover's term for voluntary partnership between business associations and government

Hoover Dam dam built by private business and paid for by the government

cooperative an organization owned and controlled by its members

Reconstruction Finance Corporation government program that provided money to banks and other institutions

Smoot-Hawley Tariff Act law passed in 1930 that placed tariffs on many imported goods

Section Summary

HERBERT HOOVER'S PHILOSOPHY

Herbert Hoover believed that government should play as small a role as possible in the affairs of business. He believed that too much government weakened the American spirit, which he called "rugged individualism." For this reason he would not give government money directly to the people. However, he also believed in cooperation. He believed that businesses should form voluntary associations to make the economy fairer and more efficient. He called the voluntary partnership between these associations and government the **associative state**.

Hoover used his idea to build **Hoover Dam**. This dam was paid for by the government but built by private businesses.

> Circle the name of the partnership between government and business.

> What was an example of Hoover's philosophy at work?
> _____
> _____

HOOVER'S RESPONSE TO THE GREAT DEPRESSION

Hoover wanted to find ways for people to help themselves. He pushed for a program of loans to strengthen farm cooperatives. A **cooperative** is an organization that is owned and controlled by its members. Using cooperatives, farmers could buy materials at lower prices and sell their crops in ways that would raise prices for them all.

> How did cooperatives help farmers?
> _____
> _____

The Great Depression Begins

Hoover also talked to businesses, asking them not to lay off workers or cut wages. Faced with economic disaster, however, businesses and individuals worried first about their own affairs. Business cut wages and jobs. State and local governments stopped building projects. Consumers stopped spending. All these actions made the Great Depression worse.

Hoover had to take direct action. In 1932 he persuaded Congress to establish the **Reconstruction Finance Corporation**. This program gave government money to banks and other institutions. Hoover also supported the Federal Home Loan Bank. The aim of this program was to encourage home building. It also tried to reduce foreclosures.

One of Hoover's actions hurt rather than helped. This was the passage of the **Smoot-Hawley Tariff Act**. A tariff is a tax on imports. The Act raised these taxes, making imports more expensive for Americans and American goods cheaper than foreign goods. Europeans responded with their own tariffs. Both these moves hurt international trade severely.

What actions made the Great Depression worse?
_____
_____
_____
_____

What was the Smoot-Hawley Tariff Act supposed to do?
_____
_____
_____

THE NATION RESPONDS TO HOOVER

Hoover tried to make people feel better by saying that the Great Depression was almost over and that things were not all that bad. People stopped believing in him. They also felt that Hoover did not really care about the suffering of ordinary people. They did not see why banks should get aid and people should not.

Hoover felt that government should always have a balanced budget. Therefore, he passed a large tax increase in 1932. This was very unpopular.

In 1930 the Republican Party lost control of the House of Representatives. By the 1932 presidential election, Hoover had very little support.

What caused Hoover to lose support?
_____
_____
_____
_____

CHALLENGE ACTIVITY

Critical Thinking: Develop How might you have responded to the Great Depression if you were president? Develop a plan for helping the country toward better economic times.

Chapter Summary

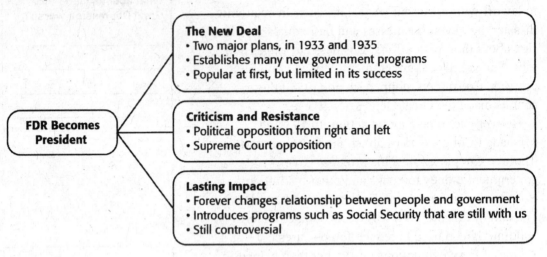

FDR Becomes President

The New Deal
• Two major plans, in 1933 and 1935
• Establishes many new government programs
• Popular at first, but limited in its success

Criticism and Resistance
• Political opposition from right and left
• Supreme Court opposition

Lasting Impact
• Forever changes relationship between people and government
• Introduces programs such as Social Security that are still with us
• Still controversial

COMPREHENSION AND CRITICAL THINKING

Use information from the graphic organizer to answer the following questions.

1. **Recall** From whom did Roosevelt face opposition on the New Deal?

_____

_____

2. **Explain** What was the lasting impact of the New Deal?

_____

_____

3. **Draw Conclusions** Why might the New Deal still be controversial today?

_____

_____

MAIN IDEA
In 1933 Franklin Delano Roosevelt became president of a suffering nation. He quickly sought to address the country's needs, with mixed results.

Key Terms and People

Franklin Delano Roosevelt president who took office during the Great Depression and led the country through World War II

public works government-funded building projects

fireside chat one of Roosevelt's radio addresses that sounded like he was sitting by your fireplace

Eleanor Roosevelt FDR's wife, who established a greater role for First Ladies

Hundred Days the first period of government activity in Roosevelt's presidency

New Deal FDR's program for ending the Great Depression

subsidy government payment

Huey P. Long Louisiana senator who said FDR was too close to banks and businesses

Father Charles Coughlin Catholic priest whose radio broadcasts attacked FDR

Dr. Francis Townsend critic who said New Deal did not do enough for older Americans

Section Summary

THE ELECTION OF 1932

Franklin Delano Roosevelt, known as FDR, became president in 1932. A Democrat, he had been governor of New York. He convinced people that he understood their hard times. He promised relief for the poor and more **public works** programs. These were building projects paid for by the government. He won by a landslide and the Democrats won control of Congress.

> **What helped convince people that FDR understood their suffering?**
> _____
> _____

A POLITICAL PARTNERSHIP

Roosevelt talked to the country by radio with his **fireside chats**. He spoke as though he was sitting in people's living rooms. FDR believed that government should solve economic and social problems.

FDR's wife, **Eleanor Roosevelt**, was her husband's "eyes and ears." She became a powerful political force. One social issue she worked on was the campaign to stop the lynching of African Americans.

> **What did FDR believe about government?**
> _____
> _____

> **How did Eleanor Roosevelt help her husband?**
> _____

Her actions helped to make the role of First Lady
more important.

ROOSEVELT TAKES ACTION

Roosevelt's first months in office were called the
Hundred Days. He began many of the programs that
made up the **New Deal**. He first rescued the banking
system. He pushed through Congress the Emergency
Banking Act, which made banks report to
government.

FDR also created the Civilian Conservation Corps.
In the CCC people were paid to work on conservation
projects. The Agricultural Adjustment Act gave
farmers a **subsidy**, a payment to grow fewer crops.
The National Industrial Recovery Act called for
businesses to act together to set wages and production
levels. The Securities and Exchange Commission was
founded to oversee the stock markets.

> **Circle the laws and programs that were part of the New Deal.**

TROUBLE FOR THE NEW DEAL

Some people were against the New Deal because they
thought it did not go far enough. These included
Louisiana Senator **Huey P. Long** and Catholic priest
Father Charles Coughlin, who criticized FDR on the
radio. **Dr. Francis Townsend** thought the New Deal
did not do enough for old people. He thought they
should receive pensions, which were payments after
retirement. One the other hand, the American Liberty
League thought the New Deal was anti-business and
had gone too far.

The Supreme Court decided that many New Deal
programs were unconstitutional because they changed
the balance of power between the president, Congress,
and courts. The Court stopped much of the New Deal.

> **Underline the names of the people and organizations that were against the New Deal.**

CHALLENGE ACTIVITY

Critical Thinking: Evaluate Do you think the New Deal went far enough
to help people, or too far? Write two paragraphs about your position.

The New Deal

MAIN IDEA
A new wave of government initiatives starting in 1935 resulted in some strong successes and stunning defeats for President Roosevelt.

Key Terms and People

Second New Deal new laws passed as part of the New Deal

Social Security government program providing a guaranteed income to older Americans

John L. Lewis head of the United Mine Workers who helped found the CIO

CIO Committee for Industrial Organization—an association of unions of unskilled workers

sit-down strike strike in which the strikers stayed at their jobs but stopped working

deficit economic condition when government spends more than it takes in

John Maynard Keynes British economist who said that limited deficit spending could help the economy

Section Summary

THE SECOND HUNDRED DAYS

In early 1935 the courts were finding that key parts of New Deal programs were unconstitutional. The economy was not getting better. With the help of a Democratic majority in Congress, FDR began many new programs, sometimes called the **Second New Deal**. It included new laws increasing government control of the banking industry and higher taxes for wealthy Americans. New relief programs began, but instead of paying Americans directly, people were required to work. The Works Progress Administration employed millions of people in projects such as building roads, subways, and airports. The WPA also created work for artists and writers.

An important part of the Second New Deal was the creation of **Social Security**. This program guaranteed an income for many Americans age 65 or older. It also included unemployment insurance.

> Circle the new laws and programs that were part of the Second New Deal.

> How were the relief plans of the Second New Deal different from those of the New Deal?
> _____
> _____

REVIVING ORGANIZED LABOR

The Wagner Act, or National Labor Relations Act, outlawed many antilabor practices. It established the National Labor Relations Board, which could conduct

The New Deal

voting in workplaces to see if employees wanted unions. It could require businesses to accept the results. Millions of Americans joined unions.

John L. Lewis, head of the United Mine Workers, helped found the **CIO**, Committee for Industrial Organization. The CIO organized the unions of unskilled workers. The following year, the United Auto Workers, part of the CIO, launched a new kind of strike. For this **sit-down strike**, workers sat at their workplaces and stopped working. They stayed there day and night. After six weeks, management recognized the union.

> **What kind of unions formed the organization called the CIO?**
>
> _____
>
> _____

THE ELECTION OF 1936

In 1936 Roosevelt won a second term in a landslide. He had halved unemployment and incomes were up sharply. His New Deal programs brought hope to millions. He had helped rural Americans by bringing electricity to remote areas. In the past, African Americans had supported the Republicans, the party of Lincoln. In this election, many African Americans voters chose Roosevelt and the Democrats.

> **What had FDR accomplished by the 1936 election?**
>
> _____
>
> _____
>
> _____
>
> _____

A TROUBLED YEAR

The courts had struck down many New Deal programs. In 1937 Congress spent most of its time on FDR's proposal to reorganize the courts. He wanted to have presidents appoint more Supreme Court justices. The Democrats were divided, and he lost the battle.

Later that year the stock market dropped and unemployment rose. FDR was worried about more spending because of the federal budget **deficit**. A deficit occurs when a government spends more money than it takes in. However, FDR followed the thinking of economist **John Maynard Keynes**. Keynes argued that deficit spending could help the economy. In the summer of 1938 the economy began to improve.

> **Why do you think FDR's proposal to reorganize the courts caused so much argument?**
>
> _____
>
> _____

CHALLENGE ACTIVITY

Critical Thinking: Design Develop a New Deal for today. Include programs for dealing with unemployment, education, the environment, health care, and poverty.

Interactive Reader and Study Guide

The New Deal

Section 3

MAIN IDEA
The Great Depression and the New Deal had a deep impact on American culture during the 1930s.

Key Terms and People

Frances Perkins Secretary of Labor; first woman to head an executive department

Black Cabinet group of black government officials

Mary McLeod Bethune director of Negro Affairs in the National Youth Administration

Dorothea Lange photographer who chronicled the Great Depression

swing a highly orchestrated type of jazz

Section Summary

NEW ROLES FOR WOMEN AND AFRICAN AMERICANS

Women's roles in public life expanded under the New Deal. The example was set by Eleanor Roosevelt, who played a large role in FDR's administration. So did other women. **Frances Perkins** served as FDR's Secretary of Labor. She was the first woman to head an executive department. She helped form many New Deal policies. However, women were still paid less than men. Many people thought women should not take jobs at all, as this might put men out of work.

African Americans also had new roles under the New Deal. FDR appointed African Americans to key positions. Included was the first black federal judge, William Hastie. These officials met as a group, nicknamed the **Black Cabinet**, and helped advise FDR. They met under the leadership of **Mary McLeod Bethune**. She was the director of Negro Affairs in the National Youth Administration.

New Deal programs, however, did not challenge racial discrimination. Roosevelt thought that to do so would make enemies of southern Democrats. Then these Democrats might block other programs.

> **What problems did women workers face during the Great Depression and New Deal?**
> _____
> _____
> _____

> **What was the Black Cabinet?**
> _____
> _____

> **Did the New Deal programs fight racial discrimination?**
> _____

TELLING THE STORY OF THE DEPRESSION

During the Great Depression artists took a new interest in social problems and activism. John

Steinbeck wrote *The Grapes of Wrath*. This novel was about a family of Okies leaving the Dust Bowl for California. Woody Guthrie wrote folk songs about the lives of ordinary people.

Photographer **Dorothea Lange** took pictures of jobless people in San Francisco. However, her most famous work included pictures of the rural poor. Starting in 1935 Lange worked for the Farm Security Administration. In 1937 the federal government began to give assistance to tenant farmers and sharecroppers. This was due in part to the photographs that raised people's awareness.

Other artists of the Great Depression included writer James Agee and photographer Walker Evans.

> How did Dorothea Lange help the rural poor?
> _____
> _____

POPULAR ENTERTAINMENT IN THE 1930S

In the 1930s seeing a movie cost an average of 25 cents. Millions of Americans went to the movies every week. Some movies dealt with the Great Depression. Most people, however, went to the movies to escape. Charlie Chaplin and the Marx Brothers made world-renowned comedies. Elegant musicals were performed by stars like Fred Astaire and Ginger Rogers. Frank Capra directed many films about the common man.

> Circle how much movies cost during the Great Depression.
> _____

Radio was very popular. Most American households had a radio. People listened to FDR's fireside chats, and also news, entertainment, and religious programming. There were also comedy and action shows. In 1938 the story *The War of the Worlds* was broadcast. It was so realistic that some listeners were convinced that spaceships from Mars were attacking Earth.

People also listened to music. Jazz became more popular. A new kind of highly orchestrated jazz came to be. It was called **swing**.

CHALLENGE ACTIVITY

Critical Thinking: Elaborate Watch a typical Fred Astaire movie from the 1930s. Write three paragraphs contrasting the world shown in the movie with the real world of the Great Depression.

Section 4

> **MAIN IDEA**
> The New Deal had mixed success in rescuing the economy, but it fundamentally changed Americans' relationship with their government.

Key Terms and People

Marian Anderson famous black singer who encountered racial discrimination

minimum wage the lowest wage an employer can legally pay a worker

incumbent the person currently holding a position

Section Summary

THE IMPACT OF THE NEW DEAL

FDR promised the nation "relief, recovery, and reform." Relief programs put billions of dollars into Americans' pockets. New Deal programs such as Social Security and unemployment insurance have lasted until today.

> **What did FDR promise the nation?**
> _____
> _____

As for recovery of the economy, however, the New Deal was less successful. Joblessness fell from 13 million in 1933 to 9 million by 1936. Wages and production moved up to their 1929 levels. However, these gains were wiped out in 1937 and 1938. By 1939, 10 million workers were still unemployed.

No one can say for sure why FDR's methods did not work as well as had been hoped. Some historians think Roosevelt's policies undermined business confidence and actually slowed the recovery. Other historians believe that the New Deal did not go far enough. They say that FDR should have spent more money and run a bigger deficit.

> **What two opposing opinions do historians hold about the New Deal?**
> _____
> _____

New Deal reforms, however, have been successful and lasted through the years. The Federal Deposit Insurance Corporation restored public confidence in the banking system and still insures bank accounts. The Securities and Exchange Commission still oversees the stock markets. Today's investors continue to rely on it.

> **What two New Deal reforms do we still rely on today?**
> _____
> _____

Finally, the New Deal left a very large physical legacy. The WPA has left us thousands of hospitals, schools, dams, bridges, roads, and public buildings, as well as murals and sculptures.

The New Deal

The New Deal changed the relationship between the American people and their government. The new relationship was based on the belief that government had a role to play in helping both businesses and individuals gain a greater level of economic security. To play this role, however, government had to get bigger, and as it did, Americans came to look regularly to the government for help.

> **How did the New Deal change the relationship between business and government?**

LIMITS OF THE NEW DEAL

Five million jobless people were not helped by the New Deal. The relief jobs themselves were only temporary, and they did not pay well. Federal programs often clashed with state programs. This resulted in different amounts of relief in different states. The New Deal also allowed racial discrimination. Although FDR appointed members of minority groups to office, he did not push for racial justice. He was afraid of losing the support of lawmakers if he did. When Eleanor Roosevelt arranged for the great African American singer **Marian Anderson** to hold a concert in Washington, D.C., it was a daring action.

> **Why were work-relief jobs not as good as regular jobs?**
> _____

THE END OF THE NEW DEAL

By 1937 FDR lost much support in his court-reorganization fight. Then came the economic downturn of 1937–1938. Many in Congress fought his policies at every step. However, FDR worked hard to have Congress pass a **minimum wage** and set the maximum hours for a work week. FDR had less success in the 1938 congressional elections. In each case, Roosevelt's candidate lost and the **incumbent**, the one presently in office, won. The American public began to turn their attention to the growing threat of war in Europe. By 1938 the New Deal era was over.

CHALLENGE ACTIVITY

Critical Thinking: Evaluate If you had lived during those times, would you have favored the New Deal? Write three paragraphs explaining your position.

Interactive Reader and Study Guide

World War II Erupts

Chapter Summary

Rise of Dictators	Aggression and War	The United States: From Isolationism to War	Mobilizing for War
Dictators, taking advantage of widespread fear, uncertainty, and despair, emerge during the post–World War I era.	Aggressive dictators use war to promote their tyrannical goals.	Isolationism gives way to the call for war when the United States comes under direct attack.	The United States musters its tremendous industrial and human might to fight the war.

COMPREHENSION AND CRITICAL THINKING

Use information from the graphic organizer to answer the following questions.

1. **Identify** What kind of leaders emerged during the post-World War I era?

_____

_____

2. **Identify Cause and Effect** What caused America's isolationism to give way to a call for war?

_____

_____

3. **Identify Cause and Effect** How did the United States respond to the challenge?

_____

_____

World War II Erupts

MAIN IDEA
The shattering effects of World War I helped set the stage for a new, aggressive type of leader in Europe and Asia.

Key Terms and People

inflation a general rise in prices

Benito Mussolini Italian leader who came to power in 1922

fascism system of government that stressed the importance and glory of the state

dictatorship government by a leader or group that holds complete power

totalitarian a type of government where no opposition is allowed

Adolf Hitler German leader who came to power in 1933

Joseph Stalin leader of the Soviet Union who came to power in the mid-1920s

Haile Selassie leader of Ethiopia when Italy conquered it

Francisco Franco Spanish leader who came to power after the Spanish Civil War

Neville Chamberlain British Prime Minister who believed in appeasing Hitler

Section Summary

EUROPE AFTER WORLD WAR I

The treaty that ended World War I left many European nations dissatisfied. Italy was angered because it did not receive any new territory. Germany felt the treaty was too harsh. It severely weakened the German economy. It also forced Germany to give up some of its land. Germany was also forced to make payments in reparation for war damage.

All these factors led to severe **inflation** in Germany. Inflation is a general rise in prices. German money came to have no value at all.

Germany tried its first democratic government in the 1920s. This was called the Weimar Republic. It was weak and unstable.

> Underline the effects on Germany of the treaty ending World War I.

> What is inflation?
> _____
> _____

TOTALITARIAN LEADERS ARISE

In 1922 **Benito Mussolini** became Italy's leader. He believed in **fascism**. Fascism is a system of government that stresses the importance of the state. This comes at the expense of the individual. Mussolini favored the use of violence against Communists and

> What was most important to Fascists?
> _____
> _____

socialists. He established a **dictatorship**. This is
government by a leader or group that holds all the
power. The Italian government under Mussolini was
totalitarian, meaning no opposition was allowed.

In 1933 **Adolf Hitler** came to lead Germany. He
led the National Socialist, or Nazi, party. He stressed
nationalism, or devotion to the state. He blamed the
Jews for Germany's problems. He used violence
against his opponents. He believed Germans were
racially superior to everyone else.

In the mid-1920s, **Joseph Stalin** came to lead the
Soviet Union. He also used violence to keep power.

> Underline the ideas that
> Hitler believed in.

TOTALITARIAN GOVERNMENTS
AND MILITARY FORCE

The totalitarian governments used force to get what
they wanted. Japan invaded the Chinese province of
Manchuria. Italy invaded Ethiopia. Ethiopia's leader,
Haile Selassie, personally asked the League of
Nations for help. The League did nothing.

In Spain there was a bitter civil war. The
nationalists, helped by Germany and Italy, won. The
new Spanish leader was **Francisco Franco**.

HITLER TAKES ACTION

Hitler began to build up the German military. He put
troops in the Rhineland, an area near France. Next, he
sent troops into Austria to unite Austria and Germany.
Then, he began to threaten the Sudetenland, an area of
Czechoslovakia. British Prime Minister **Neville
Chamberlain** and French leader Edouard Daladier
agreed to let Hitler take over the area.

> Underline Hitler's actions in
> the time between World
> War I and World War II.

CHALLENGE ACTIVITY

Critical Thinking: Make Inferences Write two paragraphs discussing
how the worldwide Great Depression might have contributed to the rise of
totalitarian governments.

World War II Erupts

Section 2

 MAIN IDEA
Far from being satisfied by the actions of France and Great Britain, Germany turned to force and triggered the start of World War II.

Key Terms and People

appeasement policy of giving in to Hitler's demands

Winston Churchill opponent of Chamberlain who later became Britain's leader

blitzkrieg lightning war: use of massive air attacks and fast-moving armored units

the Allies the alliance against Hitler of Great Britain and France

Vichy France area of France governed by French officials who cooperated with Hitler

Charles de Gaulle French leader who fled to Britain in order to continue fighting

Luftwaffe German air force

Axis Powers Germany, Japan, and Italy

Hideki Tojo Japanese Minister of War who took control of Japan

Section Summary

WORLD WAR II STARTS

British Prime Minister Neville Chamberlain believed that **appeasement** would prevent war. Appeasement meant giving in to Hitler's demands. Some disagreed. These included **Winston Churchill**, who later became the leader of Great Britain.

In March 1939 Hitler took over the rest of Czechoslovakia. Then, he signed a pact with Italy and later a non-aggression pact with the Soviet Union. Just days later, on September 1, Hitler attacked Poland. He pretended that Poland had attacked first. The German method of attack was called **blitzkrieg**. Blitzkrieg meant lightning war—massive air and land attacks that moved quickly. The Poles could not withstand the force of the attack. Britain and France declared war on Germany.

> Circle the name of the policy that involved giving in to Hitler.

> What was blitzkrieg?
> _____
> _____

GERMAN FORCES TURN TO THE WEST

The British and French, known as **the Allies**, guessed that Hitler would attack France through the Maginot Line. This was a string of bunkers and fortresses on

World War II Erupts

the border between France and Germany. Instead, Hitler first conquered Norway and Denmark. Then, in May 1940, Hitler quickly conquered the Netherlands and Belgium. From Belgium's Ardennes Forest he attacked France. By early June the Germans had trapped hundreds of thousands of Allied soldiers on the beaches at Dunkirk. Allied ships and hundreds of civilian ships rescued the soldiers.

Hitler moved on to Paris and occupied much of France. The rest, known as **Vichy France**, was governed by French officials who cooperated with Hitler. **Charles de Gaulle** and other French leaders fled to Britain to carry on the fight.

Hitler then began massive bombing raids against London. This was the start of his plan to invade Britain. However, the British had radar. This was a new technology that used sound waves to detect approaching airplanes. It helped the British fight the **Luftwaffe**, the German air force. The Londoners suffered terribly, and about 23,000 civilians died. However, the British won what came to be called the Battle of Britain. Hitler abandoned his plans to conquer Great Britain.

> **How did Hitler fool the British and the French?**
> _____
> _____
> _____

> **What new technology helped the British win the Battle of Britain?**
> _____

TENSIONS IN EAST ASIA

In Japan, the nationalists came to power. In 1937 Japan began a brutal war against China. In 1940 Japan formed a military alliance with Germany and Italy. They were called the **Axis Powers**. The French Vichy government allowed the Japanese to take over French colonies in Asia. President Roosevelt now took steps to deny Japan oil. The two countries began to hold discussions. Minister of War **Hideki Tojo** took control of Japan and would not compromise.

> **What was the name of the man who became the leader of Japan?**
> _____

CHALLENGE ACTIVITY

Critical Thinking: Elaborate What do you think it was like for Londoners to face bombing raids by the Luftwaffe night after night? Write a story of a young Londoner facing such attacks.

MAIN IDEA
Isolationist feeling in the United States was strong in the 1930s, but Axis aggression eventually destroyed it and pushed the United States into war.

Key Terms and People

pacifist person who does not believe in any use of military force

Neutrality Act law preventing the United States from being drawn into a foreign war

neutral position where you do not help either side of a conflict

Quarantine Speech FDR's speech urging Americans to isolate the aggressive nations

cash-and-carry a change in the Neutrality Act to allow countries at war to buy U.S. goods if they paid cash and collected the goods in U.S. ports

Lend-Lease Act law that allowed weapons to be sent to Great Britain even if it could not pay for them

Wendell Willkie FDR's opponent in the 1940 election

Atlantic Charter agreement in which the United States and Great Britain stated their goals of opposing Hitler and his allies

Section Summary

AMERICAN ISOLATIONISM

In the 1930s many Americans believed in isolationism. This was a desire not to be involved in foreign wars. These people were not all **pacifists**, who were against all military force. Most were willing to fight to defend their country.

President Roosevelt was not an isolationist. However, nearly all of his attention had gone to dealing with the American economy. Meanwhile, Congress had passed the **Neutrality Act** in 1935. It outlawed the sale of arms to foreign countries at war. Later, such things as loans to warring countries were also outlawed.

What was isolationism?
_____
_____

Underline the law that strengthened isolationism.

BALANCING ISOLATIONISM AND INTERVENTION

As the world's dictators became more aggressive, Roosevelt did not want to remain **neutral**, that is, not helping one side or the other. He called for Americans to help isolate the aggressors in his **Quarantine Speech** of 1937.

How did Roosevelt ask Americans to stop being neutral?
_____
_____

World War II Erupts

PREPARING FOR WAR

After Germany invaded Poland, Congress passed
FDR's **cash-and-carry** program. It allowed countries
at war to buy American goods if they paid cash and
collected the goods in U.S. ports. Roosevelt hoped
this would help the Allies. By the end of 1940,
however, German victories led the government to pass
the **Lend-Lease Act**. This allowed weapons to be sent
to Great Britain even without pay.

In the 1940 election, Roosevelt was the first
candidate to apply for a third term as president. His
opponent, **Wendell Willkie**, had similar ideas on
foreign policy. The public voted for Roosevelt.

In mid-1941 Roosevelt and Churchill agreed to the
Atlantic Charter, saying both nations opposed Hitler
and his allies. Meanwhile, German submarines began
sinking American ships carrying supplies to Britain.

> How was the Lend-Lease
> Act different from the cash-
> and-carry program?
>
> _____
>
> _____
>
> _____

JAPAN ATTACKS PEARL HARBOR

Pearl Harbor, Hawaii, was home to the U.S. Pacific
Fleet. Military leaders thought it might be attacked.
However, the forces there were not ready for what
was to come. On December 7, 1941, the Japanese
attacked Pearl Harbor. For the United States it was a
disaster. The Pacific Fleet was all but destroyed.

The following day, Roosevelt asked Congress to
declare war on Japan. Three days after that, Germany
and Italy declared war on the United States. The U.S.
now entered World War II as one of the allies.

> Why was the attack on
> Pearl Harbor such a
> disaster for the United
> States?
>
> _____
>
> _____
>
> _____

CHALLENGE ACTIVITY

Critical Thinking: Evaluate How was the attack on Pearl Harbor similar
to the events of September 11, 2001? How was it different? How was the
nation's response different? Write three paragraphs to explain your
thoughts.

Interactive Reader and Study Guide

World War II Erupts

MAIN IDEA
The outbreak of World War II spurred the mobilization of American military and industrial might.

Key Terms and People

George C. Marshall Army Chief of Staff who led America's mobilization

Oveta Culp Hobby colonel who led the Women's Army Corps

Rosie the Riveter symbol for the working women of World War II

Manhattan Project top-secret program to build an atomic bomb

J. Robert Oppenheimer leader of the Manhattan Project

atomic bomb weapon that could create an enormous explosion using the energy released by the splitting of atoms

A. Philip Randolph union leader who successfully marched on Washington to protest discrimination against African Americans

Bracero Program program that gave some Mexican workers the chance to work temporarily in the United States

zoot suit riots fight between sailors and Mexican American youths in Los Angeles in 1943

Section Summary

MOBILIZING THE ARMED FORCES

It was a massive undertaking to mobilize American forces for war. This meant getting them ready. In 1940 and 1941, the United States had increased military spending. Army Chief of Staff **George C. Marshall** helped Roosevelt plan for war. He ensured that American soldiers were well equipped and trained. Millions of Americans volunteered for war. The draft was also expanded. New military bases were built around the country. Florida and California were changed forever by the new bases.

Women were not allowed in combat, but they took over many jobs that left men free to fight. Ten thousand women joined the Women Accepted for Volunteer Emergency Service (WAVES) and 150,000 served in the Women's Army Corps (WAC). In 1943, the WAC became part of the Army. It was led by

> What gave the United States a head start on mobilizing for war?
>
> _____
>
> _____

> Underline the organizations in which women helped the war effort.

Colonel **Oveta Culp Hobby**. The Women Airforce
Service Pilots (WASP) tested and delivered aircraft.

MOBILIZING INDUSTRY AND SCIENCE

Government spending during World War II ended the
Great Depression and created millions of new jobs.
Factories were changed to produce war supplies. To
deliver these goods, industrialist Henry Kaiser
organized shipyards with assembly-line techniques.
These ships were called liberty ships.

Eight million women entered the workforce. Many
worked in industrial jobs that had never been done by
women. **Rosie the Riveter** became their symbol.

The most important U.S. scientific program of
World War II was the **Manhattan Project**. Led by
J. Robert Oppenheimer, this project's goal was to
produce an **atomic bomb**. The bomb used the energy
released by splitting atoms.

> What finally ended the Great Depression?
>
> _____
>
> _____

> What was the most important scientific program of the war supposed to create?
>
> _____

FIGHTING FOR FREEDOM AT HOME

Hundreds of thousands of African Americans served
in the war. However, they were placed in segregated
units. Their bravery was often ignored. At home,
African Americans found new jobs, but still faced
discrimination. Union leader **A. Philip Randolph**
called for a protest march. Roosevelt later outlawed
discrimination in government or defense jobs.

Many Latinos also served in the war and also faced
discrimination. The **Bracero Program** allowed many
Mexicans to become temporary farm workers. Their
arrival sometimes caused resentment. In Los Angeles,
in 1943, this resulted in the week-long **zoot suit riots.**

> What problems did African Americans face when they were helping the war effort?
>
> _____
>
> _____

CHALLENGE ACTIVITY

Critical Thinking: Drawing Inferences Draw up a list of ten materials
you think would be needed for war. Develop a plan to obtain them.

Name _____ Class _____ Date _____

The United States in World War II

Chapter Summary

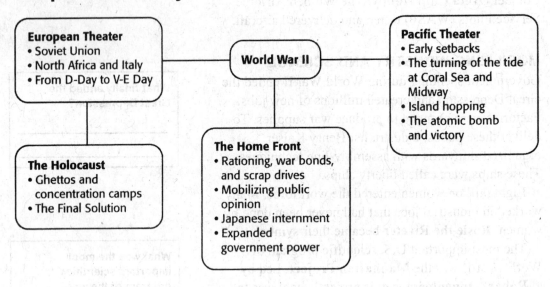

COMPREHENSION AND CRITICAL THINKING

Use information from the graphic organizer to answer the following questions.

1. **Identify** Describe the course of the war in the Pacific.

_____

_____

2. **Make Generalizations** How was the United States able to support huge military forces in both the European and Pacific theaters?

_____

_____

3. **Evaluate** In what ways do you think World War II influenced the history of the United States and why?

_____

_____

_____

Interactive Reader and Study Guide

The United States in World War II

Section 1

> **MAIN IDEA**
> After entering World War II, the United States focused first on the war in Europe.

Key Terms and People

wolf pack a group of German submarines that hunted Allied and U.S. ships

Erwin Rommel German general who commanded Nazi forces in North Africa

Dwight D. Eisenhower U.S. general who led Operation Torch and Operation Overlord

Operation Torch U.S. invasion of North Africa

Tuskegee Airmen first unit of African Americans to receive U.S. military pilot training

Operation Overlord the plan to invade the mainland of Europe

Omar Bradley U.S. general who led American troops during Operation Overlord

D-Day code name for the day Operation Overlord would begin, June 6, 1944

Battle of the Bulge battle in which Germans pushed back Americans but finally lost

George S. Patton American general in the invasion of Europe

Section Summary

THE BATTLE OF THE ATLANTIC

Using its submarines, or U-boats, Germany sank ships and supplies headed for Great Britain. The U-boats operated at night in groups called **wolf packs**. By 1941 Germany controlled the Atlantic Ocean.

After joining the war, the United States built ships and aircraft to protect convoys. Convoys are groups of ships that sail together for protection. To find the U-boats, Allied aircraft used radar. In 1941 the Allies learned how to decode German military messages. In time the Allies took control of the Atlantic Ocean.

> What four factors helped the Allies win the Battle of the Atlantic?
>
> _____
> _____
> _____
> _____

THE WAR IN THE SOVIET UNION

In summer 1941 the Nazis invaded the USSR. The Soviets were forced to retreat. Finally the Russian winter stopped the Germans. They encircled the city of Leningrad for two years but could not conquer it.

In the spring, the Germans tried to push farther. Their target was the city of Stalingrad. In some of the worst fighting of the war, the Soviets began to push the Nazis back toward Germany.

> What finally slowed the first German advance across the Soviet Union?
>
> _____

The United States in World War II

AMERICAN FORCES IN NORTH AFRICA AND ITALY

In North Africa, the British fought the Italians to protect Mediterranean shipping, especially oil. Nazi troops came to help the Italians, and both fought under General **Erwin Rommel**. U.S. soldiers, led by American Lieutenant General **Dwight D. Eisenhower**, joined the fight in **Operation Torch**, the invasion of Morocco and Algeria. It took two years to beat Rommel's forces.

In July 1943 the Allies invaded Italy. The Italian people gave up, but German forces rushed in to stop the Allies. The fighting was hard. Taking part in the fighting were the heroic **Tuskegee Airmen**, the first unit of African American pilots in the U.S. military. In June 1944 the Allies entered Rome.

> Circle the name of the person who led the U.S. soldiers in North Africa.

D-DAY: THE INVASION OF FRANCE

By early 1943 the Allies were planning **Operation Overlord**, the main invasion of Europe, to be led by General Eisenhower. For a year they collected huge amounts of troops, ships, and other materials. Eisenhower chose General **Omar Bradley** to lead the American troops.

The attack began on June 6, 1944, called **D-Day**, on the beaches of Normandy, in northern France. By late July the Allies passed the German lines in Normandy. By the end of August they had freed Paris.

Throughout the fall, the Allies moved towards Germany. That December, the Germans battled back. They pushed a bulge into the American lines, and the **Battle of the Bulge** lasted over a month. It was finally won with the help of troops brought by American Lieutenant General **George S. Patton**. By the end of January, the battle was won and the Allies continued their push into Germany.

> Why did Operation Overlord require complex planning?
> _____
> _____
> _____
> _____

CHALLENGE ACTIVITY

Critical Thinking: Design If you were part of the team planning the invasion of Normandy, what weapons, supplies, and materials would your soldiers need to make the landings and survive the first few weeks?

The United States in World War II

Section 2

MAIN IDEA
During the Holocaust, Germany's Nazi government systematically murdered some 6 million Jews and 5 million others in Europe.

Key Terms and People

anti-Semitism hatred of and prejudice against Jewish people

Holocaust the organized murder of Jews and others by the Nazis

Hermann Göering one of the top Nazi leaders

Kristallnacht a night of terrorism by Germans against Jews in November 1938

concentration camps prison camps where Jews and others were sent

ghetto a walled- or fenced-in neighborhood where Jews were forced to live

Final Solution the Nazis' plan for the widespread murder of Jews

genocide the killing of an entire people

War Refugee Board U.S. governmental organization that saved 200,000 Jews

Section Summary

NAZI ANTI-SEMITISM

Hitler claimed that Germans were superior to all other people. Of the many groups he believed were inferior, he especially hated the Jews. Hatred of Jews is called **anti-Semitism**. Hitler convinced most Germans that the Jews caused their country's problems. These hate-filled beliefs eventually led to the **Holocaust**, in which the Nazis murdered about six million Jews and five million others.

Hitler and other Nazi leaders, including **Hermann Göering**, passed many laws taking away Jews' citizenship and civil rights. They told Germans to attack Jews. One especially brutal night was called **Kristallnacht**. Later, thousands of Jews were arrested and sent to prison camps, called **concentration camps**. It was hard for Jews to leave Germany because many countries would not accept them.

> **What did Hitler believe about the Jews?**
> _____
> _____

> **Underline the words that describe the protections the Germans first took away from the Jews.**

TOWARD THE FINAL SOLUTION

As the Nazis conquered territory in Europe, more Jews came under their control. Some Jews were killed immediately, some were sent to concentration camps

Interactive Reader and Study Guide

to die of overwork and starvation, and others were forced into **ghettos**, neighborhoods they could not leave. The worst ghetto was in Warsaw, Poland. In 1943 Jews in this ghetto rebelled against the Germans. The Germans put the rebellion down and sent the survivors to concentration camps.

From the beginning of the war, there were many mass killings of Jews and others. This set the stage for the **Final Solution**, which was the Nazis' plan for the widespread murder of Jews. The killing of an entire people is called **genocide**. The Nazis built new camps especially to kill people. In the camps, people were gassed to death and their bodies burned. About three million Jews died in these camps and another three million died in other ways.

> **What was the Final Solution?**
> _____
> _____
> _____

THE AMERICAN RESPONSE

In the 1930s and through the years of the war, the U.S. government was against letting large numbers of foreigners into the country. Although by 1942 Americans were learning what was happening in the concentration camps, U.S. leaders were more concerned with fighting the war than saving Jews. Finally, in January 1944 President Roosevelt created the **War Refugee Board**. Through this board, the United States was able to rescue about 200,000 Jews.

As the Allies began advancing through Europe, they found the camps. Soldiers were horrified. They set the prisoners free and tried to help them.

At the end of the war, 22 of the Nazis who were responsible for the Final Solution, including Göering, were put on trial in Nuremberg, Germany. Some were sentenced to death and others were given long prison terms.

> **What was the purpose of the War Refugee Board?**
> _____
> _____

CHALLENGE ACTIVITY

Critical Thinking: Analyze and Predict Write a paragraph explaining why you think the German people went along with the Nazis in their anti-Jewish programs. Then write a second paragraph explaining why or why not something like the Holocaust could ever happen in the United States.

MAIN IDEA
After early defeats in the Pacific, the United States gained the upper hand and began to fight its way island by island to Japan.

Key Terms and People

Douglas MacArthur American general who led U.S. and Filipino forces

Bataan Death March five-day march the Japanese forced U.S. and Filipino prisoners to make, and on which many died

James Doolittle American lieutenant colonel who led U.S. bomber attack on Japan

Chester Nimitz American admiral who stopped Japanese advance at Battle of Coral Sea

Battle of Midway sea battle in which U.S. forces prevented Japanese invasion of Midway Island

code talkers Native Americans of the Navajo nation who sent messages in a coded version of their language for U.S. Marines in the Pacific

kamikaze Japanese pilots who crashed their bomb-filled planes into American ships

Battle of Iwo Jima battle in which U.S. forces conquered a Japanese island 700 miles from Tokyo to use for bombing raids

Battle of Okinawa battle in which U.S. forces conquered a Japanese island 350 miles from Japan to use for the final invasion of Japan

Section Summary

A SLOW START FOR THE ALLIES

After Pearl Harbor, the Japanese forced the Americans from Wake Island and Guam. Then they captured Hong Kong, Singapore, and Borneo from the British and the East Indies from the Dutch. These victories ensured an oil supply for the Japanese.

The Japanese soldiers were skilled and well-trained, with excellent equipment. The American general in the Philippines, **Douglas MacArthur**, had only a small number of U.S. soldiers and some poorly trained and equipped Filipino forces. MacArthur's forces, low on food and supplies, were forced to retreat to the Bataan Peninsula. Eventually MacArthur was ordered to leave, and the Americans and the Filipinos had to surrender. The Japanese then forced the sick and starving soldiers on a terrible march, the **Bataan Death March**, on which many soldiers died.

> **Why were their early victories important to the Japanese?**
> _____
> _____
> _____

> **What disadvantages did MacArthur face?**
> _____
> _____
> _____
> _____

The United States in World War II

FORTUNES SHIFT IN THE PACIFIC

Soon after the surrender of the Philippines, U.S. bombers, led by Lieutenant Colonel **James Doolittle**, attacked Japan. This did not do major damage but raised American spirits and worried Japanese leaders.

In May 1942 two U.S. aircraft carriers, led by Admiral **Chester Nimitz**, finally stopped the Japanese advance at the Battle of Coral Sea. Then U.S. forces dealt a huge blow to the Japanese: In the **Battle of Midway**, the Japanese had more ships and aircraft carriers, but the Americans had broken the Japanese codes and knew their attack plans. The U.S. victory at this battle greatly reduced Japanese naval power.

> How did the United States achieve victory in the Battle of Midway?
>
> _____
> _____
> _____
> _____

THE ALLIES MAKE PROGRESS

The Americans pressed on. To protect Australia, an ally, U.S. forces fought on land, sea, and air for six months to win the island of Guadalcanal. After that, this combination of forces captured island after island. They were helped by the **code talkers**, Navajo Native Americans in the Marines who used their language to invent a code the Japanese could not break.

In 1944 General MacArthur led U.S. forces back to the Philippines. The largest naval battle ever fought, the Battle of Leyte Gulf, was part of the American victory there. During the battle, the Japanese used **kamikaze** attacks, in which their pilots crashed their bomb-filled planes into ships.

By 1944 U.S. bombers were making regular raids on Japan. American forces gained a better base by winning the **Battle of Iwo Jima**. Iwo Jima is 700 miles from Tokyo. The Japanese fought to the death from caves and tunnels. In the **Battle of Okinawa**, 350 miles from Japan, U.S. forces took a base for their final invasion of Japan. It was the deadliest fighting in the Pacific. By June 1945 they had won, but with 12,000 American and 110,000 Japanese deaths.

> Circle the name of the largest naval battle ever fought.

CHALLENGE ACTIVITY

Critical Thinking: Elaborate On a map, draw lines connecting Japan with its early conquests in the Pacific. Using another color, draw lines connecting Hawaii with the American victories.

Interactive Reader and Study Guide

The United States in World War II

MAIN IDEA
While millions of military men and women were serving in World War II, Americans on the home front were making contributions of their own.

Key Terms and People

rationing limiting the amount of a certain product that each person can get

Ernie Pyle American reporter who wrote from an ordinary soldier's point of view

Bill Maudlin American cartoonist who showed ordinary soldiers in the war

internment forcing people into and keeping them in places they are not allowed to leave

Section Summary

SACRIFICE AND STRUGGLE AT HOME

In order to feed the military and the country, Americans planted backyard "victory gardens." The government was **rationing**, or only allowing each person a certain amount of coffee, butter, sugar, meat, and gasoline. Adults and children held scrap drives to collect waste metal, glass, and rubber so it could be reused. Americans also bought billions of dollars worth of war bonds. This helped the government pay for the huge numbers of weapons needed.

One of the hardest sacrifices was having loved ones far away. Millions of Americans followed the war in the newspapers. Reporter **Ernie Pyle** wrote from an ordinary soldier's point of view. Cartoonist **Bill Maudlin** showed ordinary soldiers, too.

> What were some of the things that were rationed?
>
> _____
> _____
> _____
> _____

WINNING AMERICAN SUPPORT FOR THE WAR

To raise Americans' support for the war, President Roosevelt made speeches. He began the Office of War Information, which spread propaganda, information and ideas that promote a cause. Their posters and films urged people to help the war effort. Hollywood also made patriotic films. Many Hollywood stars helped sell bonds and entertained the troops.

Some citizens felt that the push to influence attitudes went too far. In 1943 some members of a Jehovah's Witness religious group challenged a law saying students had to salute the flag. The Supreme Court, in *West Virginia Board of Education* v.

> What were some of the forms that the government used to spread propaganda?
>
> _____
> _____

Interactive Reader and Study Guide

Barnette, said that no one should be required to hold a particular belief in politics, nationalism, religion, or other issues of opinion.

JAPANESE INTERNMENT

After Pearl Harbor was attacked, some U.S. officials thought that Japanese Americans might help the enemy. They hunted for signs of spying but found nothing. Even so, President Roosevelt signed Executive Order 9066. This allowed the U.S. military to put 110,000 Japanese Americans from California, Washington, Oregon, and Arizona into **internment** camps. Two-thirds of these people were U.S. citizens. They had to live in these camps, away from their jobs and homes. Many lost both, and life in the camps was harsh. No other group was treated this way.

Many Japanese wanted to prove their loyalty. Some young men joined the 442nd Regimental Combat Team, a unit containing only Japanese Americans. While it served, it received more medals and awards than any unit its size in U.S. military history.

Many years later, the federal government formally recognized that it had been wrong. It sent apologies and payments to the survivors of the internment.

> **Why were Japanese Americans interned?**
> _____
> _____
> _____
> _____

A NEW ROLE FOR THE FEDERAL GOVERNMENT

The Great Depression, the New Deal, and World War II caused the role of the federal government to grow. Through the Office of Price Administration and the War Production Board, the government helped determine what goods people could have and what prices they would pay. The government also had to cover the cost of an expensive war. To pay for it, the government increased income tax rates. Before the war, only the wealthy paid income taxes. Now, millions of other Americans began to pay income taxes, too.

> **What happened to income tax rates during the war?**
> _____
> _____

CHALLENGE ACTIVITY

Critical Thinking: Compare and Contrast Compare and contrast life in America during World War II with life in America today.

The United States in World War II

MAIN IDEA
While the Allies completed the defeat of the Axis powers on the battlefield, Allied leaders were making plans for the postwar world.

Key Terms and People

Yalta Conference conference at which Roosevelt, Churchill, and Stalin made plans to end the war and deal with the peace that followed

occupy to take control of a place by placing troops in it

V-E Day Victory in Europe Day, May 8, 1945

Harry S Truman vice president under Franklin Roosevelt, became president when Roosevelt died

Enola Gay name of the plane that dropped an atomic bomb on the city of Hiroshima

V-J Day Victory in Japan Day, August 15, 1945

United Nations an organization meant to encourage cooperation among nations and prevent future wars

Potsdam Conference conference where Truman, Churchill, and Stalin discussed plans for the postwar world

Section Summary

WINNING THE WAR IN EUROPE

Germany could no longer defend itself. The Allies invaded Germany from the west, and the Soviets invaded from the east. In January 1945 Roosevelt, Churchill, and Stalin met at the **Yalta Conference** to discuss the war and the peace that was to follow. The leaders agreed to divide Germany into four sectors, one for each of the Allies. The Soviet sector was the entire eastern half of Germany. Berlin, Germany's capital, was also to be divided into four sectors. At Yalta, Stalin agreed to hold free elections in other countries that the Soviets would **occupy**.

Hitler ordered his forces to make a stand at the Rhine River, a key barrier to the center of Germany. He ordered the troops to blow up all the bridges across it. The Allies managed to capture one bridge and crossed the river. Thousands of Germans troops were trapped and captured.

Allied forces moved quickly across Germany, but General Eisenhower decided not to join the battle for

> **What happened to Germany at the Yalta Conference?**
> _____
> _____
> _____

> **Where did German soldiers make their last major stand?**
> _____
> _____

Berlin. He knew that Soviet troops were already much closer to the city. He also wanted to save American soldiers to fight in the Pacific.

On April 30, Hitler committed suicide, and Germany quickly surrendered. **V-E Day**, Victory in Europe Day, was declared on May 8.

WINNING THE WAR IN THE PACIFIC

The war in the Pacific took many lives. Despite the high cost, the Allies were determined to invade Japan. Even with the deadliest air raid of the entire war, Japan continued to fight. Some Japanese leaders tried to make peace. Others vowed to fight to the end.

Scientists working in the United States created the atomic bomb. President **Harry S Truman** decided to use it against Japan. In August 1945 the first bomb was dropped on the city of Hiroshima by a plane named the *Enola Gay*. Another was dropped on Nagasaki. A week later, the Japanese surrendered. **V-J Day**, Victory in Japan Day, had arrived.

> **How did the atomic bombs affect the war's outcome?**
> _____
> _____
> _____
> _____

THE CHALLENGES OF VICTORY

To try to prevent new wars, representatives of 50 countries, including the United States, met to establish the **United Nations**. Part of the UN's purpose was to encourage cooperation among nations. The leaders of the Allied nations also met at the **Potsdam Conference**. Americans were concerned that the Soviet influence would spread in the postwar world. This concern proved to be well-founded, and the conference did not help.

The United States also needed to rebuild Europe and Japan. General MacArthur directed the effort in Japan. In both Europe and Japan, war criminals were punished.

> **What were two reasons for creating the United Nations?**
> _____
> _____
> _____
> _____

CHALLENGE ACTIVITY

Critical Thinking: Predict Create two lists showing ways in which a country might be affected by a Soviet versus an American occupation. You might want to review the Soviet Union's political and economic systems.

The Cold War Begins

Chapter Summary

The Iron Curtain Falls
- Soviets fail to hold elections, install friendly governments
- Truman issues Truman Doctrine
- Marshall Plan seeks to aid Europe, stop communism
- Berlin crisis leads to Berlin Airlift
- Second Red Scare occurs in United States

Postwar Challenges

Peacetime Transition
- G.I. Bill aids adjustment of soldiers and sailors
- Truman wins re-election
- United Nations and other organizations seek a safer world

War in Korea
- Korea is divided after World War II
- Communist North Korea invades South Korea
- Back-and-forth fighting ends in stalemate
- New president Dwight D. Eisenhower ends the fighting

COMPREHENSION AND CRITICAL THINKING

Use information from the graphic organizer to answer the following questions.

1. **Recall** How did the Korean War begin?

_____

2. **Make Inferences** What did the Soviets do to create the Iron Curtain?

_____

_____

3. **Rank** How was the transition from war to peace in the United States and the rest of the world better after World War II than after World War I?

_____

_____

The Cold War Begins

MAIN IDEA
At the end of World War II, tensions between the Soviet Union and the United States deepened, leading to an era known as the Cold War.

Key Terms and People

Cold War era of high tension and bitter rivalry between the United States and the Soviet Union

Iron Curtain phrase coined by Winston Churchill to describe the division in Europe caused by communism

containment policy that called for resisting the spread of Soviet power and influence

George F. Kennan American expert on the Soviet Union who worked for containment

Truman Doctrine policy to support free nations economically to prevent the spread of communism

Marshall Plan massive American economic aid program to help Western Europe rebuild

Berlin Airlift British and American airplanes supply deliveries by air to West Berlin in response to Soviet blockade

NATO North Atlantic Treaty Organization; military alliance of 12 nations for common defense against the Soviets

Section Summary

THE ROOTS OF THE COLD WAR

The **Cold War** was an era of high tension and bitter competition between the United States and the Soviet Union. Americans were against communism. However, they fought with the Soviet Union to defeat Hitler. During World War II, Stalin pushed for an early invasion of Europe. He became angry when this was delayed. The American development of the atomic bomb also fueled Soviet distrust. The Soviets began to develop an atomic bomb of their own.

> What made Stalin angry at the other Allies during World War II?
> _____
> _____

THE IRON CURTAIN DESCENDS

At the Yalta and Potsdam conferences, Stalin had promised to hold free elections in Eastern European nations. He did not do so. Stalin wanted to have a buffer zone between Western Europe and the Soviet Union. In the nations of Eastern Europe, the Soviets jailed or killed the opponents of communism. They rigged elections. Thus they were able to put

> What promise about Eastern European nations did Stalin break?
> _____

The Cold War Begins

Communist governments in place. Churchill likened the division of Europe to an **Iron Curtain**.

THE UNITED STATES RESPONDS

The American government adopted the policy of **containment**. This policy was created by American statesman **George F. Kennan**. He believed that the United States should resist Soviet attempts to expand their influence. The **Truman Doctrine** called for providing economic aid to help free nations resist communism. The United States also began the **Marshall Plan**. This was a massive program of aid to Western Europe. It enabled the Europeans to rebuild. As a result, Western Europe was able to feed its people. It could also buy products from the United States. The Marshall Plan helped the United States build strong political support in Western Europe.

> Underline the names of the two policies the United States used in response to the increase in Soviet power.

> How did the Marshall Plan help both Europe and the United States?
> _____
> _____
> _____
> _____

THE CRISIS IN BERLIN

Germany was divided into four zones of occupation. The British, French, and Americans occupied West Germany. The Soviets occupied East Germany. The city of Berlin, in East Germany, was also divided into four zones. In 1948 the Soviets declared that they would block all rail, road, or river traffic into West Berlin. The only way left to supply the city was by air. Supplies were flown in by the British and Americans. The **Berlin Airlift** continued for almost a year.

The conflict with the Soviet Union worried many Western Europeans. Five nations joined in a system of common defense. Then the United States and six other nations joined the original five. They formed the North Atlantic Treaty Organization (**NATO**). The nations of NATO pledged to defend each other against a Soviet attack.

> Why was NATO formed?
> _____
> _____
> _____

CHALLENGE ACTIVITY

Critical Thinking: Design What if your city or town was blockaded as Berlin was? Make a list of all the things you can think of that would have to be brought in by air.

The Cold War Begins

MAIN IDEA
Following the end of World War II, U.S. military forces—and the rest of the country—faced the challenge of returning to life during peacetime.

Key Terms and People

GI Bill law aimed at helping veterans make a smooth entry into civilian life

baby boom dramatic rise in the birthrate after World War II

Fair Deal Truman's plan for the United States in the tradition of the New Deal

Universal Declaration of Human Rights UN document specifying basic human rights all people should have

World Bank postwar organization aimed at helping poor countries build their economies

International Monetary Fund postwar organization formed to encourage economic policies that promoted international trade

General Agreement on Tariffs and Trade international organization to promote trade

Section Summary

LIFE IN AMERICA AFTER WORLD WAR II

Some people worried that the American economy would be in trouble when the war ended. Suddenly there was no need for factories to produce war materials. Also, most men and women in the armed forces would be returning to civilian life. In 1944 President Roosevelt signed the **GI Bill**. This bill aimed at helping veterans make a smooth change to being civilians. The bill provided money for veterans who wanted education. It gave them loans to buy homes, farms, or businesses. It also helped veterans find work and provided unemployment benefits for those who could not. During the war, the government had controlled what factories could produce. When the war ended, people had money to spend on consumer items. Also, there was a large increase in the birthrate after World War II. This was called the **baby boom**. Demand for consumer goods rose sharply. The economy shifted from providing tools of war to products of peace.

After the war, the power of labor unions was reduced by law. Truman opposed this unsuccessfully. He had more success on behalf of minorities. Truman

> **Underline the reasons why the American economy might have had trouble after World War II.**

> **What did the GI Bill do for veterans?**
> _____
> _____
> _____
> _____
> _____

ended segregation in the armed forces by executive order. Both African Americans and Hispanics began to make gains after the war.

POLITICS IN POSTWAR AMERICA

Harry Truman faced huge challenges when he became president. He had to lead the Allies through the end of the war. He had to guide the nation back to peace. He faced much criticism. Most people thought he would lose the election of 1948. He surprised many by winning. He then put forward his **Fair Deal**. It included a number of programs in the tradition of the New Deal. Congress defeated most of his proposals. Meanwhile, problems arose in Korea.

> How did Congress treat the Fair Deal?
> _____
> _____
> _____

TRYING TO BUILD A BETTER WORLD

After two world wars, many people wanted to prevent another war. Representatives of 50 nations formed the United Nations, or UN. Member nations agreed to live in peace and to unite to provide security. The UN Commission on Human Rights published the **Universal Declaration of Human Rights**. This document set high goals for all member nations. It said that all human beings were born free and equal. It called for an end to slavery and torture. It also demanded a variety of civil rights including the right to assembly and the right to access to courts.

> Underline what the Universal Declaration of Human Rights said.

Poor financial relationships between countries had helped cause the Great Depression. Representatives of the world powers formed the **World Bank** and the **International Monetary Fund** (IMF). The World Bank aimed to help poor countries build their economies. It provided grants and loans. The IMF encouraged economic policies that promoted international trade. The **General Agreement on Tariffs and Trade** (GATT) also promoted trade. It aimed to reduce tariffs and other trade barriers.

> Circle the names of the three organizations that were formed to help countries have better financial relationships.

CHALLENGE ACTIVITY

Critical Thinking: Analyze Write two paragraphs explaining what happened to the American economy following the war. What factors affected the postwar economy?

Interactive Reader and Study Guide

The Cold War Begins

MAIN IDEA
The start of the Cold War and events at home helped trigger a second Red Scare in the late 1940s and early 1950s.

Key Terms and People

Chiang Kai-shek leader of the Chinese Nationalists

Mao Zedong leader of the Chinese Communists

House Un-American Activities Committee Congressional committee to investigate radical groups in the United States; also known as HUAC

Hollywood Ten group of writers and directors who were jailed for refusing to answer questions before HUAC

Alger Hiss government official accused of being part of a plot to place Communists inside the U.S. government

Joseph McCarthy senator from Wisconsin who became known as the nation's top Communist fighter

McCarthyism Joseph McCarthy's tactics of spreading fear and making baseless charges

Section Summary

GROWING FEAR OF COMMUNISM

After the war Americans were worried about the spread of communism in Europe. Then the Soviet Union developed an atomic bomb. Soon afterwards, the United States learned that Communists had gained nearly full control of China. The Nationalist government led by **Chiang Kai-shek** retreated from mainland China to the island of Taiwan. Chiang had been loyal to the Allies during World War II. He and the United States claimed that the Nationalist government was the one true government of all China. **Mao Zedong** led the Chinese Communists. China became the People's Republic of China.

> Underline the name of the country that developed the atomic bomb after World War II.

> Circle the name of the island to which the Nationalist Chinese retreated.

FIGHTING THE SPREAD OF COMMUNISM AT HOME

Anti-Communist feeling was strong in the United States. The House of Representatives had formed a **House Un-American Activities Committee** (HUAC) in the 1930s. This committee was to investigate all

Interactive Reader and Study Guide

The Cold War Begins

radical groups. However, it soon came to focus on the threat of communism.

In 1947 the committee wanted to investigate possible Communist influence in the entertainment industry. Ten writers and directors were called before the committee. They refused to answer questions about their beliefs or the beliefs of others. Known as the **Hollywood Ten**, these people were jailed for their refusal. After that, many people provided names of friends and colleagues to the committee. Those who refused were blacklisted. This meant their names were on a list and Hollywood employers would not hire anyone on the list. In 1948 President Truman used the Smith Act to convict some leaders of the Communist Party in the United States. They were convicted for their thoughts, not their actions. Then Congress passed the McCarran Act over Truman's veto. This act made it illegal for Communists and other radicals to enter the United States.

Spy cases helped fuel the fear of communism. **Alger Hiss** was a government official accused of plotting to put Communists in the government. He served several years in prison. Ethel and Julius Rosenberg were convicted of spying and executed.

> Why were the members of the Hollywood Ten jailed?
> _____
> _____
> _____

> Underline the two spy cases that frightened Americans.

SENATOR JOSEPH MCCARTHY

Joseph McCarthy was a senator from Wisconsin. He came to national attention by pretending to have lists of Communists in the government. Americans believed him even though he never showed the lists. McCarthy attacked many people as Communists without evidence. He used fake photographs to defeat one of Truman's strongest supporters. His tactic of spreading fear and making baseless charges was called **McCarthyism**. McCarthyism spread to government, universities, labor unions, and private businesses. People could lose their jobs simply for having radical ideas. Thousands of people were fired for political reasons.

> How did McCarthy come to national attention?
> _____
> _____
> _____
> _____

CHALLENGE ACTIVITY

Critical Thinking: Contrast Write two paragraphs contrasting McCarthyism and the Communist hunts of the 1940s and 1950s with our treatment of suspected terrorists today. Note the similarities and differences between today and the 1940s and 1950s.

The Cold War Begins

Section 4

MAIN IDEA
Cold War tensions finally erupted in a shooting war in 1950. The United States confronted a difficult challenge defending freedom halfway around the world.

Key Terms and People

38th parallel dividing line between North Korea and South Korea

Kim Il Sung first leader of North Korea

Syngman Rhee first president of South Korea

police action term used to refer to the UN effort in Korea, where war was never officially declared

Inchon port city in Korea; site of an important battle

Panmunjom Korean town that was the site of peace negotiations

Section Summary

KOREA BEFORE THE WAR

Japan controlled the Korean peninsula until World War II ended. The Allies agreed that Korea should be free after the war. Temporarily, however, they divided the peninsula in half. The division was made at the **38th parallel**. This was the line at 38° north latitude. The Soviet Union would control Korea north of that line. The Americans would have control south of it. Communist **Kim Il Sung** was the first leader of North Korea. South Korea's president, **Syngman Rhee**, had dictatorial control. Both leaders wanted to reunite Korea, but they had different ideas about how to do it. Efforts toward reunification led to war.

> **Who controlled Korea during World War II?**
> _____

THE START OF THE KOREAN WAR

On June 25, 1950, North Korean troops invaded South Korea. They were armed with Soviet weapons and tanks. The attack surprised most leaders in the United States. Truman believed that South Korea had to be defended. The United States had to take a stand against Communist aggression. Not to do so might lead to another world war. The North Koreans quickly pushed to the capital city of Seoul and took it. Truman asked the UN to approve the use of force. The UN Security Council agreed because the Soviet

> **What country armed the North Korean troops?**
> _____

The Cold War Begins

representative was absent. Instead of officially declaring war, the fighting was called a **police action**. The United States and 15 other nations sent ground troops to fight. The commander of the United Nations force was American General Douglas MacArthur.

> Circle the name of the American leader of the UN forces.

KEY BATTLES OF THE KOREAN WAR

The North Koreans pushed the UN forces to the southern tip of South Korea. UN forces were told to hold the port city of Pusan at all costs. They held the city and the Communist attack became stalled. This gave time for more UN troops and supplies to arrive. MacArthur's plan was to land behind North Korean lines at the port city of **Inchon**. His daring plan was successful. The UN forces quickly moved out from Inchon to recapture Seoul. The UN forces drove the North Koreans out of South Korea.

> Why was MacArthur's plan daring?
> _____
> _____
> _____

MacArthur wanted to take North Korea. However, a large Chinese army came into North Korea. The UN forces had to retreat. MacArthur thought that the UN had to attack China and possibly use atomic bombs. But he was wrong. A force led by Lieutenant General Matthew Ridgway stopped the Chinese and pushed them back to the 38th parallel. MacArthur still demanded an invasion of China. Truman had to fire MacArthur because he would not obey presidential orders.

FIGHTING ENDS IN KOREA

Peace talks began in 1951 in the Korean town of **Panmunjom**. They dragged on for two years, until after Eisenhower became president in 1953. Over 36,000 American soldiers had died. Almost 60,000 UN troops from other countries had died. Communist forces had 2 million casualties. As many as 3 million Korean civilians were killed or injured.

> Circle the numbers of all the casualties of the war. In total, how many people were hurt or killed?
> _____

CHALLENGE ACTIVITY

Critical Thinking: Evaluate Was Truman right to fire MacArthur? Write two paragraphs explaining your position.

Postwar America

Chapter Summary

```
┌─────────────────────────────┐            ┌─────────────────────────────┐
│ Eisenhower's Presidency     │            │ Arms Race Anxiety           │
│ • Elected in 1952,          │            │ • Soviets and Americans     │
│   re-elected in 1956        │            │   engage in arms race       │
│ • Presidency focuses heavily│            │ • Foreign policies built    │
│   on Cold War issues        │            │   around nuclear weapons use│
│ • "Hot spots" include       │            │ • New technologies emerge,  │
│   Eastern Europe, Southeast │            │   including massive hydrogen│
│   Asia, and the Middle East │            │   bombs                     │
└─────────────────────────────┘            │ • Public prepares for worst │
                    ┌─────────────────┐    └─────────────────────────────┘
                    │ The United States│
                    │ in the 1950s     │
                    └─────────────────┘
              ┌──────────────────────────────┐
              │ Television and Cultural Change│
              │ • Television arrives in full  │
              │   force                       │
              │ • Scientific advances, such as│
              │   vaccines, change life       │
              │ • Population grows and moves   │
              └──────────────────────────────┘
```

COMPREHENSION AND CRITICAL THINKING

Use information from the graphic organizer to answer the following questions.

1. **Recall** What were the "hot spots" during Eisenhower's presidency?

_____

2. **Evaluate** How did the arms race affect America?

_____

_____

3. **Rank** Which of the developments above had the greatest influence on American culture? Why?

_____

_____

Interactive Reader and Study Guide

Postwar America

MAIN IDEA
The presidency of Dwight D. Eisenhower was shaped in large part by the Cold War and related conflicts.

Key Terms and People

Richard M. Nixon vice president under President Eisenhower

John Foster Dulles secretary of state under Eisenhower

brinkmanship policy of getting to the brink, or verge, of war without going to war

massive retaliation use of great force to settle serious conflicts

CIA Central Intelligence Agency; formed to spy on foreign governments

Nikita Khrushchev leader of the Soviet Union after Stalin's death

Warsaw Pact military alliance of the Soviet-dominated countries of Eastern Europe

summit meeting of heads of government

SEATO Southeast Asia Treaty Organization; alliance against Communist aggression

Eisenhower Doctrine declaration of the right of the United States to help any nation in the Middle East trying to resist Communist aggression

Section Summary

THE ELECTION OF 1952

In 1952 Dwight D. Eisenhower was the Republican candidate for president. In his campaign he criticized Truman's handling of the Korean War. The war was dragging on. Thousands of Americans were being killed. Eisenhower's vice presidential running mate was **Richard M. Nixon**. During the campaign Nixon was accused of being dishonest. He went on television to defend himself. Eisenhower went on to a solid win.

> **What war was going on when Eisenhower became president?**
> _____

THE COLD WAR CONTINUES

Eisenhower visited Korea and got the stalled peace talks going again. Peace finally came in 1953. Secretary of State **John Foster Dulles** helped Eisenhower with his foreign policy. Dulles believed in a policy of **brinkmanship**. This means getting close to war without going to war. For it to work, the United States had to have enough nuclear weapons for **massive retaliation**. This meant being ready to use great force to settle serious conflicts. The Central

> **What policy would take the United States close to war?**
> _____

  Interactive Reader and Study Guide

Postwar America

Intelligence Agency, or **CIA**, was formed to spy on foreign governments. It also took part in secret actions against foreign governments.

In 1953, Stalin died. The new Soviet leader was **Nikita Khrushchev**. Under him, the Soviet Union created the **Warsaw Pact**. This was a military alliance of Eastern European countries. An anti-Communist revolt in Poland was put down by force. When Hungary rebelled, the Soviets invaded with tanks. Despite these problems, the United States and the Soviet Union had their first **summit** meeting in 1955. A summit is a meeting of the heads of government.

> Circle the name of the man who came to power in the Soviet Union after Stalin died.

> In which two Eastern European nations did rebellions take place?
>
> _____

COLD WAR "HOT SPOTS"

In 1954 France withdrew from its former colony Vietnam. During peace talks, Vietnam was divided in two. The north came under Communist control. There was supposed to be an election to allow the Vietnamese people to decide what kind of government to have. Eisenhower and Dulles worried that they would choose a Communist government. If that happened, they reasoned, other nations in the area would follow. They helped form **SEATO**, the Southeast Asia Treaty Organization. SEATO and the United States supported the creation of an anti-Communist nation, South Vietnam. However, the leader of this nation angered his people with his harsh government.

> How were the Vietnamese supposed to choose their government?
>
> _____
> _____
> _____

In the Middle East there was tension between Israel and its Arab neighbors. In 1956 Egypt took control of the Suez Canal from Britain and France. Israel, Britain, and France attacked Egypt. The Soviets threatened to help Egypt. Eisenhower ordered the attackers out of Egypt. Egypt kept control of the canal. Eisenhower issued the **Eisenhower Doctrine**. It said that the United States had the right to help any nation in the Middle East trying to resist Communist aggression.

CHALLENGE ACTIVITY

Critical Thinking: Evaluate Based on the evidence, how much of a threat do you think the Soviets really posed to the United States? Write two paragraphs explaining your position.

Interactive Reader and Study Guide

Postwar America

MAIN IDEA
The growing power of, and military reliance on, nuclear weapons helped create significant anxiety in the American public in the 1950s.

Key Terms and People

hydrogen bomb a bomb that gets its power by fusing together hydrogen atoms

ICBM intercontinental ballistic missiles; missiles with nuclear weapons attached that could travel thousands of miles to strike their targets

satellite an object in orbit around Earth

Sputnik the first artificial satellite; launched by the Soviet Union

NASA National Aeronautics and Space Administration; agency in charge of U.S. space programs

nuclear fallout particles of radioactive material produced by nuclear explosions

Section Summary

THE HYDROGEN BOMB

Atomic bombs ended World War II. The United States searched for even more powerful weapons. Nuclear testing took place in several states. Americans also worked on an entirely new type of bomb. This was the **hydrogen bomb**. It got its power from fusing hydrogen atoms together. This fusion is the same process that creates the energy of the sun and stars. Americans thought this bomb would give them an advantage over the Soviet Union. Soon, however, the Soviets developed their own hydrogen bomb.

> **What new type of bomb did Americans develop?**
> _____

THE ARMS RACE

Both the United States and the Soviet Union built up stockpiles of nuclear weapons. The United States worked less on its traditional military plans and more on nuclear ones. By 1954 all the problems with the hydrogen bomb had been worked out. The bombs could be carried on planes. Then missiles were developed that could carry nuclear weapons thousands of miles. These were called intercontinental ballistic missiles, or **ICBMs**. Scientists also found out how to use nuclear power to run submarines.

> **How did American military strategy change?**
> _____
> _____
> _____

> **Underline the two ways that nuclear bombs could be delivered to their targets.**

Postwar America

In 1957 the Soviets launched the first artificial **satellite** into space. It was called *Sputnik*. A satellite is an object in orbit around Earth. The launch of *Sputnik* caused concern in the United States. It seemed that Soviet scientists had greater technical skill than American ones. Americans worried that the Soviets would create better weapons. The United States created **NASA**, the National Aeronautics and Space Administration, to take charge of its space programs. In 1958 Congress passed the National Defense Education Act. It provided hundreds of millions of dollars for education.

> **Circle the name of the first artificial satellite.**

AMERICANS REACT TO THE THREAT OF NUCLEAR WAR

Americans were afraid of the destruction caused by nuclear weapons. Many people were also afraid of **nuclear fallout**. Fallout is particles of radioactive material produced by nuclear explosions. Fallout can cause burns and increase the risk of future health problems. These include cancer and birth defects. To prepare for a nuclear attack, the Truman administration created the Federal Civil Defense Administration (FCDA). The FCDA distributed pamphlets and educational films. Schoolchildren and workers practiced what to do in an emergency. Some people built bomb shelters in their backyards. Many communities installed air raid sirens. People lived in fear of a nuclear attack.

> **What problems can fallout cause?**
> _____
> _____
> _____

When Eisenhower was leaving office, he warned of a new danger. He pointed out that there was now an arms industry that stayed in business during peacetime. He called this the military-industrial complex. He warned that it posed a threat to freedom.

CHALLENGE ACTIVITY

Critical Thinking: Design Bomb shelters were designed for people to stay inside without leaving or opening a door for several weeks. Make a list of all the things you would have to put in a bomb shelter to live there for several weeks.

Interactive Reader and Study Guide

MAIN IDEA
Television was a major influence on American culture in the 1950s, mirroring larger changes in technology and culture.

Key Terms and People

Lucille Ball popular comic actress who was a pioneer in the television industry

transistor device that replaced vacuum tubes to make electronic devices, such as radios and computers, smaller and better

integrated circuit a single piece of material that includes a number of transistors and other electronic components

Jonas Salk developer of the polio vaccine

vaccine a preparation that uses a killed or weakened form of a germ to help the body build its defenses against that germ

Levittown a suburban development of the 1950s that featured affordable homes

Sunbelt the southern and western portions of the United States

Interstate Highway System network of high-speed roads across the United States

Section Summary

TELEVISION CHANGES AMERICAN LIFE

By the end of World War II, television was ready for the home. By 1959 more than 40 million Americans had TVs. Politicians learned to use television to communicate with people. Advertisers also learned to use it to reach people with messages about their products. There were many popular television programs. **Lucille Ball** made the move from movies to television. Some people began to question television's influence. They especially worried about its impact on children. The television industry adopted its own standards. Law enforcement would always be shown in a positive light. Criminals would always be shown as "bad guys." Congress decided not to take any action to control television programming.

> Circle the number of Americans who had TVs by 1959.

> What did people worry about in regard to television?
> _____
> _____
> _____

OTHER TECHNOLOGICAL DEVELOPMENTS OF THE 1950S

In the 1940s the first computers were built. They were very large. In 1947 the **transistor** was invented. It was

Interactive Reader and Study Guide

a device that took the place of vacuum tubes. The invention of the transistor led to much better electronics. Transistors allowed smaller and better computers to be built. Another development was the **integrated circuit**. It was a single piece of material that included a number of transistors and other electronic components. Integrated circuits are also called computer chips. They helped speed the development of computers.

In 1952, **Jonas Salk** developed a **vaccine** against polio. A vaccine is a preparation that uses a killed or weakened form of a germ to help the body build its own defenses against that germ. The vaccine was used widely by the mid-1950s. The number of cases of polio dropped sharply.

What were two inventions that made computers better and smaller?
_____
_____

What vaccine changed American life?
_____

CULTURAL CHANGE IN THE 1950S

The American economy did well in the 1950s. The baby boom also continued. New suburban housing communities like **Levittown** were built. They included affordable single-family homes. The new homes were filled with new appliances. New TVs urged people to buy even more. Millions of people bought cars. Many Americans moved to the **Sunbelt**. This is the southern and western portions of the United States. The nation started building the **Interstate Highway System**. It is a network of high-speed roads that crisscross the country.

Many Americans were well off. But there were also many poor Americans. Michael Harrington wrote about them in *The Other America*. William H. Whyte wrote *The Organization Man*. It was about the push toward "sameness" among business workers. Among many writers and artists, rebellion was fashionable. The so-called Beat generation posed as outsiders. Young people expressed their rebellion through rock and roll music. The rebels were mostly males, however. Women still tended to fill traditional roles.

How did young people express their rebellion?
_____

CHALLENGE ACTIVITY

Critical Thinking: Predict How do you think your life would be different if there was no television? Write three paragraphs explaining your thoughts.

The New Frontier and the Great Society

Chapter Summary

January 1961: Kennedy takes office as the youngest elected president

March 1961: Kennedy announces Alliance for Progress program

April 1961: Bay of Pigs invasion fails in Cuba

August 1961: East German Communists build Berlin Wall

August 1963: Limited Nuclear Test Ban Treaty signed

November 1963: Kennedy is assassinated; Johnson becomes president

February 1965: Active U.S. involvement in Vietnam War begins

April 1965: Johnson sends marines to Dominican Republic

July 1965: Congress creates Medicare and Medicaid programs

August 1965: Congress passes Voting Rights Act

January 1968: North Korea captures *Pueblo* and crew

1961	1962	1963	1964	1965	1966	1967	1968

October 1962: Cuban missile crisis threatens war with USSR

January 1964: Johnson announces War on Poverty

July 1964: Congress passes Civil Rights Act

August 1964: Congress passes Economic Opportunity Act

November 1964: Johnson defeats Goldwater in landslide

April 1967: Outer Space Treaty is signed

COMPREHENSION AND CRITICAL THINKING

Use information from the graphic organizer to answer the following questions.

1. **Recall** How did Lyndon Johnson become president?

_____

2. **Identify Cause and Effect** What event on the time line might have persuaded the United States to favor the Limited Nuclear Test Ban Treaty?

_____

3. **Analyze** What kind of programs and legislation were created during the Johnson administration?

_____

The New Frontier and the Great Society

Section 1

MAIN IDEA
President Kennedy continued the Cold War policy of resisting the spread of communism by offering help to other nations and threatening to use force if necessary.

Key Terms and People

John F. Kennedy president of the United States from 1961 to 1963

Robert Kennedy brother of the president; served as attorney general

Fidel Castro Communist dictator of Cuba

Bay of Pigs invasion unsuccessful attempt by the United States to overthrow Castro

Lyndon B. Johnson Kennedy's vice president who went to West Berlin

Cuban missile crisis conflict between the United States and the Soviet Union over Soviet missiles in Cuba

Peace Corps U.S. group that trained volunteers and sent them to poorer nations to be teachers, health care workers, and to do other helpful work

Alliance for Progress Kennedy's program for aid to Latin America

flexible response Cold War strategy that involved strengthening non-nuclear U.S. forces so that there would be choices for response other than nuclear war

Section Summary

KENNEDY BECOMES PRESIDENT
John F. Kennedy ran against Richard Nixon for president in the 1960 election. Kennedy called his plans for changing the nation the New Frontier. He spoke out about changes, but he also spoke out against communism. He won by a small majority of the popular vote. Kennedy had young, smart advisers, including the attorney general, who was his brother, **Robert Kennedy**.

> Circle the name of the man who ran against Kennedy in 1960.

THE BAY OF PIGS INVASION
In 1960 the CIA had been training exiled Cubans to invade Cuba. They wanted to remove **Fidel Castro**, the Communist dictator of Cuba. He had ties to the Soviet Union. The invasion, called the **Bay of Pigs invasion**, began during Kennedy's early days in office. Many things went wrong and the invasion was a failure. Cuba grew closer to the Soviet Union.

> Which country did Castro have ties to?
> _____

Interactive Reader and Study Guide

The New Frontier and the Great Society

THE BERLIN CRISIS

Kennedy met with Nikita Khrushchev, the Soviet leader, in 1961. Khrushchev demanded that the United States recognize East Germany as an independent nation and remove its troops from West Berlin. West Berlin was an island of freedom surrounded by East Germany. Kennedy reacted by sending more troops.

Thousands of East Germans were escaping to West Berlin. To stop them, the East Germans closed the borders and built a high wall around Berlin. Anyone caught crossing the wall was shot. Vice President **Lyndon B. Johnson** visited West Berlin and told its people they would not be abandoned. Two years later, Kennedy, too, visited Berlin and repeated the promise.

> **Why did the East Germans build a wall around West Berlin?**
> _____
> _____
> _____

THE CUBAN MISSILE CRISIS

The **Cuban missile crisis** began in October 1963, when U.S. spy planes found that the U.S.S.R. had put nuclear missiles in Cuba. These could strike anywhere in the United States. In response, Kennedy blockaded Cuba by sea. He put U.S. forces on full alert. Soviet ships carrying missile parts approached the American ships. Fortunately, at the last minute they turned back. Khrushchev agreed to remove the missiles from Cuba if the United States promised never to invade Cuba.

> **The United States and the Soviet Union almost came to nuclear war during the Cuban missile crisis. How was this avoided?**
> _____
> _____

KENNEDY'S FOREIGN POLICY

Kennedy created several programs to help poorer nations. The **Peace Corps** trained volunteers to serve as teachers and health care workers in poor countries. The **Alliance for Progress** gave aid to Latin America. However, it often tied the aid to anti-Communist dictators who were not supported by the people. Kennedy's strategy was the **flexible response**. This meant strengthening non-nuclear forces so there were choices other than nuclear war.

> **Why was Kennedy's strategy called "flexible?"**
> _____
> _____
> _____

CHALLENGE ACTIVITY

Critical Thinking: Compare and Contrast Conduct some research into everyday life in East Berlin and West Berlin. How was it the same in both parts of the city? How was it different?

The New Frontier and the Great Society

MAIN IDEA
John F. Kennedy brought energy, initiative, and important new ideas to the presidency.

Key Terms and People

Jacqueline Kennedy First Lady to President John F. Kennedy

New Frontier Kennedy's plans to change the country

mandate permission to act

Earl Warren chief justice of the Supreme Court; author of many important decisions

Warren Court the Supreme Court for the 21 years that Earl Warren was chief justice

Lee Harvey Oswald assassin of President Kennedy

Warren Commission commission led by Earl Warren to investigate Kennedy's assassination

Section Summary

KENNEDY'S NEW FRONTIER

Kennedy was skilled at using the media to project the image he wanted. He showed himself as young and athletic. Actually, he had many health problems. First Lady **Jacqueline Kennedy** was attractive and from a wealthy family. She supported the arts and made the White House the nation's unofficial cultural center.

Kennedy wanted to improve the nation with his **New Frontier** plans. However, he did not have a clear **mandate**. The election of 1960 was too close to be seen as permission for him to act. Kennedy urged Congress to reduce taxes in order to fight unemployment. He proposed federal aid for education and creation of a health plan for the elderly. Congress acted on none of these ideas. Kennedy did convince Congress to pass financial help for poor areas of the country. Congress also created a job retraining program and raised the minimum wage.

In 1961 the Soviet Union caught Americans by surprise. It launched the first human into space. Kennedy proposed that within 10 years the United States should land a human on the moon. The space race began.

> How was Kennedy's image different from reality?
> _____
> _____

> What were three ideas President Kennedy had to improve the nation?
> _____
> _____
> _____

> Circle the year the first human was launched into space.

The New Frontier and the Great Society

THE WARREN COURT

During Kennedy's presidency, the Supreme Court made major changes in U.S. society. Led by Chief Justice **Earl Warren**, the court made many important decisions about the laws of the land. The court became known as the **Warren Court**. In 1954 the court banned racial segregation in schools. In 1962 the court required the states to redraw the boundaries of their legislative districts when populations changed. In 1964 it decided that a person has a right to a lawyer during police questioning. The court also prohibited formal prayers and daily Bible readings in public schools. The justices said that the government may not make any one religion the nation's "official" religion.

> Circle the date when the Supreme Court outlawed racial segregation in schools.

> Why did the court prohibit formal prayers in public schools?
>
> _____
>
> _____
>
> _____

THE KENNEDY ASSASSINATION

On November 22, 1963, Kennedy was working to build support for his re-election campaign in Texas. He was in Dallas, riding in an open car on his way to deliver a speech. Suddenly shots were fired and Kennedy was killed. Within hours, Vice President Lyndon Johnson was sworn in as the next president.

Just hours after Kennedy was shot, the police arrested **Lee Harvey Oswald**, a troubled man with connections to Cuba and the Soviet Union. As Oswald was being moved to the county jail, he was shot to death by Jack Ruby, a man with ties to organized crime. These occurrences caused people to wonder if Oswald had acted alone. President Johnson named Earl Warren to head the **Warren Commission** to investigate the assassination. It concluded that Oswald and Ruby had each acted alone.

> What did the Warren Commission decide about the assassination?
>
> _____

Kennedy offered great promise to Americans. In world affairs he had won friends for the nation through the Peace Corps and bettered relations with the Soviet Union. At home, however, he was not able to accomplish all he set out to do.

CHALLENGE ACTIVITY

Critical Thinking: Evaluate Would you rate Kennedy as a successful president? Write two paragraphs explaining your position.

MAIN IDEA
President Johnson used his political skills to push Kennedy's proposals through Congress and expanded them with his own vision of the Great Society.

Key Terms and People

War on Poverty set of programs designed to reduce poverty in the United States

Job Corps work-training program for unemployed youth of the United States

VISTA Volunteers in Service to America; the domestic Peace Corps

Great Society Johnson's programs to improve American society

Barry Goldwater Johnson's opponent in the presidential election of 1964

Medicaid government program to provide free medical care to the poor

Medicare government program to provide medical care to the elderly

Johnson Doctrine foreign policy guideline that called for the United States to step in if a Communist dictator came to power in Latin America

***Pueblo* incident** capture of a U.S. Navy spy ship by the North Koreans

Section Summary

JOHNSON BECOMES PRESIDENT

Johnson had been a congressman, a senator, and Senate majority leader. By 1960, when he became vice president, he had more influence in Washington, D.C., than any other Democrat. He had great political skills and great compassion for the underprivileged.

> **What positions did Johnson hold before he became vice president?**
>
> _____
>
> _____

ENACTING KENNEDY'S AGENDA

Johnson told the nation that he would carry on Kennedy's programs. He asked Kennedy's advisers to stay. One of Kennedy's plans was to fight poverty. Johnson called it the **War on Poverty** and gave it high priority. He got Congress to pass the Economic Opportunity Act. It created the **Job Corps**, a work-training program for unemployed youth, and **VISTA**, Volunteers in Service to America. VISTA was a domestic Peace Corps. Kennedy's tax cut bill was passed and the economy grew while unemployment fell. Johnson also got Congress to finally pass the Civil Rights Act.

> **Underline the programs first developed by Kennedy that Johnson got passed.**

Interactive Reader and Study Guide

The New Frontier and the Great Society

THE GREAT SOCIETY

Johnson's plans for the country went beyond those of Kennedy. He wanted to create the **Great Society**, a society with abundance, liberty, and justice for all. In the 1964 election, Johnson faced conservative **Barry Goldwater**. Goldwater suggested using nuclear weapons in Vietnam and thought that government programs to help people were similar to communism. Johnson won the election by a landslide.

With a mandate to act, Johnson pushed Congress into action. In 1965 it passed the first large-scale program of government aid to public schools. Other programs created the first federal college scholarships and Head Start, a preschool education program. The Department of Housing and Urban Development was created. Congress approved the money for **Medicaid**. This provided free health care for poor people. **Medicare**, a health care program for the elderly, was also begun. In 1967 Johnson also signed laws to improve the environment and to create the Corporation for Public Broadcasting.

> **What Great Society programs were begun between 1964 and 1967?**
>
> _____
>
> _____
>
> _____
>
> _____
>
> _____

JOHNSON'S FOREIGN POLICY

Progress on the Great Society slowed by the end of 1966. One reason was that the government was spending $2.5 billion per month on the Vietnam War. Johnson was determined not to lose ground to the Communists. In 1965 he had sent troops to the Dominican Republic to end a revolt. The development of the **Johnson Doctrine** said that the United States had a right to step in if a Communist dictatorship might be established. In 1967 Johnson signed the first direct treaty with the Soviet Union in 50 years. Also, the United States, the Soviet Union, and 58 other nations agreed to ban weapons in outer space. In a 1968 crisis, the North Koreans captured the U.S. Navy spy ship *Pueblo*. Johnson negotiated a settlement for the *Pueblo* incident. North Korea released the crew but kept the ship.

> **To which foreign country did the United States send troops in 1965?**
>
> _____
>
> _____

CHALLENGE ACTIVITY

Critical Thinking: Analyze Why do you think Johnson was more successful than Kennedy at passing new programs through Congress?

Interactive Reader and Study Guide

Name _____ Class _____ Date _____

The Civil Rights Movement

Chapter Summary

Fighting Segregation	Freedom Now!	Voting Rights	Changes and Challenges	The Movement Continues
• Early civil rights groups included the NAACP and CORE. • In 1954 the Supreme Court ordered an end to racial segregation in public schools. • A bus boycott in Montgomery, Alabama, launched the SCLC and the modern civil rights movement.	• Sit-ins and Freedom Rides provoked violent reactions from some white southerners. • Violent response to marches in Birmingham, Alabama, shocked the nation. • The March on Washington helped lead to the Civil Rights Act of 1964.	• Some white southerners tried to block efforts of African Americans to vote. • African Americans in Mississippi organized to increase their political power. • A brutal attack on a protest in Selma, Alabama, helped win support for the Voting Rights Act of 1965.	• Civil rights leaders began attacking de facto segregation in the North in the mid-1960s. • Differences within the civil rights movement weakened it and led to the rise of Black Power. • The assassination of Martin Luther King Jr. caused urban unrest.	• King's death and the Poor People's Campaign helped lead to the decline of SCLC. • Internal divisions and an FBI campaign weakened some civil rights groups. • The civil rights movement resulted in important gains for African Americans.

COMPREHENSION AND CRITICAL THINKING
Use information from the graphic organizer to answer the following questions.

1. **Recall** What did the Supreme Court do in 1954 that favored civil rights?

2. **Identify Cause and Effect** What event led to the Voting Rights Act of 1965?

3. **Evaluate** Which tactics and strategies of the civil rights movement were most successful?

Interactive Reader and Study Guide

The Civil Rights Movement

MAIN IDEA
In the mid-1900s, the civil rights movement began to make major progress in correcting the national problem of racial segregation.

Key Terms and People

CORE Congress of Racial Equality; civil rights group devoted to nonviolent protest

Jackie Robinson first African American major league baseball player

Thurgood Marshall lead lawyer in landmark 1954 school desegregation case

Little Rock Nine the nine African American students blocked from entering school by the Arkansas National Guard in 1957

Rosa Parks NAACP member whose arrest for refusing to give up her seat on a bus launched the Montgomery bus boycott

Montgomery bus boycott boycott of the Montgomery, Alabama, bus system by African Americans to protest racial discrimination

Martin Luther King Jr. Baptist minister who became the leader of the SCLC

SCLC Southern Christian Leadership Conference; civil rights group committed to nonviolent protest

Section Summary

THE CIVIL RIGHTS MOVEMENT PRIOR TO 1954

The fight for equal rights for African Americans began with the struggle against slavery. Former slaves enjoyed some rights during Reconstruction. However, once Reconstruction was over legalized racism returned to the South. In 1896 the Supreme Court ruled that segregation was legal.

Circle the date when the Supreme Court ruled that segregation was legal.

Some progress was made in the 1940s. Discrimination in defense-related work was banned. The Congress of Racial Equality, or **CORE**, was formed. It was dedicated to nonviolent protest. In 1947 **Jackie Robinson** became the first African American major league baseball player. In 1948 the armed forces were desegregated.

Who was Jackie Robinson? _____ _____

The NAACP began to work for civil rights through the courts. It fought the concept of "separate but equal." **Thurgood Marshall** was a leader in court battles to end legalized racism.

BROWN V. BOARD OF EDUCATION

Lower courts upheld segregation of the schools. Thurgood Marshall and the NAACP took a case known as *Brown* v. *Board of Education of Topeka, Kansas*, to the Supreme Court. The Court heard many arguments. It also used research that said that segregation made black children feel inferior. The Court ruled that segregation violated the Constitution's guarantee of equal protection under the law. At the time, 21 states had segregated schools. In some of these there was strong resistance to integration. In Virginia officials practiced massive resistance. With this tactic, officials at all levels pledged to block integration. Schools that planned to integrate were closed. In Little Rock, Arkansas, the governor ordered the National Guard to keep African American students out of school. President Eisenhower sent federal troops to end the crisis. The students—the **Little Rock Nine**—had to put up with much abuse at school.

> **What did the Supreme Court's research say about segregation?**
> _____
> _____

> **Why did Eisenhower have to send federal troops to Little Rock?**
> _____
> _____

A BOYCOTT BEGINS IN MONTGOMERY, ALABAMA

In addition to schools, many other public places were segregated. In Montgomery, Alabama, African Americans could only ride in the back of buses. They had to give up their seats to white people. One day **Rosa Parks** refused to give up her seat. She was arrested. This led to the **Montgomery bus boycott**. Local Baptist minister **Martin Luther King Jr.** was one of the leaders. In the boycott, African Americans refused to ride Montgomery's buses for a year. The boycott only ended when the Supreme Court ruled that segregated buses were unconstitutional. The success of the boycott led to the forming of the Southern Christian Leadership Conference (**SCLC**). Martin Luther King Jr. was its leader. SCLC was committed to mass, nonviolent action.

> **Who led the Montgomery bus boycott?**
> _____
> _____
> _____

CHALLENGE ACTIVITY

Critical Thinking: Develop Develop a plan for using a boycott to make public your views on an issue of your choice. Consider what to boycott, how to mobilize protestors, and how to use the media.

The Civil Rights Movement

MAIN IDEA
The quest for civil rights became a nationwide movement in the 1960s as African Americans won political and legal rights, and segregation was largely abolished.

Key Terms and People

James Farmer American civil rights leader

Mohandas Gandhi leader of India's nonviolent struggle for independence

SNCC Student Nonviolent Coordinating Committee; formed to hold nonviolent protests

Freedom Riders groups of people who took buses through the South to try to integrate public accommodations

James Meredith first African American to enroll at the University of Mississippi

Medgar Evers head of Mississippi NAACP; shot dead in his front yard

Civil Rights Act of 1964 bill banning discrimination in employment and public accommodations

Section Summary

SIT-INS AND FREEDOM RIDES

African American civil rights leaders like **James Farmer** and Martin Luther King Jr. borrowed the tactic of nonviolence from **Mohandas Gandhi**. Gandhi had used it as he led India's struggle for independence from Great Britain. African American protesters began a sit-in movement aimed at segregated restaurants. They would take a seat and order food. The restaurants would refuse to serve them. The protesters would then not leave until the police arrived and arrested them. Protesters faced abuse and ended up in jail, but the tactic worked. Sit-in leaders formed **SNCC**—the Student Nonviolent Coordinating Committee.

CORE aimed to integrate bus stations. They sent **Freedom Riders** on buses in the South. African American Freedom Riders would try to use whites-only restrooms and lunch counters. Often they faced angry mobs. Attorney General Robert Kennedy sent federal marshals to protect them. In 1961 the government forced bus and train stations to integrate.

> **What was a sit-in?**
> _____
> _____
> _____

> **Why did the attorney general send federal marshals to protect the Freedom Riders?**
> _____
> _____
> _____

INTEGRATING HIGHER EDUCATION

The NAACP tried to integrate universities and colleges. By 1961 it had a court order for the University of Georgia to admit two black students. Like them, **James Meredith**, who tried to enroll in the University of Mississippi in 1962, was threatened. He arrived with 500 federal marshals but faced 2,500 protesters. Troops had to be sent in to control the riot.

> Who tried to integrate the University of Mississippi?
> _____

ALBANY AND BIRMINGHAM

In Albany, Georgia, SNCC protested when local officials did not integrate bus stations. The campaign, called the Albany Movement, filled local and surrounding jails with protesters, including King. The tactic failed, though, as King's SCLC took control of the campaign and local officials would only negotiate with local leaders. In Birmingham, Alabama, King used children as protesters. The police used fire hoses to break up a march. Hundreds of protesters were jailed. Federal negotiators pressured the city to give in to King's demands. King's motel was bombed.

> What did the police use against the protesters in the Birmingham campaign?
> _____

THE CIVIL RIGHTS ACT OF 1964

President Kennedy wanted a law ending segregation in public accommodations. These are facilities that serve the public, such as hotels and restaurants. When **Medgar Evers**, head of the NAACP in Mississippi, was assassinated, many whites saw how serious the situation was. In August 1963 more than 200,000 people attended the March on Washington for Jobs and Freedom. There, King gave his "I Have a Dream" speech. The next month a Birmingham church was bombed, and three months later Kennedy was dead. But President Johnson pushed for the **Civil Rights Act of 1964**. It banned discrimination in employment and public accommodations.

> What did the Civil Rights Act of 1964 ban?
> _____
> _____
> _____

CHALLENGE ACTIVITY

Critical Thinking: Elaborate Write a short story about a young civil rights protester who had to face fire hoses and other abuse.

MAIN IDEA
In the 1960s, African Americans gained voting rights and political power in the South, but only after a bitter and hard-fought struggle.

Key Terms and People

Voter Education Project a civil rights campaign aimed at registering African American voters

Twenty-fourth Amendment amendment banning states from taxing citizens to vote

Freedom Summer hundreds of volunteers went to the South to register voters and teach

Mississippi Freedom Democratic Party (MFDP) African American delegation to the Democratic National Convention

Fannie Lou Hamer poor sharecropper and a leader of the MFDP

Voting Rights Act of 1965 law protecting the voting rights of minorities

Section Summary

GAINING VOTING RIGHTS

In 1962 SNCC, CORE, and other groups founded the **Voter Education Project** (VEP). Their aim was to register southern African Americans to vote. Marches to register voters were attacked by mobs or broken up by police. Some workers were killed. Still, the VEP was a success.

Some African Americans were kept from voting by poll taxes, taxes that some states charged for voting. In 1962 Congress passed the **Twenty-fourth Amendment**. It banned poll taxes in elections for president or Congress. It was ratified and went into law in 1964.

Freedom Summer was a project that sent hundreds of white college students to Mississippi in 1964. They were trained by SNCC workers to register voters and teach in schools. When it was discovered that two CORE workers and a Freedom Summer volunteer were murdered, many volunteers went home. Those who stayed faced attacks and arrests. Despite the violence, 17,000 blacks applied to vote. The state accepted only about 1,600 of these applications. A federal law was needed.

> **What was the aim of the VEP?**
> _____
> _____

> **What did the 24th Amendment prevent?**
> _____
> _____

> **What did the Freedom Summer volunteers hope to accomplish?**
> _____
> _____
> _____

The Civil Rights Movement

Section 3

POLITICAL ORGANIZING

African American leaders supported President Johnson in the 1964 election. Many of them agreed not to hold protests until after election day. SNCC, however, did not. They wanted to rid the Democratic Party of its own racism. SNCC helped organize the **Mississippi Freedom Democratic Party** (MFDP). It sent 68 delegates to the Democratic National Convention. They were to replace the delegates sent by Mississippi's all-white Democratic Party. **Fannie Lou Hamer**, an MFDP leader, presented their case. President Johnson offered a compromise that allowed two delegates to vote. The NAACP and SCLC supported the compromise; SNCC and the MFDP did not. This helped split the civil rights movement.

> Whose place at the 1964 Democratic National Convention did the Mississippi Freedom Democratic Party want to take?
>
> _____
>
> _____

THE VOTING RIGHTS ACT

The SCLC now focused on voting rights for African Americans. The campaign began in 1965 with marches in Selma, Alabama. More than 2,000 marchers were arrested. When Martin Luther King Jr. was arrested, the national media arrived. Pictures of mass arrests and children being jailed appeared on televisions across the country.

> Where did the 1965 campaign for voting rights begin?
>
> _____

In another march, a state trooper killed a marcher. To protest the actions of the police, King announced a march from Selma to Montgomery. Six hundred African Americans began the 54-mile march. Before they could leave Selma, city and state police attacked them with tear gas, clubs, and other weapons. Many people saw this violence on TV. When the march went on two days later, hundreds of black and white northern supporters joined them. The march was halted again but without violence. Finally, protected by federal troops, 25,000 marchers arrived in Montgomery. A week later President Johnson proposed a tough new voting rights law. The **Voting Rights Act of 1965** was passed by a large majority.

> How did TV coverage help the civil rights movement?
>
> _____
>
> _____
>
> _____

CHALLENGE ACTIVITY

Critical Thinking: Elaborate African Americans and women both fought for the vote. Yet today many Americans don't bother to vote. Write three paragraphs on why this is and what could be done about it.

The Civil Rights Movement

Section 4

MAIN IDEA
Continued social and economic inequalities caused many young African Americans to lose faith in the civil rights movement and integration and seek alternative solutions.

Key Terms and People

de jure segregation segregation by law

de facto segregation segregation by custom and practice

Kerner Commission commission formed to study the causes of 1960s riots in U.S. cities

Stokely Carmichael leader of SNCC who founded the Black Power movement

Black Power civil rights movement that rejected nonviolence and integration and called for separate, African Americans–only, political and economic organizations

Black Panther Party organization inspired by Black Power movement; called for blacks to control their own communities; members carried guns

Malcolm X Nation of Islam leader and minister who called for revolution and was assassinated after changing his views

Section Summary

EXPANDING THE MOVEMENT

The civil rights movement had done much to end segregation by law, or **de jure segregation**. However, there was still much **de facto segregation**. This is segregation that exists through custom and practice. De jure segregation ends when laws are changed. De facto segregation is much harder to overcome. Many African Americans outside the South faced de facto segregation, especially in housing. African Americans were often shut out of white neighborhoods. Banks often made it hard for African Americans to borrow money. Black neighborhoods had high unemployment and poverty.

From 1964 to 1967 violence erupted in more than 100 U.S. cities. In the Watts neighborhood of Los Angeles, a six-day riot destroyed entire blocks. More than 3,000 people were arrested and 34 people were killed. In Detroit, 43 died in riots. President Johnson appointed the **Kerner Commission** to study the causes of the riots. It reported that poverty and discrimination were the causes. Northern riots convinced Martin Luther King Jr. to campaign in

> How did de facto segregation affect African Americans in the North?
>
> _____
> _____
> _____

> Circle the number of U.S. cities that experienced rioting in the mid 1960s.

Chicago. The campaign failed as Chicago's blacks' concerns were economic, not political, and its police reacted with nonviolence.

FRACTURES IN THE MOVEMENT

Although the civil rights movement seemed unified, it was made up of many separate groups. After SNCC and CORE workers were harassed during Freedom Summer, some members of these organizations began to reject nonviolence. Under the leadership of **Stokely Carmichael**, SNCC itself rejected nonviolence. Carmichael started the **Black Power** movement. It rejected nonviolence and integration. It wanted separate, African Americans–only, political and economic organizations.

The Black Power movement inspired some blacks to create the **Black Panther Party**. It called for a revolution to change American society. Its leaders were usually armed. Most people who believed in Black Power were Black Muslims. They were members of the Nation of Islam, a group founded in 1930 and based on the religion of Islam. One of its leaders and ministers was **Malcolm X**. He first called for revolution and criticized nonviolence. Later he softened his views. He was killed by Black Muslims after he appealed for the races to get along.

> What caused some members of the civil rights movement to reject nonviolence?
>
> _____
>
> _____

> Why do you think some Black Muslims would be unhappy with Malcolm X's call for the races to get along?
>
> _____
>
> _____
>
> _____
>
> _____

THE ASSASSINATION OF KING

In 1968 Martin Luther King led a march in Memphis. He was supporting striking sanitation workers. They were protesting discrimination in the city's work and pay policies. King also spoke at a rally. The next day he was killed by a white sniper. Angry riots erupted in 120 cities. Troops were called in to restore peace. One leader noted that King would have been upset by the violent reaction to his death.

> Circle the year in which Martin Luther King was assassinated. What happened after the assassination?
>
> _____
>
> _____

CHALLENGE ACTIVITY

Critical Thinking: Evaluate Explain why various civil rights groups used different methods. Why were there divisions within the civil rights movement? Write a two-paragraph evaluation.

MAIN IDEA
The civil rights movement was in decline by the 1970s, but its accomplishments continued to benefit American society.

Key Terms and People

Poor People's Campaign King and the SCLC's campaign to fight poverty

Ralph Abernathy leader of SCLC after the assassination of Martin Luther King

Civil Rights Act of 1968 law banning discrimination in housing; also called the Fair Housing Act

affirmative action programs that gave preference to minorities and women in hiring and admissions

John Lewis civil rights activist and former SNCC head who was elected to Congress from Georgia

Andrew Young Georgia's first black member of Congress since Reconstruction

Jesse Jackson adviser to Martin Luther King and founder of Operation PUSH

Section Summary

A CHANGE IN GOALS

The **Poor People's Campaign** was an expansion of the civil rights movement. Laws had given African Americans more rights. But Martin Luther King Jr. knew that poverty kept many African Americans from achieving equality. After King's death, **Ralph Abernathy** took over the SCLC. Without King's leadership, the campaign did not succeed.

> Why did the civil rights movement take on the problem of poverty?
>
> _____
>
> _____

THE DECLINE OF BLACK POWER

The civil rights movement took place during the height of the Cold War. FBI director J. Edgar Hoover believed that civil rights groups were led by Communists. In 1956 Hoover created a secret program to spy on groups involved in unrest. FBI agents were to disrupt and interfere with the activities of these groups. The FBI spread false rumors about the Black Panthers. It also forged letters, posters, and leaflets. The FBI made the Black Panthers look more violent than they really were. Police raided Panther headquarters. There were gun battles. Many Panther

> What else was the nation facing during the civil rights movement?
>
> _____

> Underline the ways the FBI weakened the civil rights movement.

leaders died or went to prison. The FBI also helped destroy SNCC in the early 1970s.

NEW CHANGES AND GAINS

President Johnson signed the **Civil Rights Act of 1968**. It is also called the Fair Housing Act. This law banned discrimination in the sale or rental of housing. Some people felt that school integration was progressing too slowly. The courts ordered that students be bused from their neighborhood schools to other schools. Many people were violently opposed to busing, especially in the North. Forced busing caused some whites to leave the cities for the suburbs. The blacks in the cities soon gained political power. By 1974 several large cities had elected African American mayors, including Los Angeles and Atlanta.

Starting in the late 1960s, **affirmative action** programs gave preference to minorities and women in hiring and admission to college. The backlash against these programs cost the Democrats support. Many southern whites and urban, working-class whites became Republicans.

African Americans took over some elected offices in the South. Many who had played a role in the civil rights movement served the nation. Thurgood Marshall became the Supreme Court's first African American justice. **John Lewis**, a civil rights activist, was elected to Congress from Georgia. **Andrew Young** had been a staff member of SCLC. He was elected to Congress from Georgia. Later he was the U.S. ambassador to the United Nations. **Jesse Jackson** had been an adviser to Martin Luther King. He founded the civil rights organization Operation PUSH. He became an activist for poor and oppressed peoples around the world. At home, he ran for the Democratic presidential nomination in 1984 and 1988.

> **Why did the courts order children to be bused to schools that were out of their neighborhoods?**
> _____
> _____
> _____

> **Which civil rights worker became Ambassador to the United Nations? Which ran for the presidential nomination?**
> _____
> _____

CHALLENGE ACTIVITY

Critical Thinking: Evaluate Some people have argued that affirmative action programs are no longer necessary, or that they are "reverse discrimination." What do you think? Write three paragraphs explaining what affirmative action is and what you think about it.

The Vietnam War

Chapter Summary

1965 First major U.S. combat troops arrive in Vietnam to fight the Vietcong and NVA; first national antiwar protest is held in Washington, D.C.

1972 Nixon orders the Christmas bombings on Hanoi and Haiphong after peace talks with North Vietnam break down.

1960 President Eisenhower sends military advisers to train South Vietnam's army.

1968 Vietcong launch the Tet Offensive; President Johnson decides not to seek re-election.

1973 United States and North Vietnam sign a truce; the U.S. withdraws its troops from Vietnam.

1960	1963	1966	1969	1972	1975

1964 Congress approves the Tonkin Gulf Resolution, giving President Johnson more war-making powers in Vietnam.

1970 President Nixon orders invasion of Cambodia to destroy NVA bases; antiwar protests erupt on American college campuses.

1971 Release of the Pentagon Papers reveals that government officials had misled the public about the war.

1975 North Vietnam takes over Saigon; the United States airlifts U.S. embassy staff and 120,000 South Vietnamese supporters to safety.

COMPREHENSION AND CRITICAL THINKING

Use information from the graphic organizer to answer the following questions.

1. **Recall** What congressional act gave President Johnson more war-making powers?

_____

2. **Describe** Trace the course of U.S. actions in Vietnam and Cambodia.

_____

_____

3. **Make Judgments** The Pentagon Papers revealed that the government had misled the public about the war. The person who released this information did not have the government's permission to do so. Do you think he did the right thing? Why or why not?

_____

_____

MAIN IDEA
Concern about the spread of communism led the United States to become
increasingly involved in Vietnam.

Key Terms and People

Ho Chi Minh leader of the drive for Vietnamese independence; leader of North Vietnam

Vietminh Vietnamese group that resisted the Japanese occupation in World War II

domino theory theory that if one Southeast Asian country fell to communism, others
would follow

Dien Bien Phu site of France's last stand to keep Vietnam a French colony

Geneva Conference conference to work out a peace agreement for Indochina

Ngo Dinh Diem corrupt and brutal South Vietnamese leader

Vietcong military forces in South Vietnam who united to overthrow Diem

Tonkin Gulf Resolution resolution that enabled President Johnson to use "all necessary
measures to repel any armed attack"

Section Summary

COLONIAL VIETNAM

Vietnam came under Chinese control in about 200
BC. The Vietnamese struggled against the Chinese
until they won independence in the 1400s. Then in the
1800s the French took over Vietnam. After World
War I their leader, who came to be known as **Ho Chi
Minh**, tried unsuccessfully to get President Wilson to
apply his Fourteen Points to Southeast Asia. In World
War II, the Japanese controlled Vietnam. The
Vietnamese resistance fighters were called the
Vietminh. Many were Communists. They claimed
independence.

Who ruled Vietnam from about 200 BC to the AD 1400s?
_____

Who took control of Vietnam during World War II?
_____

VIETNAM AFTER WORLD WAR II

After World War II France, with U.S. support, took
back control of Vietnam. The Vietnamese fought
back. President Eisenhower believed in the **domino
theory**. This theory said that if one Southeast Asian
nation fell to communism, others would follow.
Despite massive U.S. aid, the French lost. Their last
stand occurred at **Dien Bien Phu**.

The Vietnam War

A peace agreement was reached at the **Geneva Conference**. This called for a temporary division of Vietnam into north and south. Free elections were supposed to take place in 1956. The north, led by Ho Chi Minh, was Communist. Communist countries were the only ones who would help him fight for independence.

> At the time of the Geneva Conference, which part of Vietnam was Communist?
>
> _____

GROWING CONFLICT IN VIETNAM

South Vietnam was ruled by **Ngo Dinh Diem**. He was corrupt and brutal. He persecuted Buddhists. His government helped the wealthy landowners and not the poor farmers. He knew the people would vote for Ho Chi Minh in the 1956 election, so Diem refused to allow an election. The Communist leaders of North Vietnam sent supplies to rebels in the south. The Vietminh in South Vietnam formed the **Vietcong** to fight Diem. Most of the Vietcong were Communists. Soldiers from North Vietnam slipped into South Vietnam to help fight Diem. President Eisenhower decided to send military advisers and special forces.

> Why were the South Vietnamese unhappy under Diem?
>
> _____
>
> _____
>
> _____

INCREASING U.S. INVOLVEMENT

President Kennedy sent more advisers and special forces. By 1963 nearly 500 Americans had been killed in Vietnam. Then Diem was murdered and the South Vietnamese government came close to falling. By March 1964 the Vietcong controlled about 40 percent of South Vietnam. President Johnson wanted to act but needed Congress's support. He presented inaccurate evidence that a U.S. ship had been fired on without having fired first. Congress approved the **Tonkin Gulf Resolution**. This enabled the president to take "all necessary measures to repel any armed attack" on U.S. forces. It was as if the president was given the power to make war without declaring war.

> Why do you think President Johnson presented inaccurate evidence to Congress?
>
> _____
>
> _____
>
> _____
>
> _____

CHALLENGE ACTIVITY

Critical Thinking: Draw Conclusions Review the system of checks and balances of the U.S. government. Write a paragraph explaining why Congress has the power to declare war, while the president has the power to wage war.

Interactive Reader and Study Guide

MAIN IDEA
As the United States sent increasing numbers of troops to defend South Vietnam, some Americans began to question the war.

Key Terms and People

Operation Rolling Thunder bombing campaign in North Vietnam in 1965

Ho Chi Minh Trail network of paths and tunnels that began in North Vietnam and ended in South Vietnam

William Westmoreland commander of U.S. ground troops in South Vietnam

pacification U.S. policy aimed at winning the support of the South Vietnamese people

doves people who opposed the war

hawks people who supported the war

J. William Fulbright head of the Senate Foreign Relations Committee who criticized the war openly

Section Summary

THE AIR WAR

In March 1965 President Johnson ordered **Operation Rolling Thunder**. This was a bombing campaign in North Vietnam. U.S. forces bombed military targets and also bridges, roads, railways, and power plants. To clear the jungle, U.S. planes sprayed it with Agent Orange, a chemical that caused plants to drop their leaves. It caused disease and disability in humans. Napalm, or jellied gasoline, was used to make firebombs. Pilots also did carpet bombings. These were strings of bombs dropped from high altitude to destroy large areas with no specific target. The Vietcong continued moving soldiers and supplies along the **Ho Chi Minh Trail**, a network of paths and tunnels that led from North Vietnam into South Vietnam.

Why was the Ho Chi Minh Trail important?
_____
_____
_____
_____

THE GROUND WAR

By 1967 there were 486,000 American troops in Vietnam. They were commanded by General **William Westmoreland**. Westmoreland ordered thousands of search-and-destroy missions. In these, ground troops would locate the enemy and then call in air strikes to

Circle the number of U.S. troops in Vietnam by 1967.

Interactive Reader and Study Guide

destroy it. The United States then began the policy of
pacification. If a village was close to the Vietcong,
the Americans moved the villagers to secure camps.

U.S. FORCES MOBILIZE

More than 2.5 million Americans served in the
Vietnam War. The United States used the draft to get
enough soldiers. Men who went to college could put
off their military service. This meant young men from
higher-income families were less likely to be drafted.
In 1969 the government began to use a lottery for the
draft. In 1973 the draft was ended. About 10,000
women also served in the war.

> Why did fewer young men from higher-income families fight in the war?
>
> _____
> _____
> _____

PUBLIC OPINION SHIFTS

Television coverage brought the Vietnam War into
people's living rooms. President Johnson was
criticized by **doves**. These were people opposed to the
war. **Hawks** were in favor of the war. However, many
criticized the way the war was fought. Senator
J. William Fulbright was head of the Senate Foreign
Relations Committee. He criticized the war. There
was a large antiwar movement. Some people said the
majority of the Vietnamese did not want the war. One
of the most vocal antiwar groups was the Students for
a Democratic Society. They led the first national
antiwar demonstration.

> What were people who criticized Johnson called?
>
> _____

> Who led the first national antiwar demonstration?
>
> _____
> _____

CHALLENGE ACTIVITY

Critical Thinking: Evaluate If you lived during the Vietnam War, would
you have been a hawk or a dove? Would your position on the war have led
you to join a movement? a political party? Write three paragraphs telling
what you would have done as a citizen during the Vietnam War.

MAIN IDEA
As the Vietnam War dragged on and increasingly appeared to be unwinnable, deep divisions developed in American society.

Key Terms and People

Tet Offensive a series of massive, coordinated attacks by the Vietcong across South Vietnam

Robert S. McNamara secretary of defense for both Presidents Kennedy and Johnson

Eugene McCarthy candidate for Democratic presidential nomination in 1968

Hubert Humphrey Democratic nominee for president in 1968

George Wallace independent candidate for president in 1968

Section Summary

THE TET OFFENSIVE

The **Tet Offensive** was a series of massive coordinated attacks by the Vietcong throughout South Vietnam. It occurred in 1968. It surprised U.S. commanders. They had noticed more activity on the Ho Chi Minh Trail. However, they thought it was related to a major battle at Khe Sanh. Instead, it led to attacks on 12 U.S. bases and over 100 cities. The North Vietnamese hoped the offensive would inspire the South Vietnamese to rise up against their government. It did not.

> Why did the Tet Offensive surprise the Americans?
>
> _____
>
> _____
>
> _____

EFFECTS OF THE TET OFFENSIVE

With the Tet Offensive Americans gave up the idea that the United States was winning the war. Even Walter Cronkite, the anchor of *CBS Evening News*, changed his mind. President Johnson then knew that people would listen to Cronkite and public opinion would turn against the war. Public criticism of the war grew. By 1968 roughly 3 out of 4 Americans were against Johnson's Vietnam policies. **Robert S. McNamara**, secretary of defense for both Kennedy and Johnson, began looking for ways to make peace.

> Why could Americans no longer believe that they were winning the war?
>
> _____
>
> _____
>
> _____

The Vietnam War

JOHNSON SEEKS A SOLUTION

General Westmoreland wanted more troops in Vietnam. Johnson's advisers could not agree on a strategy. Some thought that North Vietnam should be invaded. Others thought that was too extreme. In March 1968 Johnson declared that he would seek a peace agreement. In that same speech he announced that he would not run for president again. Peace talks began in Paris, but the two sides could not agree.

> **Why do you think President Johnson's advisers could not agree on a strategy to win the war?**
>
> _____
>
> _____
>
> _____
>
> _____

THE ELECTION OF 1968

Early in the 1968 election campaign, Senator **Eugene McCarthy** challenged President Johnson for the Democratic presidential nomination. So did Robert Kennedy, senator from New York. When Johnson withdrew from the race, his vice president, **Hubert Humphrey**, also entered the race. He was linked to policies supporting the war. McCarthy and Kennedy were against the war. The war was a key issue.

> **Underline the names of the presidential challengers who were against the war. Circle the one who was not. Who started out as the Democrats' favorite?**
>
> _____

Kennedy was the Democratic favorite, but after winning the California primary he was assassinated. When the Democratic Party held its convention in Chicago that August, many antiwar protesters came to demonstrate. Chicago mayor Richard Daley used police and the National Guard to maintain order. The situation exploded into violence. Humphrey was nominated.

The protests showed that there was a divide between young people and their parents, a "generation gap." Young people accused the older generation of valuing money and comfort ahead of justice. Older Americans urged them to trust the government to do best. The Democratic Party was deeply divided.

> **What is a generation gap?**
>
> _____
>
> _____
>
> _____

The Republicans nominated Richard Nixon for president. **George Wallace** ran as the candidate of the American Independent Party. Wallace had gained national attention by opposing civil rights. With the Democrats divided, Nixon won.

CHALLENGE ACTIVITY

Critical Thinking: Elaborate The riots at the Democratic convention led to the trial of the Chicago Seven. Write a report that explains who the Chicago Seven were and why they were prosecuted.

MAIN IDEA
President Nixon eventually ended U.S. involvement in Vietnam, but the war had lasting effects on the United States and in Southeast Asia.

Key Terms and People

Henry Kissinger President Nixon's national security adviser

Vietnamization policy of turning over the fighting to the South Vietnamese

silent majority people who disapproved of the protesters and generally supported the war

My Lai massacre the killing of at least 450 civilians by U.S. soldiers in Vietnam

Pentagon Papers secret documents that revealed that the government had been misleading the American people

George McGovern Democratic nominee for president in 1972; opposed the war

Twenty-sixth Amendment amendment reducing the voting age from 21 to 18

Khmer Rouge brutal Communist group that controlled Cambodia for four years

War Powers Act U.S. law limiting the president's war-making abilities

Section Summary

WIDENING THE WAR

President Nixon's national security adviser, **Henry Kissinger**, began secret peace talks with the North Vietnamese. Nixon also started **Vietnamization**. This policy turned the fighting over to the South Vietnamese. Nixon began withdrawing U.S. forces. Nixon believed he had the backing of the **silent majority**. These were people who disapproved of antiwar protesters and supported the war. Nixon also secretly expanded the war. He ordered the bombing of Cambodia and sent U.S. troops into Cambodia and Laos to destroy North Vietnamese army bases. He also started bombing North Vietnam.

> Circle the name of Nixon's national security adviser.

> Underline the ways Nixon expanded the war.

INCREASING PROTESTS

As the war dragged on, antiwar protests got bigger. At Kent State University, four students were shot by the National Guard. Two more were killed at Jackson State College. People on hundreds of college campuses went on strike. Trade unionists, veterans, and the clergy helped the movement. Meanwhile, in

Vietnam, the **My Lai massacre** occurred in 1968 but
was hushed up. American soldiers shot at least 450
women, children, and elderly men while on a search-
and-destroy mission. When the public found out, it
further weakened support of the war. By late 1969
more than half of Americans were against the war. In
1971 the *New York Times* published the **Pentagon
Papers**. These secret documents showed that the
government had been misleading the American people
for years about the success of the war.

> **Why were the Pentagon Papers important to American democracy?**
> _____
> _____
> _____
> _____

END OF U.S. INVOLVEMENT

In the presidential election of 1972, Nixon's
Democratic challenger was Senator **George
McGovern**. He was openly and strongly against the
war. Many of his supporters were young people,
especially since the ratification of the **Twenty-sixth
Amendment**. It lowered the voting age from 21 to 18.
A week before the election, Kissinger announced
"Peace is at hand," and Nixon won the election by a
landslide. In January 1973 the peace deal was signed.

> **What was McGovern's position about Vietnam?**
> _____
> _____
> _____

THE LEGACY OF VIETNAM

In 1975 North Vietnam conquered South Vietnam and
set up a Communist government. That same year
Communist forces called the **Khmer Rouge** took over
Cambodia. They killed 1.5 million people. Vietnam
invaded Cambodia in 1979 to get rid of the Khmer
Rouge and stayed until 1989. The Vietnam War killed
over 1.5 million Vietnamese. It devastated the
environment. About 58,000 Americans were killed
and about 300,000 wounded, many seriously. The war
cost $150 billion. It caused many Americans to
mistrust their government. Congress passed the **War
Powers Act** in 1973. The act limits the president's
ability to make war.

> **What were the results of the Vietnam War for the Vietnamese? Did America win the war?**
> _____
> _____
> _____
> _____

CHALLENGE ACTIVITY

Critical Thinking: Cause and Effect The U.S. government spent $150
billion on the Vietnam War. Do some research to find out about the
American economy and what effect the war spending had.

A Time of Social Change

Chapter Summary

| 1961 Declaration of Indian Purpose is issued | 1965 The Delano grape strike begins | 1969 Woodstock Music and Art Fair is held in Bethel, New York | 1972 Passage of the ERA in Congress |
| | 1968 AIM is founded | | |

| **1960** | **1963** | **1966** | **1969** | **1972** |

| 1963 Publication of Betty Friedan's *The Feminine Mystique* | 1966 NOW is founded | 1967 José Angel Gutiérrez and other students form MAYO | 1970 La Raza Unida wins elections in several Texas cities |

COMPREHENSION AND CRITICAL THINKING

Use information from the graphic organizer to answer the following questions.

1. **Recall** Who wrote *The Feminine Mystique?*

_____

2. **Identify** When did the Delano grape strike begin?

_____

3 **Analyze** How many years after *The Feminine Mystique* was published was NOW founded? How many years after that did the ERA pass?

_____

A Time of Social Change

MAIN IDEA
In the 1960s women and Native Americans struggled to achieve social justice.

Key Terms and People

Betty Friedan author of *The Feminine Mystique*; first president of NOW

feminism belief that women and men should be socially, politically, and economically equal to men

National Organization for Women (NOW); women's rights group

Equal Rights Amendment proposed amendment to the Constitution to guarantee women equal rights with men

Phyllis Schlafly opponent of the Equal Rights Amendment

Roe v. *Wade* the Supreme Court case that ruled women had the right to abortion

American Indian Movement (AIM); Native Americans' rights group

Russell Means leader of American Indian Movement

Section Summary

REVIVAL OF THE WOMEN'S MOVEMENT

By 1963 one-third of American workers were women. However, on average they earned about 60 percent of what men earned. At that time it was common to think that women belonged in the home. **Betty Friedan** surveyed women who had graduated from college. Most were not satisfied with their lives as homemakers. In 1963 she wrote a book called *The Feminine Mystique*. The book started a debate about women's roles. Women formed discussion groups called consciousness-raising sessions.

> Circle the title of the book that sparked debate over women's roles.

THE WOMEN'S LIBERATION MOVEMENT

In the late 1960s and 1970s, the movement for women's rights grew. Its core belief was **feminism**. This is the conviction that women and men should be socially, politically, and economically equal. The **National Organization for Women**, or NOW, was formed. Members lobbied government and filed lawsuits in favor of women's rights. They campaigned for the **Equal Rights Amendment**. It would put equal rights for women into the Constitution. Opponents

> What is the core belief of the women's rights movement?
>
> _____

such as **Phyllis Schlafly** kept it from being ratified. The women's movement helped women earn more money and land better jobs. Some women campaigned for abortion rights. In a 1973 case called *Roe v. Wade*, the Supreme Court ruled that state laws banning abortion were illegal.

How did the women's movement help women? _____ _____

THE LIVES OF NATIVE AMERICANS

Many Native American tribes suffered hardships. These included high rates of unemployment, poverty, disease, and alcoholism. The government tried to improve Native American life with the policy of termination. This was designed to cut the ties between the federal government and Native Americans. All it did was cut services and relocate 200,000 Native Americans to cities. D'Arcy McNickle wrote the Declaration of Indian Purpose to protest termination and state Native American goals.

Underline the hardships faced by Native American tribes.

NATIVE AMERICANS FIGHT FOR FAIRNESS

In 1969 a group of Native Americans occupied Alcatraz Island as a protest against the termination policy. It inspired the **American Indian Movement** (AIM), which called for a renewal of Indian cultures and recognition of Native Americans' rights. One of the movement's leaders, **Russell Means**, discussed the importance of AIM in a television show in 2002. AIM sometimes used strong tactics. They marched on Washington and took over the Bureau of Indian Affairs. They occupied Wounded Knee, South Dakota. The occupation ended violently. Other organizations also focused on Native American needs. The National Indian Education Association fought to improve education for Native Americans. The Native American Rights Fund provided legal services. Congress in the 1970s passed laws to enhance education, health care, voting rights, and religious freedom for Native Americans.

What were the tactics used by AIM? _____ _____ _____

CHALLENGE ACTIVITY

Critical Thinking: Analyze Study the incident at Wounded Knee in 1890. Write a brief summary. Why was this place important to AIM?

MAIN IDEA
In the 1960s Latinos struggled to achieve social justice.

Key Terms and People

social justice the fair distribution of advantages and disadvantages in society

César Chávez leader of the National Farm Workers Association

Chicano a shortened form of *Mexicano*; expresses ethnic pride

Rodolfo "Corky" Gonzales leading figure in Chicano movement

José Angel Gutiérrez founder of Mexican American Youth Organization

La Raza Unida Party political party for Latinos

boricua term that Puerto Ricans use for themselves expressing ethnic pride

Section Summary

THE LIVES OF LATINOS

Latino is a term for people of Latin American descent.
Hispanic means all Spanish-speaking people. By 1960
one-third of Mexican American families lived below
the poverty line. Twice as many Mexican Americans
as white Americans were unemployed. Latinos did not
have the same educational opportunities. State
legislatures drew election districts so as to decrease
Latino power.

> Underline problems that
> Mexican Americans
> encountered.

LAUNCHING THE STRUGGLE FOR SOCIAL JUSTICE

Latinos began to struggle for **social justice**. This is the
fair distribution of advantages and disadvantages in
society. Many migrant agricultural workers were
Latino. They received very low pay and did
backbreaking work. In 1965, farm workers went on
strike in Delano, California. The National Farm
Workers Association joined the strike. **César Chávez**
was one of the leaders. The workers urged consumers
to stop buying grapes to support the strike. The strike
was successful. Chávez became famous for his
commitment to nonviolence and to helping farm
workers.

> Why did agricultural
> workers go on strike?
>
> _____

A Time of Social Change

MOVEMENTS FOR LATINO RIGHTS

Some Mexican Americans called themselves
Chicanos, which is a shortened form of *mexicanos*.
The name carried a meaning of ethnic pride and a
commitment to political activism. Reies López
Tijerina led the Alianza Federal de Mercedes (Federal
Alliance of Land Grants). This organization worked to
regain lands lost by Mexican Americans to the U.S.
government. Other political organizations also began
forming, some more militant than others.

In 1966 **Rodolfo "Corky" Gonzales**, a leader in
the Chicano movement, founded Crusade for Justice, a
group that promoted Mexican American nationalism
and helped the poor. In Texas, **José Angel Gutiérrez**
and other students formed the Mexican American
Youth Organization (MAYO). MAYO organized
school walkouts and mass protests against
discrimination. At Crystal City, students successfully
boycotted the school. They wanted Mexican American
teachers and bilingual education. MAYO helped
improve conditions in many schools.

Gutiérrez went on to found **La Raza Unida Party**,
(RUP). The party called for bilingual education,
improved public services, education for migrant
children, more jobs for bilingual government
employees, and an end to job discrimination. RUP
elected candidates in several cities in Texas. It also
expanded into Colorado and California. In the late
1970s disagreements among the leaders caused RUP
to break up.

One of the most militant organizations in the
Chicano movement was the Brown Berets. They lent
their support to many issues that other groups were
fighting for. They also worked with African American
civil rights groups.

Other Latino groups also struggled for equality.
Boricua is a term that Puerto Ricans use for
themselves and expresses ethnic pride. In the 1950s
and 1960s boricua groups began their struggle for
change.

> What meaning did the word *Chicano* carry?
>
> _____
> _____

> How did Mexican Americans begin to improve their conditions?
>
> _____
> _____
> _____

> Underline the goals of La Raza Unida Party.

CHALLENGE ACTIVITY

Critical Thinking: Elaborate César Chávez became a national figure.
Write a report discussing his strategies and commitment to nonviolence.

Interactive Reader and Study Guide

A Time of Social Change

Section 3

 MAIN IDEA
The counterculture that emerged in the 1960s and 1970s left a lasting impact on American life.

Key Terms and People

counterculture a rebellion of teens and young adults against mainstream American society

Establishment mainstream of American society

Free Speech Movement student movement on campuses to protest injustices

flower children self-descriptive term used by hippies

Summer of Love summer of 1967; height of the hippie movement

pop art new style of art that made use of popular culture themes

Section Summary

RISE OF THE COUNTERCULTURE

The **counterculture** of the 1960s was a rebellion of teens and young adults against mainstream American society. These young Americans were called hippies. They believed that society's values and priorities were wrong. They called the mainstream the **Establishment**.

Because of the baby boom after World War II, there were many more teens in the 1960s than ever before. They blamed their parents' generation for problems such as the threat of nuclear war, racial discrimination, and the Vietnam War. On college campuses, students rebelled against school policies they thought were unjust. In 1964 students at the University of California at Berkeley launched a major protest. It came to a peaceful end. This was the beginning of the **Free Speech Movement**. Across the country, students used civil disobedience to protest injustice.

> **What did hippies believe about mainstream America?**
> _____

> **Why were there so many teens and young adults during the 1960s?**
> _____
> _____

LIFE IN THE COUNTERCULTURE

In the 1960s thousands of teens and young adults left school and jobs for a new way of life. They rejected materialism, that is, owning more and more. Some hippies formed communities in urban areas. The best-known of these was the Haight-Ashbury district in San Francisco. Other hippies formed rural communes. They wanted to build communities based on peace and love. Some hippies believed in Eastern religions such as Buddhism. Others used illegal drugs such as marijuana and LSD, or "acid." Hippies expressed their freedom by wearing casual, colorful clothing. Since they often put flowers in their hair, sometimes they called themselves **flower children**. The height of the hippie movement was the summer of 1967. This was called the **Summer of Love**. Hippies celebrated love and peace. However, the hippie lifestyle sometimes caused problems. Some died from overdoses of drugs. Sometimes the lack of rules led to chaos and violence.

> The hippies were against materialism. What were they for?
> _____
> _____

MAINSTREAM SOCIETY REACTS

Some critics of the counterculture felt that hippies did not live up to their ideals. Others viewed the counterculture as threatening and disrespectful. FBI director J. Edgar Hoover felt it was a serious threat to America. The TV show *All in the Family* expressed both establishment views and counterculture views.

> Underline the name of the TV show that expressed two sides of the issues.

THE COUNTERCULTURE'S LEGACY

Many Americans became more casual in dress and more open-minded. In the arts, people explored topics that had once been forbidden, including sex and violence. A new style of art called **pop art** appealed to popular tastes. It took inspiration from popular culture. The film industry adopted its own rating system. In music, the counterculture was expressed in rock and roll. The Woodstock Music and Art Fair, called simply Woodstock, attracted more than 400,000 people to three days of music and community.

> How did people change as a result of the counterculture?
> _____
> _____
> _____

CHALLENGE ACTIVITY

Critical Thinking: Elaborate How do you think society has progressed since the counterculture days? Did the movement accomplish anything valuable? Write three paragraphs explaining your views.

Name _____ Class _____ Date _____

A Search for Order

Chapter Summary

```
                    ┌─────────────────────┐
                    │  The Search for Order │
                    │      1968–1980       │
                    └─────────────────────┘
```

Nixon's Presidency
- Conservative policies included New Federalism.
- Liberal policies included support for environment, and wage and price controls.
- Seeks détente with the Soviets, dialogue with the Chinese.
- Shuttle diplomacy helped end Yom Kippur War and oil embargo.
- Moon landing a highlight.

Watergate and Ford
- Scandal with roots in 1972 presidential campaign haunted Nixon.
- Nixon eventually forced to resign for lying and covering up White House crime.
- Ford became president, but lost support for pardoning Nixon.

Carter's Presidency
- Elected for honesty and integrity.
- Focused on saving energy.
- Foreign policy built around human rights.
- Helped secure Camp David Accords.
- Response to Soviet actions in Afghanistan and Iran hostage crisis seen as weak.

COMPREHENSION AND CRITICAL THINKING

Use information from the graphic organizer to answer the following questions.

1. **Recall** What were Nixon's liberal policies?

_____

_____

2. **Contrast** How was Carter's presidency different from Nixon's?

_____

_____

3. **Evaluate** Which of the foreign policy issues during this era have had the greatest impact on our lives today?

_____

_____

Interactive Reader and Study Guide

> **MAIN IDEA**
> Beyond the ongoing turmoil of the Vietnam War, the Nixon administration did enjoy some notable success.

Key Terms and People

realpolitik the basing of foreign policies on realistic views of national interest rather than on broad rules or principles

détente policy that eased tensions between Cold War enemies

SALT I talks between the United States and the Soviet Union to limit the building of offensive weapon systems

shuttle diplomacy shuttling from group to group to work out agreements between parties that refuse to meet

OPEC Organization of Petroleum Exporting Countries; a group of many of the oil-producing nations of the world

Apollo 11 NASA flight to the moon and back in July 1969

Neil Armstrong astronaut on *Apollo 11*; first human being to set foot on the moon

Section Summary

NIXON'S POLITICS AND DOMESTIC POLICIES

Richard Nixon was known as a conservative who was strongly anti-Communist. He believed the federal government was too large. He had been in favor of civil rights. However, as president he started a "southern strategy" to get support from those against the civil rights movement. He tried to weaken the 1965 Voting Rights Act. He urged a slowing down of forced integration. He also opposed busing. On the other hand, Nixon's more liberal policies led him to increase funding for food stamps and Social Security payments. He signed the Clean Air Act. He worked to establish the Environmental Protection Agency. He helped create the Occupational Health and Safety Administration. He also encouraged affirmative action, extending it to cover women.

> **What was Nixon's "southern strategy"?**
> _____
> _____
> _____

> **Underline the steps Nixon took to help improve the environment.**

NIXON'S FOREIGN POLICIES

Nixon's national security adviser was Henry Kissinger. Later Kissinger became secretary of state. His policy was called **realpolitik**. This meant basing

A Search for Order

foreign policy on realistic views of what was good for the country rather than on rules or principles.

Nixon took steps to ease tensions with America's Cold War enemy, the Soviet Union. This easier relationship was called **détente**. Nixon held the Strategic Arms Limitation Talks (**SALT I**) with the Soviet Union. These talks aimed at limiting the building of new offensive weapons. Nixon also made a surprising visit to China and met with Chinese leader Mao Zedong. He wanted to ease relations between the two nations.

> **What foreign nation did Nixon visit and why?**
> _____
> _____
> _____

TROUBLE IN THE MIDDLE EAST

Israel had occupied Arab territory since a 1967 war. The United Nations wanted Israel to leave the territories and debated the issue until there was another war in 1973. At that point the Soviet Union offered support to the Arabs. The United States supported the Israelis. To negotiate a ceasefire, Kissinger used **shuttle diplomacy**. This meant traveling back and forth between the parties, since they refused to meet.

During the war, the Arab members of the Organization of Petroleum Exporting Countries (**OPEC**) agreed not to ship oil to the United States and some other countries. This was in response to American support for Israel. The United States depended heavily on OPEC oil. This caused an energy crisis in the United States. There was not enough gasoline or heating oil and prices rose sharply.

> **Why was the OPEC oil embargo damaging to the United States?**
> _____
> _____
> _____

MAJOR EVENTS AT HOME

In July 1969 the *Apollo 11* spacecraft landed on the moon. Astronaut **Neil Armstrong** was the first human to set foot on the moon.

At home, inflation and unemployment were very high. Nixon announced a 90-day freeze on wages and prices. It halted inflation, but only temporarily. The oil crisis would soon send prices higher.

> **Why did Nixon order a freeze on wages and prices?**
> _____
> _____

CHALLENGE ACTIVITY

Critical Thinking: Contrast How did realpolitik and détente differ from containment and brinkmanship? Write two paragraphs of explanation.

A Search for Order

> **MAIN IDEA**
> The Nixon presidency became bogged down in scandal, leading to the first presidential resignation in American history and the administration of Gerald Ford.

Key Terms and People

Watergate scandal scandal involving a break-in at the Watergate

executive privilege policy that holds that the president must be able to keep official conversations and meetings private

Saturday night massacre Nixon's order to fire the special prosecutor, which caused the attorney general and his assistant to resign

transcript a written record of a spoken event

Gerald R. Ford president after Nixon; first person to become president without being elected either president or vice president

Section Summary

THE ELECTION OF 1972

Nixon wanted desperately to win the 1972 election. In the past his supporters had used underhanded tactics. Two of Nixon's advisers created a special group to find out who was giving out secret information and to investigate Nixon's political enemies. This group, called the "Plumbers," broke into Daniel Ellsberg's psychiatrist's office. Ellsberg had given out secret documents about the Vietnam War. The Plumbers were looking for information to embarrass Ellsberg.

During the re-election campaign, Nixon's team sent burglars into the headquarters of the Democratic National Committee. The headquarters were in the Watergate hotel-office complex. The burglars were caught and arrested, but the connection to the president was still unknown. Reporters Bob Woodward and Carl Bernstein began to investigate the burglary. The burglary did not bother voters. Nixon was re-elected by one of the largest majorities in history.

> **Why did the Plumbers want to embarrass Daniel Ellsberg?**
> _____
> _____
> _____

> **Underline the names of the two reporters who investigated the Watergate burglary.**

THE SCANDAL UNFOLDS

Ties to the White House came out during the burglars' trials. People wondered if Nixon had known about the

A Search for Order

wrongdoing and helped hide it. Nixon ordered an investigation of the **Watergate scandal**. His top aides and the attorney general resigned. Then he fired John Dean, the investigating lawyer. Democrats called for Nixon to appoint what is now called a special prosecutor, an investigator who is not part of the administration. Archibald Cox was appointed.

Meanwhile, the Senate began its own investigation. It found that Nixon had taped his conversations. To get the tapes, Cox issued a subpoena, a legal order requiring a person to bring something to court. Nixon claimed the tapes were secret because of **executive privilege**, the president's right to keep official conversations and meetings private. He also responded by ordering the attorney general to fire Cox. The attorney general refused and resigned, as did his assistant. Cox was eventually fired, ending what is called the **Saturday night massacre**. But the nation now questioned Nixon's honesty. Nixon released a **transcript** of some of the tapes. This written record of spoken events, however, did not prevent a probable impeachment. Facing this, Nixon resigned.

> **Why did Democrats want Nixon to appoint a special prosecutor?**
> _____
> _____
> _____

> **What did Nixon not want to release to the special prosecutor?**
> _____

GERALD FORD'S PRESIDENCY

Nixon's original vice president, Spiro T. Agnew, had resigned in disgrace. Nixon chose the Republican leader of the House, **Gerald R. Ford**, to be vice president. When Nixon resigned, Ford became president. Ford granted Nixon a full pardon, or formal, legal forgiveness for a crime. The public was outraged. In office, Ford tried to slow inflation by reducing government spending. Congress refused to let Ford aid South Vietnam or to step in against Communists in Angola. At election time, Ford won the Republican nomination only after a struggle.

> **How did Ford outrage the American public?**
> _____
> _____

CHALLENGE ACTIVITY

Critical Thinking: Elaborate Watch and give a report on the movie *All the President's Men*, about reporters Woodward and Bernstein's investigation of these events. The movie is based on their book.

A Search for Order

 MAIN IDEA
Jimmy Carter used his reputation for honesty to win the presidency in 1976, but he soon met challenges that required other qualities as well.

Key Terms and People

James Earl "Jimmy" Carter president of the United States from 1977 to 1981

SALT II treaty between the United States and the Soviet Union that called for limits on certain kinds of nuclear weapons

Camp David Accords peace agreement between Israel and Egypt, guided by Jimmy Carter

Ayatollah Ruholla Khomeini Islamic religious leader who came to political power in Iran after the shah was overthrown

Section Summary

CHALLENGES FACING THE NATION

James Earl "Jimmy" Carter won the presidency in 1976. He appealed to voters as a trustworthy, honest man. One of his first actions in office was to pardon thousands of American men who had avoided the draft during the Vietnam War. Inflation and unemployment were high. Carter worked to create new jobs. However, he was unable to bring down inflation. He developed a national energy policy and urged Americans to conserve energy. He pushed automakers to build more energy-efficient cars. Carter promoted other kinds of energy besides oil, such as wind and solar power. Carter was also concerned about the environment and faced two environmental crises. At a nuclear power plant at Three Mile Island an accident threatened to leak radiation and some nearby people were evacuated. At Love Canal buried chemicals seeped up through the ground and caused birth defects in the community.

> **Why did Carter appeal to voters?**
> _____
> _____

> **Underline the ways in which Carter dealt with the problem of finding enough energy to supply the country's needs.**

CARTER'S FOREIGN POLICY

Jimmy Carter had no real foreign-policy experience and brought new ideas and people to Washington. His ambassador to the United Nations was Andrew Young, whose background was in the civil rights

A Search for Order

movement. Carter appointed many African Americans, women, and Hispanic Americans to office. He was committed to human rights and tried to tie his foreign policies to them. In 1979 the United States and the Soviet Union signed **SALT II**. This treaty limited certain kinds of nuclear weapons. Carter also agreed to give Panama control of the Panama Canal in 1999, ending conflict between the countries. He formally recognized the government of the Communist People's Republic of China. His greatest foreign policy achievement was the **Camp David Accords**. Carter invited the leaders of Israel and Egypt, which had long been enemies, to the presidential retreat at Camp David, Maryland. There he guided them to a peace agreement.

> How did Jimmy Carter's concern for human rights show itself in his actions?
>
> _____
> _____
> _____
> _____
> _____

INTERNATIONAL CRISES

In 1979 the Soviets invaded Afghanistan to support a new pro-Soviet government. Carter responded by blocking grain shipments to the Soviets and withdrawing U.S. participation from the 1980 Moscow Olympics. In some ways these responses hurt the United States, for they made the country appear weak. In 1979 the Iranians overthrew their leader, known as the shah. Among Iranians he had a reputation for cruel repression. The United States had supported the shah. A religious leader, **Ayatollah Ruholla Khomeini**, took power. When the American government allowed the shah to come to the United States for cancer treatment, Iranians were angry. A mob attacked the American embassy and dozens of Americans were captured. They were held hostage for more than a year. Carter was unable to end the hostage crisis. In one speech, Carter said the United States faced a crisis in confidence. He was right. Many Americans blamed him for the crisis.

> Why did Iranians attack the embassy and take Americans hostage?
>
> _____
> _____
> _____

CHALLENGE ACTIVITY

Critical Thinking: Analyze Carter won passage of several energy and environmental laws. Yet we still depend on foreign oil and produce air pollution. Write three paragraphs on why these problems still exist.

A Conservative Era

Chapter Summary

Reagan's First Term
- Under President Reagan, people have renewed confidence in America
- Conservative policies begin, such as smaller government and increased defense spending
- Supply-side economics, lower taxes, and big deficits occur

Reagan's Foreign Policy
- Soviet Union becomes a partner in arms control
- Staunch anti-communism leads to Granada invasion, Iran-Contra scandal

A Conservative Era

The New World Order
- George H. W. Bush becomes president
- Soviet empire collapses, although China remains Communist
- "New world order" proves dangerous, as United States goes to war with Iraq

Life in the 1980s
- Good economic times, though not for all
- Social issues divide society and lead to Supreme Court battles

COMPREHENSION AND CRITICAL THINKING

Use information from the graphic organizer to answer the following questions.

1. **Recall** List two examples of Reagan's conservative policies.

   _____

   _____

2. **Contrast** How did the relationship between the United States and the Soviet Union change under Reagan?

   _____

   _____

3. **Analyze** After the Soviet Union collapsed a "New World Order" was proclaimed. Was it any safer than the old one? Why or why not?

   _____

   _____

A Conservative Era

MAIN IDEA
In 1980 Americans voted for a new approach to governing by electing Ronald Reagan, who powerfully promoted a conservative agenda.

Key Terms and People

Ronald Reagan president of the United States from 1981 to 1989

New Right collection of thinkers, writers, research companies, and Christian groups who wanted to return to conservative values

Jerry Falwell television preacher who was a leader of the New Right

Nancy Reagan First Lady who headed the "Just Say No" antidrug program

David A. Stockman Reagan's budget director who later disagreed with Reagan's economics

supply-side economics Reagan's economic theory

budget deficit when the government spends more money than it takes in

Section Summary

A NATION READY FOR CHANGE

After the changes in American society in the 1960s and the government scandals in the 1970s, the nation seemed depressed and uneasy. In a 1979 speech, President Carter called it America's "crisis of confidence." However, 1980 presidential candidate **Ronald Reagan** seemed to be cheerful about the future. He said the country needed to return to a simpler time. He wanted lower taxes, smaller government, and a stronger military. He had conservative values. The conservative movement was against abortion, school integration, welfare, and affirmative action. Many people agreed with the movement and Reagan won the 1980 election.

> **How did Ronald Reagan appeal to voters?**
> _____
> _____
> _____
> _____
> _____
> _____

THE REAGAN REVOLUTION

Reagan became the hero of a growing movement called the **New Right**. It was a collection of conservative thinkers and writers, research companies (called think tanks), and Christian groups. One of its leaders was television preacher **Jerry Falwell**. The

> **Underline the groups that belonged to the New Right.**

New Right wanted prayer in schools. It wanted tax cuts and a smaller government. It wanted a stronger military. It did not want gun control laws or abortion. It was against gay rights and school busing to achieve desegregation. It did not want the Equal Rights Amendment or affirmative action. It wanted to turn back liberal policies in government, the economy, and social programs.

> Underline the policies favored by the New Right. Circle the things it was against.

Reagan was a good speaker. He had been a movie actor before going into politics. He was called the Great Communicator. In his first few months as president, he convinced Congress to cut taxes and social programs. He cut the budgets of many federal agencies. He passed the biggest peace-time increase in the defense budget. When 13,000 air traffic controllers went on strike, Reagan fired all of them. His wife, First Lady **Nancy Reagan**, started an antidrug program called "Just Say No."

> List four of Reagan's accomplishments in his first few months in office.
>
> _____
> _____
> _____
> _____

REAGAN'S ECONOMIC PLAN

Reagan's economic plan was called Reaganomics. The budget director, **David A. Stockman**, convinced Congress that tax cuts for wealthy Americans and businesses would give them more money, and that money would eventually "trickle down" to all levels of society. This was called **supply-side economics**. Stockman later rejected the plan. Critics said the tax breaks would only make the rich richer. The tax cuts, together with increased military spending, produced a huge **budget deficit**. This is when the government spends more than it takes in. In 1981 and 1982 the nation had the worst economy since the Depression. Congress was forced to pass the Balanced Budget and Emergency Deficit Control Act. It required budget cuts. In 1983 the economy began to quickly improve. However, this growth mostly helped the wealthy.

> Who benefited most from supply-side economics?
>
> _____

CHALLENGE ACTIVITY

Critical Thinking: Draw Conclusions Many of the things the New Right stood for are still debated today. Choose one issue and write three paragraphs explaining what you think about it. Discuss whether the groups on your side of the issue have made their case well.

A Conservative Era

MAIN IDEA
President Reagan took a hard line against communism around the world.

Key Terms and People

Strategic Defense Initiative Reagan's plan to use space weapons to protect the United States from Soviet missiles

Lech Walesa union leader in Poland; founder of Solidarity

Solidarity independent union that became a freedom movement in Poland

Mikhail Gorbachev leader of the Soviet Union who came to power in 1985

INF Treaty Intermediate Nuclear Forces treaty; first treaty to actually reduce nuclear arms

apartheid South Africa's official policy of extreme racial segregation

Iran-Contra affair scandal involving Reagan staff members who disobeyed Congress to support anti-Communists in Nicaraguan civil war

Oliver North military man who helped run the Iran-Contra affair and took the blame

Section Summary

REAGAN AND THE COLD WAR

President Reagan broke from the previous U.S. policy to leave the Soviet Union as it was and try to get along with it. He wanted to destroy communism. He called the Soviet Union an "evil empire." He increased U.S. military spending by about $100 billion to add thousands more nuclear weapons. New nuclear missiles were put in Europe. Reagan wanted to create a system of space weapons to keep out any missiles that might come from the Soviet Union. This was called the **Strategic Defense Initiative**. Some people were against the plan. They said it would not work and would cost too much.

> What was the "evil empire"?
> _____

The Soviet Union weakened. Its economy was not managed well. It was inefficient. In Poland, **Lech Walesa** led a huge strike. His union became the freedom movement called **Solidarity**. **Mikhail Gorbachev** became the head of the Soviet Union. Reagan met with him to talk about nuclear weapons cuts. They agreed to the **INF Treaty**, which ordered many nuclear weapons destroyed.

> Underline two factors that led to the weakening of the Soviet Union.

A Conservative Era

TROUBLE SPOTS ABROAD

Reagan tried to stop communism in the Americas. He supported a moderate leader in the civil war in El Salvador. In Nicaragua, a rebel group supported by Cuba overthrew the country's dictator. Reagan cut off aid to that country because of the rebels' Communist beliefs. In 1981 he approved $20 million for the CIA to set up a group to fight the rebels. The group was called the Contras. When Congress found out that the CIA was conducting secret operations to help the Contras, it banned all U.S. support for them. Still, Reagan told his staff to find a way to help the Contras.

A debate began about the role of the U.S. military in troubled parts of the world. In 1983 U.S. Marines joined an international peacekeeping force to calm the situation in Lebanon. However, a suicide bomber destroyed a barracks and killed 241 U.S. soldiers. Reagan withdrew the troops from Lebanon.

In South Africa, the government's policy was called **apartheid**. This was extreme racial segregation. While some urged the removal of U.S. investments there, Reagan tried to work with and reform the government there.

> **Why did Reagan approve millions of dollars for the Contras?**
> _____
> _____

> **Why did Congress ban U.S. support for the Contras?**
> _____
> _____
> _____

THE IRAN-CONTRA AFFAIR

In 1985 Reagan agreed to sell arms to Iran in order to get some U.S. hostages released in Lebanon. This was against U.S. policy of not selling arms to Iran or negotiating with terrorists. The **Iran-Contra affair** unfolded when members of the National Security Council, including **Oliver North**, secretly gave the money from the arms sales to the Contras. When the scheme was revealed in 1986, Reagan admitted approving the arms sales but said he didn't know the funds were given to the Contras. The full details are not known because many key documents were destroyed and members of Reagan's staff lied to Congress.

> **Why are the full details of the Iran-Contra affair not known?**
> _____
> _____
> _____

CHALLENGE ACTIVITY

Critical Thinking: Draw Conclusions Investigate and write a report on the Iran-Contra affair. Include your own conclusion as to how much President Reagan was involved and provide support for your conclusion.

Interactive Reader and Study Guide

A Conservative Era

MAIN IDEA
In 1988 Reagan's vice president, George H. W. Bush, won election to a term that saw dramatic changes in the world.

Key Terms and People

George H. W. Bush president of the United States from 1989 to 1993

glasnost allowing more openness in Soviet society

perestroika restructuring the Soviet government and economy

velvet revolution nonviolent revolution in Czechoslovakia that removed the Communists from power

Boris Yeltsin leader of the Russian Republic

Tiananmen Square massacre killing of hundreds of protesters in China

Saddam Hussein dictator of Iraq who invaded Kuwait

Operation Desert Storm war to drive Iraq out of Kuwait

Nelson Mandela political prisoner in South Africa; first president under non-apartheid elections

Section Summary

THE ELECTION OF 1988

George H. W. Bush, vice president during the Reagan years, was chosen as the Republicans' presidential candidate for the 1988 election. African American civil rights leader Jesse Jackson ran to be the Democratic candidate. In the end, however, Governor Michael Dukakis of Massachusetts was chosen. Voter turnout was low, in part because people disliked the bad things the candidates said about each other. Bush won, however, after promising "no new taxes."

> Circle the name of the African American who ran for the Democratic presidential nomination in 1988.

THE OPENING OF THE USSR

As the Soviet system weakened, Soviet leader Mikhail Gorbachev announced a new policy of openness. It was called *glasnost*. At last people were allowed to say what they wanted to about the government. Gorbachev also began trying to change the way the government worked. This was called *perestroika*. He also worked to improve the economy. In 1989 he

> What new Soviet policy allowed criticism of the government?
>
> _____

Interactive Reader and Study Guide

A Conservative Era

allowed the first free elections in the USSR since 1917.

In 1986, however, the Soviets tried to cover up an accident at a nuclear power plant in Chernobyl, near Kiev, the capital of the Ukraine. As the deadly radiation drifted across Europe, the truth came out. The accident caused death and illness and the site is still not safe.

> **What happened at Chernobyl?**
> _____
> _____

THE SOVIET EMPIRE COLLAPSES

The USSR could not afford to keep troops in Eastern Europe. The countries of Eastern Europe jumped at the chance for freedom. Like Czechoslovakia in its nonviolent **velvet revolution**, they got rid of their Communist governments. The Berlin Wall was torn down, and in 1990 East and West Germany reunited. In the Soviet Union, Gorbachev was about to allow partial freedom to the Soviet republics when old-style Communists tried to overthrow him. He was rescued by **Boris Yeltsin**, the leader of the Russian Republic. Yeltsin led a revolt and the Communists failed. The 14 non-Russian republics declared independence, and the USSR was gone.

> **Why do you think the change of government in Czechoslovakia was called a "velvet revolution?"**
> _____

OTHER BUSH-ERA CONFLICTS

With democracy on the rise, many people joined a large protest in Beijing, China, for democracy there, too. In the **Tiananmen Square massacre**, Chinese tanks killed hundreds of protesters.

In 1990 Iraq's dictator, **Saddam Hussein**, invaded Kuwait. The U.S.-led **Operation Desert Storm** freed Kuwait. South Africa also worked towards democracy. In 1994 **Nelson Mandela**, a black political prisoner, was elected president and apartheid ended.

> **Who was the first black president of South Africa?**
> _____

CHALLENGE ACTIVITY

Critical Thinking: Describe The Iraqi army caused a lot of harm to the environment in Kuwait by setting fire to oil wells. Conduct research on this event and describe it while showing pictures of it to your classmates.

Interactive Reader and Study Guide

A Conservative Era

MAIN IDEA
The 1980s and early 1990s saw major technological, economic, and social changes that produced both progress and intense conflicts.

Key Terms and People

Steve Jobs inventor and founder of Apple Computer

Bill Gates inventor and founder of software company Microsoft

space shuttle first spacecraft to be able to go into space, return to Earth, and be reused for more space flights

Alan Greenspan chairman of the Federal Reserve Board

savings and loan crisis many savings and loans went bankrupt from making bad loans

Sandra Day O'Connor first woman Supreme Court Justice

Clarence Thomas Supreme Court Justice who was accused of sexual harassment

Section Summary

THE SPACE SHUTTLE BLASTS OFF

The 1980s saw great advances in technology. The computer revolution brought computers to the home and workplace. **Steve Jobs** started Apple Computer and made the first personal computer. **Bill Gates** started Microsoft and made computers easier to use with his software. The 1980s also changed space travel. Using rocket power, previous spaceships could only be used once. In 1981 the first **space shuttle** took off. It could fly into space, return to Earth, and be reused again. In 1986, however, the space shuttle *Challenger* exploded after liftoff. After more research, shuttle flights resumed.

> Underline the two entrepreneurs who started the computer revolution.

THE ECONOMY OF THE 1980S

The gross domestic product, or GDP, is the value of goods and services produced by the nation. From 1982 to 1989 GDP grew at an average of 3.5 percent. This was the longest period of U.S. peacetime economic growth up to that time. Inflation and unemployment stayed low. On the other hand, not everyone benefited from the strong economic growth, especially farmers. The recession of 1982–83 hit many businesses hard, and many people lost their jobs and homes. The

> Who did not benefit from the strong economic growth in the 1980s?

Interactive Reader and Study Guide

budget deficit nearly tripled. The national debt grew to more than four times its size in 1980. To prevent inflation or further recession **Alan Greenspan**, the chairman of the Federal Reserve Board, took a more active role in managing the money supply.

One of Reagan's economic policies was to have fewer government regulations for businesses. The savings and loan industry made too many loans. When the economy weakened, people could not pay back their loans creating the **savings and loan crisis**. This cost taxpayers about $152 billion. In addition, a recession that began in late 1990 forced President Bush to break his promise of "no new taxes."

> **Why did the Federal Reserve Board take a more active role in managing the money supply?**
> _____
> _____

CHANGES AND CHALLENGES IN AMERICAN SOCIETY

During the 1980s women began to vote in greater numbers, sometimes more than men. Politicians began to pay attention to what women wanted. President Reagan appointed **Sandra Day O'Connor** to become the first woman on the Supreme Court. Later, President Bush appointed **Clarence Thomas** to the Court. He finally was allowed to join the Court after defending himself against charges of sexually harassing a woman he used to work with.

> **Why was the appointment of Sandra Day O'Connor to the Supreme Court important?**
> _____
> _____
> _____

Court rulings during the Reagan and Bush years also showed the divide between the country's liberals and conservatives. Many of these cases had to do with how much power the government had to enter people's private lives.

The early 1980s also saw the first cases of AIDS, as thousands died and doctors could do nothing. Gradually much was learned about it and the virus that caused it—the human immunodeficiency virus (HIV). Doctors found that the virus is spread through body fluids. Millions of men and women around the world now have AIDS.

CHALLENGE ACTIVITY

Critical Thinking: Design By choosing Supreme Court judges who share their beliefs, presidents can make their policies last. Write a profile of the person you would select if you wanted your ideas to influence the Court.

Into the Twenty-First Century

Chapter Summary

The Clinton Administration
- Welfare reform was achieved, but health-care reform was not.
- The nation was drawn into conflicts in Somalia, Haiti, and the former Yugoslavia.
- Despite impeachment, President Clinton completed his two terms.

Terrorism and War
- The attacks of September 11, 2001, shifted national focus to terrorism.
- In the war on terror, the United States attacked Afghanistan and Iraq.
- The United States created the Department of Homeland Security and passed new laws to fight terrorism.

The 1990s and Beyond

The Bush Administration
- President Bush won a controversial election in 2000 and re-election in 2004.
- His domestic policy focused on tax cuts, education, and Medicare reform.
- His foreign policy was dominated by response to the terrorist attacks of September 11, 2001.

Looking Ahead
The twenty-first century should bring:
- demographic changes — greater diversity and an aging population.
- technological changes in communication, medicine, agriculture, and space exploration.
- challenges in health care, energy, and the environment.

COMPREHENSION AND CRITICAL THINKING

Use information from the graphic organizer to answer the following questions.

1. **Recall** Whose presidency was marked by impeachment?

_____

2. **Identify** Which two countries did the United States attack as part of the war on terror?

_____

3. **Predict** Make two predictions about what the twenty-first century will bring in health care and defense.

_____

MAIN IDEA
Bill Clinton was a new type of Democrat, and his administration faced challenges for a new millennium—and scandals as old as politics.

Key Terms and People

Bill Clinton U.S. president from 1993 to 2001

Hillary Rodham Clinton Clinton's First Lady, and a lawyer and politician in her own right

Al Gore vice president under Clinton

Contract with America program many Republicans campaigned with in 1994

terrorism the use of violence by individuals or small groups to advance political goals

NAFTA North American Free Trade Agreement; trade treaty between the United States, Canada, and Mexico

Section Summary

BILL CLINTON'S POLITICAL RISE

Bill Clinton was the nation's youngest governor at age 32. As a centrist he was a new kind of Democrat; not as conservative in his views as many Republicans and not as liberal in his views as many Democrats. Clinton was the Democratic candidate for president in 1992. He said the country needed a national health-care plan and tax cuts for the middle class. His wife, **Hillary Rodham Clinton**, was one of the top lawyers in the country. Clinton made it clear that he would use her skill and guidance. He chose Senator **Al Gore** as his vice president. Clinton won the election.

> **What is a centrist?**
> _____
> _____

DOMESTIC POLICY ISSUES

Because of the huge budget deficit, Clinton was forced to raise taxes instead of cutting them. Republicans criticized him, but in 1993 the country prospered. The nation had a long period of low unemployment and interest rates. Clinton proposed a major new health-care plan but it was defeated. The taxes and the failed health-care plan helped the Republicans win many seats in Congress in 1994. They campaigned with a document they called the **Contract with America**. It was a plan to balance the budget, fight crime, and cut taxes. It included welfare

> **Why couldn't Clinton cut taxes?**
> _____
> _____

> **What three things helped the Republicans win many seats in Congress in 1994?**
> _____
> _____
> _____

reform. Clinton proposed a different welfare-reform program, and it passed in 1996. Clinton also helped the country cope with tragedy after a terrorist attack in Oklahoma City. **Terrorism** is the use of violence by individuals or groups to advance political goals.

FOREIGN POLICY CHALLENGES

One of the high points of Clinton's first term was his White House ceremony in which Israel and the Palestinians signed a peace agreement called the Oslo Accords. Although much of the plan was not carried out, it set the stage for more peace talks.

Clinton was also heavily involved in stopping the wars in the former Yugoslavia. The ethnic groups that had been held together by a dictator now fought each other for independence. In 1995 he helped end the fighting in Bosnia-Herzegovina with the Dayton Accords. In 1999 he urged NATO to act in Serbia. NATO actions stopped the Serbian army from forcing ethnic Albanians out of the province of Kosovo.

Clinton promoted international trade by getting Congress to pass **NAFTA**, the North American Free Trade Agreement. It made Canada, the United States, and Mexico one large free-trade zone. Some people thought that Americans would lose jobs because of it.

> What are three accomplishments of President Clinton's foreign policy?
>
> _____
>
> _____
>
> _____
>
> _____
>
> _____

SCANDAL AND IMPEACHMENT

During his first term as president, Clinton faced an investigation about a property investment he and his wife made in the 1970s. No charges were brought against him. He was also investigated for sexual harassment of a female state employee while he was governor. Information came out about an improper relationship with a 21-year-old White House worker and this, too, was investigated. The House of Representatives voted to impeach Clinton. The Senate did not have enough votes to remove him from office.

> Underline the three things Clinton was investigated for.

CHALLENGE ACTIVITY

Critical Thinking: Evaluate Many people were worried that NAFTA would be bad for the U.S. economy. Write a report on what happened after NAFTA was passed.

Into the Twenty-First Century

MAIN IDEA
Following a troubled election, Republican George W. Bush won the White House and strongly promoted his agenda.

Key Terms and People

budget surplus when the government takes in more money than it spends

George W. Bush elected president in 2000 and 2004

Bush v. Gore Supreme Court case that decided in favor of Bush in the 2000 election

dot-com pioneer Internet companies

dividend a payment companies sometimes make to their stockholders

Condoleezza Rice national security adviser for Bush

Donald Rumsfeld secretary of defense for Bush

Section Summary

THE ELECTION OF 2000

The election of 2000 was one of the closest in U.S. history. Under Clinton, the economy had done well. The government had a **budget surplus**. This meant that the government was taking in more money than it spent. But Clinton's administration had faced scandals. Vice President Al Gore was the Democratic candidate in 2000. He tried to distance himself from Clinton's scandals. However, he wanted to take credit for some of the presidency's successes. **George W. Bush** had been governor of Texas. He was the Republican candidate. The election was very close. Whoever won in Florida would be president.

Bush had a tiny lead. The votes were recounted by machine. Democrats saw problems in the way the machines read the ballots and asked for a recount by hand. The Republicans did not want recounts. There were lawsuits back and forth. The case of **Bush v. Gore** went to the Supreme Court. The Court ruled in favor of Bush and against recounts. It said there were no clear standards for counting by hand. Bush became only the fourth person in U.S. history to have won the presidency in spite of having received fewer popular votes than his opponent.

> Did Clinton leave the country with a budget deficit or a budget surplus? What does this say about the economy at this time?
>
> _____
> _____
> _____
> _____

> Which state did the outcome of the 2000 election depend on?
>
> _____

Into the Twenty-First Century

BUSH'S DOMESTIC POLICY

The economy had begun to weaken when Bush took office. During the 1990s there were many new Internet companies. Many of these companies, called **dot-coms**, began to fail. Scandals also hit some large corporations, causing stock prices to fall.

Bush had promised tax cuts. He argued this would strengthen the economy. The Republican-controlled Congress passed the cuts. The economy did not improve. Instead it went into recession, a long slowing of business activity. In 2003 Bush pushed for tax cuts on **dividends**. These are payments that companies sometimes make to stockholders.

Bush tried to improve education. In 2001 his No Child Left Behind Act went into effect. It directed states to develop academic standards and to test students yearly to make sure they were meeting the standards. In 2003 he added a new benefit to help those using Medicare to afford prescriptions.

In 2004 Bush ran for re-election against Democratic senator John Kerry. Kerry criticized Bush's handling of the economy, but Bush won in another close election.

> **What did Bush think would strengthen the economy? Did it?**
> _____
> _____
> _____

> **Underline the two goals of the No Child Left Behind Act.**

BUSH'S FOREIGN POLICY

When Bush took office in 2001, he chose Colin Powell as secretary of state. He named **Condoleezza Rice** as national security adviser. He appointed **Donald Rumsfeld** as secretary of defense. When Bush was re-elected, Condoleezza Rice became secretary of state after Colin Powell resigned.

After a review of the armed forces, Bush cancelled the 1972 Anti-Ballistic Missile Treaty because Russia was no longer a nuclear threat. Instead, Bush planned to develop a missile defense system against terrorist states. Bush promoted the Middle East peace plan called the road map. The events of September 11, 2001, greatly affected Bush's foreign policy.

> **Circle the name of the person who became secretary of state in Bush's second term.**

CHALLENGE ACTIVITY

Critical Thinking: Elaborate Investigate how the peace process is going in the Middle East. Has progress been made on the road map? Report to your classmates.

MAIN IDEA
A horrific attack on September 11, 2001, awakened the nation to the threat of terrorism and changed America's view of the world.

Key Terms and People

9/11 date of massive terrorist attacks against the United States

Rudolph Giuliani mayor of New York during 9/11

Osama bin Laden terrorist believed to have planned the 9/11 attacks

al Qaeda bin Laden's terrorist network

Taliban strict Islamic government of Afghanistan; supported terrorists

Department of Homeland Security cabinet-level organization formed after 9/11

USA PATRIOT Act law that made it easier for law enforcement agencies to secretly collect information about suspected terrorists

Section Summary

SEPTEMBER 11, 2001

On September 11, 2001, two airplanes crashed into the Twin Towers of the World Trade Center in New York City. The towers started to burn. Police and firefighters rushed into the building. Then the towers collapsed. Meanwhile, another airplane crashed into the Pentagon. There was a fourth crash in the Pennsylvania countryside. Nearly 3,000 people died in all. The events of **9/11** made the nation sad and angry. People were also proud of the heroism of the rescue workers. They admired the leadership of **Rudolph Giuliani**, the mayor of New York. Americans donated to blood banks and gave millions of dollars to charities. Patriotic feelings soared.

> **What happened on September 11, 2001?**
> _____
> _____
> _____
> _____

BACKGROUND TO THE ATTACKS

Investigators found out that a terrorist named **Osama bin Laden** had planned the attacks. He was a wealthy Saudi Arabian. His goal was a worldwide Islamic revolution. He claimed this required the destruction of United States.

Bin Laden formed a worldwide terrorist group called **al Qaeda**. It participated in several terrorist attacks. Bin Laden had links to a 1993 bombing at the

> **Who was Osama bin Laden?**
> _____
> _____
> _____

Into the Twenty-First Century

Section 3

World Trade Center. In 1998 al Qaeda was behind the attack on U.S. embassies in Africa. In early 2000 terrorists enrolled in U.S. flight schools to learn how to fly airliners. On September 11, 2001, they boarded as passengers, took over the planes, and then flew them into the buildings.

THE UNITED STATES RESPONDS

President Bush blamed not only the terrorists but also the countries that allowed them to live and train there. In Afghanistan a group called the **Taliban** had taken over. They governed according to very strict Islamic law. Women were not allowed to go to school or leave their homes without a male relative.

> How did the Taliban treat women?
> _____
> _____
> _____

The Taliban supported bin Laden. In October 2001 the United States and Great Britain attacked Afghanistan. The Taliban were defeated quickly. However, bin Laden was not found.

At home in the United States, the **Department of Homeland Security** was created. This was a cabinet-level organization formed to fight terrorism at home. The **USA PATRIOT Act** was passed. This law made it easier for law-enforcement agencies to secretly collect information about suspected terrorists.

WAR IN IRAQ

After the 1991 Gulf War, Iraq had agreed to destroy its weapons of mass destruction. The UN put weapons inspectors there to make sure they did this. Each year, Iraq's leader, Saddam Hussein, became less cooperative. The UN removed its inspectors from Iraq in 1998. Bush thought that Hussein was a terrorist threat. Along with Great Britain and several other countries, the United States attacked Iraq in March 2003. Saddam's regime quickly fell. Rebuilding Iraq, however, caused many problems, including violence that continued for a long time.

> Circle the country that was the ally of the United States in Iraq.

CHALLENGE ACTIVITY

Critical Thinking: Design If you were in charge of rebuilding a country damaged by war, what issues would you have to think about? Write a plan giving a rough outline of what would have to be done.

MAIN IDEA
The dawn of a new century found the United States facing a new era of opportunity and challenge.

Key Terms and People

Antonio Villaraigosa elected in 2005, the first Hispanic American mayor of Los Angeles since 1872

IT computerized information technology

genetic engineering altering the genes of an organism to produce certain features

Section Summary

AMERICA'S CHANGING FACE

America has grown richer and stronger as it has become more diverse. In 2005 **Antonio Villaraigosa** became the first Hispanic American mayor of Los Angeles since 1872. There were 1.7 million Latinos in Los Angeles in 2005, about half the city's population.

Today minority groups make up 30 percent of the U.S. population. This includes such groups as African Americans, Hispanic Americans, and Asian Americans. By 2050 minority groups will make up 50 percent, or one-half, of the population.

There have already been reactions to this changing population. For example, some Americans have been against affirmative action. Other changes include the choice of where people will live. The South and West are expected to grow faster than the rest of the country. People and businesses move there for warm weather and lower energy costs. Another change is that Americans are getting older. People over 64 are the fastest-growing age group. This has affected programs such as Social Security. It may not have enough money to pay everyone.

> What percentage of the population is made up of minorities today? What is it expected to be in 2050?
>
> _____
>
> _____

THE PROMISE OF TECHNOLOGY

Computerized information technology, or **IT**, has made American businesses able to sell or share information. They can be more efficient. Technology has also brought us **genetic engineering**. This is the changing of an organism's genes to make it into

> What effect has IT had on American business?
>
> _____
>
> _____

something different than the way it was before. Some
people worry that the changes in the genes will cause
harm to humans. Genetic engineering is already
producing crops that are resistant to pests.

CHALLENGES FOR THE FUTURE

People are expected to live longer. Medical
researchers have learned a great deal about how to
treat and cure diseases. Health care also has
challenges, though. The cost of health care is going up
quickly. Many Americans do not have health
insurance because it is expensive. The growing
number of older Americans who will need more
health care makes the problem worse. Some diseases
still are a problem. HIV/AIDS continues to spread
widely in this country and in the rest of the world.

What is happening to the cost of health care?
_____

The American economy is the largest in the world.
To keep this economy going requires a great deal of
energy. In fact, the United States is the world's largest
user of energy. Most of the oil it uses is from other
countries. It is expected to import 70 percent of its oil
by 2025. The United States depends on fossil fuels
such as oil and coal. Burning these makes pollution.
The search continues for energy sources that are
cleaner and easier to get. A possible solution might be
the hydrogen fuel cell. It uses hydrogen to produce
energy with producing pollution. NASA has used fuel
cells for many years, but they are still not useful and
affordable for ordinary consumers.

What percentage of its oil is the United States expected to import by 2025?
_____

Natural disasters continue to challenge the United
States. Hurricane Katrina caused great destruction in
August 2005. The city of New Orleans was flooded,
as were large parts of Alabama, Mississippi, and
Louisiana. More than 1,000 people died and hundreds
of thousands were made homeless. Still, few doubt the
region will recover. The story of the United States is
the story of a people who rise to every challenge.

CHALLENGE ACTIVITY

Critical Thinking: Elaborate Choose one of the resources discussed in
this chapter. Make a collage illustrating how this resource is used and the
steps that are being taken to conserve it.